Prof. Dr. Keun-Won Park
Hankuk Theological Seminary
129 Suyudong, Dobongku
Seoul 132, Korea

FORMATION AND REFLECTION

FORMATION AND REFLECTION

The Promise of Practical Theology

Edited by
    LEWIS S. MUDGE
        and
    JAMES N. POLING

FORTRESS PRESS   Philadelphia

Library of Congress Cataloging-in-Publication Data

Formation and reflection.

Bibliography: p.
  1. Theology, Practical. I. Mudge, Lewis Seymour, 1929–   .
II. Poling, James N. (James Newton), 1942–
BV3.F66 1987   230   86–46412
ISBN 0–8006–2054–2

2997D87   Printed in the United States of America   1–2054

Contents

Foreword

This book has emerged from a series of seminars sponsored by the Issues Research program of the Association of Theological Schools. The editors received a joint grant under this program to gather an ongoing group of discussants representing the then Chicago Cluster of Theological Schools and the Divinity School of the University of Chicago. The purpose was to probe new inquiries going on under the rubric of "practical theology" and especially to weigh their significance for theological education. The chosen format continued and broadened a dialogue previously carried on at the Divinity School under the leadership of Professor Don Browning. Issues connected with the M.Div. curriculum and with the experience of practitioners were to be added to an already-rich dialogical mix.

The initial working hypothesis was twofold. First, we felt that the field of "practical theology," if indeed it was a field, needed to be mapped. What possible approaches were included and how were they related to each other? Where were the boundaries and why? Second, we believed that distinctive insights could be gained by introducing theorists to practitioners, by relating research methods to practical styles. The focus of this present book, as it has turned out, is related to those earlier notions, but it has also shifted significantly. The terms "formation" and "reflection" not only reverse the originally assumed *ordo cognoscendi* (order of knowing), they relate the debate on "practical theology," as the Introduction shows, to several of the salient struggles in contemporary Christian thought.

The ATS grant made possible invitations—over a period of two years—to an array of distinguished scholars and practitioners from outside Chicago as well as from within. A faithful core of local participants ensured continuity in the dialogue. These local colleagues also formed a progressively more sophisticated and aggressive audience to meet each new famous but unwary visiting speaker! The essays in this book represent a selection of the papers given on these occasions. The Editors' Introduction and Epilogue offer commentary on the fundamental issues—we think the most significant ones—in the papers and in the conversations responding to them.

In many ways this dialogue has taken on new aspects since the working sessions concluded. The editorial process has enabled eight presenters to reread each other's pieces, and in some cases to read them for the first time. Genuine surprises, of course, have been few: nearly all the essayists have published well-known books elsewhere. But the eight essays chosen go beyond previous work. They have constituted a field of friendly contention in their own right. Several of our writers have materially altered their texts in response to having read the others. Drafts of the editors' introductory and concluding pieces have been included in the discussion. The result is a book with significant conceptual roots whose present form reflects the current state of the "practical theology" question.

A word is needed about editorial method. True to the original intention of the seminar series, one of the editors, James Poling, is a scholarly practitioner (in the field of pastoral care), and the other, Lewis Mudge, is a theologian (with interests in biblical hermeneutics). The question whether practitioners and theorists can talk to each other was thus put in practical terms at every editorial meeting. The answer in most cases turned out to be yes. The editors' normal procedure was first to discuss the issues, identifying the chief points to be made. Poling then produced a draft reflecting this discussion in the light of his pastoral and clinical experience. Mudge then rewrote, recasting to some extent and bringing philosophical and theological resources to bear. Both editors stand behind the Introduction and the Epilogue. Lewis Mudge took final responsibility for shaping their language to express a common intent.

Warm appreciation goes to all those colleagues, too numerous to name, who took part in our discussions, and especially to those whose papers or presentations were not chosen for this book. Some of these have found their way to print elsewhere. The Rev. Jeff Finkbeiner, then a student at Bethany Theological Seminary, served as organizer, coordinator, and active participant. Thanks are due, too, to Leon Pacala, Executive Director, and his associates at the Association of Theological Schools, at whose initiative the Issues Research program came to be.

Foreword

Robert Lynn and Fred Hofheinz of the Lilly Endowment deserve also to be remembered here for having had the good sense to listen to Leon Pacala and to fund his project. Fortress Press deserves praise for its confidence in this project, and editor Davis Perkins likewise for his encouragement and for his skills. Kathy Wohlschlaeger, indefatigable secretary to the dean at McCormick Theological Seminary, had to put up with more than she bargained for here. Both editors are grateful. McCormick, whose facilities were used for the original series of meetings, and Bethany Theological Seminary, whose treasurer managed the grant funds for the program, deserve thanks for their courtesies.

Formation and Reflection is thus launched, in the hope that it will take its place in the larger dialogue whose continued unfolding makes "practical theology" a significant movement in theological education today.

Chicago, June 1987   Lewis S. Mudge
                                                          James N. Poling

The Contributors

DON S. BROWNING is Alexander Campbell Professor of Religion and Psychological Studies at the Divinity School of the University of Chicago. He is author of several books, among them *The Moral Context of Pastoral Care; Pluralism and Personality: William James and Some Contemporary Cultures of Psychology;* and *Religious Thought and the Modern Psychologies: A Critical Conversation in the Theology of Culture.*

REBECCA S. CHOPP is Assistant Professor of Theology at the Candler School of Theology of Emory University. She is the author of the recent book *The Praxis of Suffering: An Interpretation of Liberation and Political Theologies.*

EDWARD FARLEY is Professor of Theology at the Divinity School of Vanderbilt University. He is author of *Ecclesial Man: A Social Phenomenology of Faith and Reality; Ecclesial Reflection: An Anatomy of Theological Method;* and *Theologia: The Fragmentation and Unity of Theological Education.*

THOMAS H. GROOME is Associate Professor of Theology and Religious Education at Boston College and author of *Christian Religious Education: Sharing Our Story and Vision.*

LEWIS S. MUDGE is Dean of the Seminary and Professor of Theology at San Francisco Theological Seminary and in the Graduate Theological Union. He is the author of *One Church: Catholic and Reformed,* and *The Crumbling Walls.* He is editor of *Essays on Biblical Interpretation* by Paul Ricoeur.

The Contributors

JAMES N. POLING is Professor of Pastoral Theology at Colgate Rochester Divinity School and co-author (with Donald Miller) of *Foundations for a Practical Theology of Ministry.*

DAVID TRACY is Professor of Theology in the Divinity School of the University of Chicago, and the author of *Blessed Rage for Order: The New Pluralism in Theology; The Analogical Imagination: Christian Theology and the Culture of Pluralism;* and most recently, *Pluralism and Ambiguity: Hermeneutics, Religion, Hope.*

JAMES D. WHITEHEAD is consultant to the Center for Pastoral and Social Ministry at the University of Notre Dame. With Evelyn Eaton Whitehead he is co-author of *Christian Life Patterns: Psychological Challenges and Religious Invitations in Adult Life,* and *Method in Ministry: Theological Reflection and Christian Ministry.*

CHARLES E. WINQUIST is Thomas J. Watson Professor of Religion at Syracuse University. He is author of *Practical Hermeneutics: A Revised Agenda for Ministry,* and *Epiphanies of Darkness: Deconstruction in Theology.*

Editors' Introduction

What is the relation between "theology" as an academic discipline and living, worshiping, serving communities of faith? Despite good intentions that it should be otherwise, many today would say that little relationship exists. On the one hand, the academic theological world seems preoccupied with its own problems of methodological coherence and reality reference. On the other, faith communities—whether oriented to the center, the left, or the right—function with scant attention to theology of the scholarly, critical kind. Nuances and qualifications aside, traditional Western assumptions about the relation between church and theology, between faith lived and faith thought-through, seem by and large to be evaporating before our eyes.

This does not bode well for the Christian faith. It is not that academicism is necessary to discipleship: far from it. But if faith by its nature seeks understanding, if conviction must stand up to critical, publicly responsible reflection, then the canons of critical inquiry as they have grown up in the West are indispensable until we have something better. Yet the professional theological community—located in institutions and faculties that see themselves as part of the academic world of doctoral programs, tenure, and all the rest—is now under attack from every side. Never entirely trusted by secularly minded colleagues, the theologians seem even less trusted today by congregations of believers. Although center, left, and right are distrustful for different reasons, the effect is the same. At the "mainline" center, there is a loss of ecclesial and cultural identity and also a slide toward intellectual decay. "Mainline" congregations want to be told who they are in a world that seems to have passed them by. They believe that seminary professors either do not understand them or deliberately make matters more complex than they need to be. The religious right believes this last point too, but also tends to think that many theologians are not believers in a sense which simple Christians can understand. The left, on the other hand, sees the theological community as unduly privileged: isolated in a position of relative power remote from the battles for justice and peace which faith communities must fight.

In this volume, eight theologians from various sectors of the academic world acknowledge these criticisms yet seek to reaffirm their responsibility to, and within, the community of faith. The vehicle of this reaffirmation is a convergence of concerns, variously identified by different observers, which may soon deserve to be called a movement. The editors have chosen to use the term "practical theology," not because the expression is without drawbacks (some of our writers in fact are uncomfortable with it), but because for better or for worse it indicates a direction, and may suggest a genre.

By "practical theology" we mean that movement among seminary and university and divinity-school faculty which makes the process of *formation* of Christian community and personhood in the world thematic for critical *reflection*. Reflection can be *about* the formation of the community of faith, and it can also be, in another form, an element *within* this process of formation. There are other ways in which the practical theology movement can be described. Our reasons for describing the movement in these particular terms will become evident in what follows.

This book eschews the current romanticism that theology simply is "the work of the people of God." Of course it is. But any pastor knows that if a typical congregation of Christian people is simply told to go and "do theology," what will come out will be a mishmash of favorite scripture verses quoted out of context, superstitions, fragments of civil religion, vague memories of poorly taught Sunday-school lessons of long ago, and the like. Not an inspiring picture. The polls of "religious beliefs" indicate enormous confusion among professed Christians about the content and implications of their faith. If the people are to be the theologians, as they must be, theology as a fully responsible enterprise must teach them what it is to do theology in the community of faith. They must be taught, so that they can then surpass their teachers.

RECENT LITERATURE

Recent publications bear witness to the depth and breadth of these concerns. A movement, one supposes, may be defined by its bibliography. But this movement is hard to circumscribe that way. Works relevant to our theme range giddily across the Library of Congress classifications. The most important books, interestingly enough, tend to be by people writing somewhat outside their normal professional fields. They show their backgrounds at the point of method, but reach out to meet new discussion partners, attempt new things. No exhaustive list of "practical theology" books can probably exist. But the editors may suggest the genre in mentioning works by which they have been influenced. Endnotes to the different articles greatly expand this list.

Two works by contributors to this volume already have grandparent status for the books and articles being published today. They are *Christian Religious Education* by Thomas H. Groome,[1] and *Method in Ministry* by James D. Whitehead and Evelyn Eaton Whitehead.[2] These are works in the "practical" area of the curriculum which began forcefully to break beyond the traditional limitations of that "field." Thousands of students and pastors have learned from them. Another, much too little noticed, book by a contributor to our collection was *Practical Hermeneutics: A Revised Agenda for the Ministry* by Charles E. Winquist.[3] But the volume which began to turn polite conversation in the curriculum committee into a spirited interchange across the academic disciplines as well as between seminaries and their constituencies was no doubt Edward Farley's *Theologia*,[4] a study commissioned by the Association of Theological Schools. Farley analyzes the development of the present departmental structure of most theological faculties, carefully unpacks the questions to be asked, and seeks to recover an integral understanding of theology's role in the life of faith. The sponsorship of this book, as well as its quality, ensured widespread attention. Shortly thereafter there appeared *Practical Theology: The Emerging Field in Theology, Church, and World*, edited by Don S. Browning.[5] Besides being a landmark, this work demonstrated that its area of concern is far from limited to discussions among those who teach the "practical" disciplines in our seminaries. The majority of contributors to the Browning symposium are, in fact, theologians or ethicists by trade.

Carl S. Dudley's *Building Effective Ministry*[6] approached the matter another way. Disguised by its publisher's choice of title as a "how-to-do-it" potboiler for the parish, this work in fact gathers commentaries representing different academic disciplines around a case study of a particular congregation seen in its own way as a culture developing over time in the midst of the larger culture. James Poling and Donald Miller's *Foundations for a Practical Theology of Ministry*[7] then traced an emerging methodological consensus in this field. The metaphor of faith community provides a field for integration of faith and praxis. More recently, Robert Schreiter has published his *Constructing Local Theologies*,[8] a study which explores how circumstances—of culture, of political environment, of economic class, and the like—shape our response to the gospel and thus give rise to forms of theological reflection specific to the localities in which they appear. And there is more. Joseph Hough and John Cobb have conveyed the results of an intense faculty dialogue at the School of Theology in Claremont with *Christian Identity and Theological Education*.[9] This work brings to focus a vision for theological education as it seeks to produce leaders who themselves will be "practical theologians." And Charles M. Wood offers *Vision and Discernment*,[10] in which he presses toward a comprehensive understanding of the theological curriculum that can, in turn, illumine the relationship between scholarly inquiry and the training of church leadership. No doubt we are culpably ignorant of work done in other countries. But a book from Britain has just now appeared which clearly belongs in this dialogue. It is *The Foundations of Pastoral Studies and Practical Theology*, edited by Paul H. Ballard.[11]

Much has inevitably been left out. The number of journal articles now exceeds the possibility of coverage in a work such as this. And we have not begun to mention the different liberation theologies, which obviously have very important implications for our theme. The point is that the dialogue is already rich and rapidly becoming richer. We hope it is doing so without hardening too soon into schools of thought. This book seeks to keep the debate open, to move it forward still more.

FINDING LEVERAGE ON THE PROBLEM

Given that we wish to close the gap between theological "academics" and the shared life of faith, how may we gain leverage on the problem? The usual means have not worked very well. As Thomas Ogletree puts it in *Practical Theology*, "We encourage the academically oriented to venture some practical life applications of the knowledge they have gained, and we urge the practically minded to draw more widely on the resources of the academic disciplines in 'reflecting' on the meaning of concrete human involvements."[12] But this, as the editors of the present book know from personal experience as theological educators, asks the student to perform feats of intellectual and practical integration that no one on the faculty seems prepared to demonstrate. The sense dawns that there are underlying questions here that have to do with our very conception of the theological task, with the conceptual equipment the church uses in thinking, and in thinking *about* its thinking. As Ogletree puts it, "What we need is a reconstruction of our understandings of the relation between theory and practice in our theological work, and of the distinctions and connections between theoretical and practical knowledge that figure in that relation."[13]

Any approach to such a reconstruction must begin with some frame of reference, some knot in the thread. This makes the work possible and simultaneously limits its scope. The terms "formation" and "reflection" taken together serve this purpose for us. What do these words mean? How are they related?

The word "formation" is widely used of course, particularly in Roman Catholic circles, to refer to the training in disciplined spirituality received by a future priest or member of an order. But it has further meanings. One may speak of intellectual formation, ethical formation, personal formation, community formation, and so on. Formation may mean the *act* of giving shape to something, or the manner in which it *is* formed: by its past, its circumstances, its inherent structure. Thus formation may be a conscious process, as in a religious community, or the word may point to personal or cultural depth structure: present and powerful although we do not know it. As used in this book (and also where the notion is implied although different words are used) "formation" is the total process by which a given expression of Christian faith—as a company of persons in community in a given setting—comes to be and perdures in the world. Formation is partly under conscious control as an exercise in leadership, but it is also partly a matter of materials, assumptions, tendencies already present in the situation. To be grasped, the complex elements in any given case of Christian formation must be teased out by use of the appropriate images, models, and concepts.

Hence, the element of "reflection." This word is at least as multivalent as "formation." The notion, naturally, has a history. The word may simply mean deliberation, a conscious standing aside from the march of events to pass alternative possibilities in review. Or it may mean, in a more sophisticated sense, an act by which we objectify our own processes of thought in order to examine their logical validity or their claim to generate knowledge. Taken to a still further stage, reflection may mean thinking designed to grasp symbolically the force or desire that comes to expression in the self. Or reflection may be transcendental (asking, say, on what conditions a world like this is possible), or metaphysical (asking what fundamental reality lies behind the world of flux and change). The essays in this book nowhere offer a philosophical reflection on reflection, for which the reader may be duly thankful. But all are *examples* of reflection in that they seek ways of sorting out what happens as the community of faith takes its shape in the world. To talk *about* this is to be engaged in a reflective process. Reflection necessarily means putting some kind of a grid over the material in order to get it into manageable categories. One may choose various conceptual means for doing this, thereby producing different descriptive characterizations. One may say, for example, that the process of formation is best thought of in "praxis" terms, or that it is, in essence, a "hermeneutic of situations." Or one may argue that it should be treated as a form of ethical deliberation in which one may distinguish different levels. Or that it is essentially correlative, or essentially emancipatory. Ultimately, theology must ask what lies behind the witness of the people of God as such, reaching toward what Schubert Ogden calls "fully reflective understanding."[14]

This variety of possibilities, both in the definition of our terms and in our understanding of their relationship, offers rich resources for understanding the essays in this book. It does so, we trust, without limiting or distorting what the writers seek to say.

POTENTIAL AGREEMENTS AND
EMERGING QUESTIONS

If issues are to be defined there must be agreement sufficient to permit meaningful questions to be posed. A certain consensus is beginning to appear about the terrain we are seeking to map. Our authors would probably agree in general to the following three propositions although each would wish to put each point in his or her own way: (1) that the contexts and ways in which Christian community and personhood are formed today have become almost unmanageably diverse: to the extent that one may doubt that any single style of theological reflection can hold them together, much less defend rationally the proposition that they represent one faith; (2) that today's academic theological disciplines are ill-equipped even to begin the needed reflection on formation: they have lost their grounding in the thought and experience of contemporary faith communities and in consequence have also lost clarity about their methods and reasons for being; and (3) that the traditionally conceived relationships between theory and practice, tradition and faith-enactment, need to be radically rethought in the light of the ways in which these polarities are transformed in actual communities of worship and service. Let us examine each of these propositions more closely.

The Varieties of Formation: Pluralism and Contextuality

How are Christian persons and communities actually being "formed" today? The question is vitally important, especially for those, such as Stanley Hauerwas,[15] who believe that Christian faith can only be sustained in a secularized and pluralistic society through the formation of "communities of character" in which Christian behavior and conviction are bred, not argued, into sustainable existence. Of late this point has been forcefully made in an article by William Willimon. While our forebears "assumed that the culture would help prop up the church," he writes, "almost no one believes that today." Willimon argues that the church must take seriously "the task . . . of intentionally forming a peculiar people."[16] If the church does not take this seriously, we may add, the surrounding media-dominated culture, with whatever it assumes Christian faith to be, will do the job, making millions impervious to the gospel because they assume they already know what it is.

Indeed, formation is already going on everywhere. We are conditioned from birth to the world view of our surroundings. Cognitive powers are programmed or coded below the level of consciousness. "Reason" is a product of socialization, from oedipal resolution to graduate school and beyond. We should expect, in the light of this, that the manner in which Christian community and personhood take form will depend upon the context. And with the success this faith has had in leaping national and cultural boundaries, formation has taken on many styles and shapes.

The formative interaction between tradition and situation now takes place simultaneously in a host of contexts: of class, race, gender, geography, ethnicity, nationality, and so on. The East vies with the West, the Northern hemisphere with the Southern. Few human beings can rest content in their own group's version of the faith without at least being aware of other versions. Moreover, there seems to be no center, no context of faith whose form is normative. Clearly, the first question to ask about any manifestation of Christian faith is not, What are these peoples' beliefs? but What, concretely, does their Christian faith mean to them as a form of life? In this context the question arises: What do these formations have in common? Despite family resemblances of language and liturgy, is this one faith or many? What is to be regarded as of its "essence"?

Perhaps an example from outside the sphere of Christianity will help make this phenomenon vivid. In his book *Islam Observed*,[17] Clifford Geertz studies Islam as a cultural reality in two utterly different modern settings. In Morocco, Islam is legalistic, warlike, political. In Indonesia, it is relaxed, almost playful, intrinsic. To the outsider it is difficult to see that the same phenomenon is under study in the two places because the common factor between the two, the Qu'ran, is only the same book in the most abstract sense. What a book *is* is the tradition of its interpretation. Surely Christians, comparing the "Bible" of North American evangelicalism with the "Bible" of Latin American liberation theology would have to say the same.

Pluralism of one sort or another has long been with us, of course. The New Testament itself is a collection of documents from different contexts displaying important differences of presupposition, perception, and rhetorical method. The reality has been around for millennia, but the *concept* of pluralism is of recent vintage. The appearance of a concept means that it has become important to *mark* the reality: to insist that it be taken into account. "Pluralism" now means something different from its older cousins "indifferentism" and "toleration." It does not say that differences of religious belief and practice are unimportant, or that we may permit what we do not necessarily endorse or approve. "Pluralism" says that something important has happened to society such that the perennial reality of fundamental difference among human beings and cultures has become salient, and thus claims our attention.[18]

What is this claim on our attention? Some are saying that it is a moral claim. Our planet has become a "multicultural global village." The easy communications we enjoy appear to have intensified the themes of individuality and group identification. At the moment at which the sense of the whole planet Earth and the whole human race is more evident to us than ever before, we are coming to realize that humanity is many communities, self-identified and discerned on the basis of many different rationales, each legitimately insisting on the right to be on its own terms, to be heard by others, to take its part in the councils of the human race. No longer may the dominant groups in society define reality so as to deny the identity of others and make their own ordering of the world seem equivalent to natural law. Reality itself is many things, depending on the angle from which we view it. And we feel moral pressure, not merely intellectual fascination, in these demands.[19]

This new recognition of pluralism has made its companion theme "contextuality" a matter to be reckoned with as well. If one can no longer take for granted that the formative interaction between tradition and one's own context is simply normative, one must ask *how* such interactions take place and how "other" interactions are to be regarded. The copious evidence of pluralism and contextuality throughout Scripture and church history begins to be seen in a new light. Above all, we want to know how radical the reality of pluralism is, how total the dependence of faith-formation upon context. On the one hand, we may hold to the view that tradition and faith are one despite their many forms. On this showing, all that is needed is skill in adapting the *depositum fidei* (tradition of faith) to the conditions that obtain in any given case. At the other extreme, we may conclude that we are faced with what amounts to an irreducible diversity of forms of Christian faith and life. If so, there may be no "one gospel for the whole world," or at least not one that can be articulated or conceptualized as a single, identifiable entity.

Perhaps the truth lies somewhere in between. Still the intellectual and spiritual challenge is formidable. The church faces life-or-death issues, issues around which cluster questions of basic integrity and faithfulness to the gospel. But the issues in different parts of the world, in different cultures, are not the same. In the West, the "crisis of cognitive claims" continues to be very real. But in Latin America, the issue is between the Christianity of the rich and the Christianity of the poor. And what of South Africa, Eastern Europe, or Asia? It is not merely a question of adaptation or application of the gospel to circumstances, but rather fundamental differences of perspective, divergent ways of conceiving what the gospel is about. When pluralism reaches a certain point, contextuality begins to become more important than tradition, more important than any ideal or essential unity the faith may possess. How far along this path is it legitimate to go?

The Rootlessness and Ineffectuality of "Theology"

"Theology," as we know it, is not ready to deal with the situation described. Just at the moment in time when clarifying, unifying reflection on the myriad forms of the church is most needed, the theological community has reached a point of confusion about its own methodological coherence and sense of direction.

By "theology" here we mean not merely "systematic theology" but the entire academic enterprise within which critical reflection is carried on and pastors are trained: that is, theology in the sense of "faculty of theology" or "theological seminary." Complaints about "theology," as Edward Farley notes, are as old as the theological disciplines themselves. The critics have more often than not contended "that theology effects a distanciation from the experientiality and activity of faith."[20]

Theology is seen as "intrinsically problematic because it fails to address the primacy and integrity of the individual human self, the church's actual situation, the concreteness of living language, the minister's pathos, the world's politics and oppressions."[21]

These critical allegations are justified in varying degrees, depending on the type and social location of the institutions and persons concerned. On the one hand, today's seminary faculties are probably more involved in and knowledgeable about the life of the church than their predecessors of a generation ago. But at the same time, a very impressive proportion of today's theological scholarship is being produced in university and college departments of religious studies which have no formal connection with the church and, for the most part, little concern about it. In neither case has the relation between scholarship and the community of faith really been thought through. The "guild mentality," with its powerful hold on the mechanisms of professional advancement, tends to inhibit the thought that is needed.

Yet, particularly in Protestantism, it is precisely these academic theologians in their isolated and alienated disciplines who are primary transmitters and interpreters of tradition. Protestant pastors, at least, tend to look back to seminary for their theological orientations rather than to ecclesiastical authority per se. Of course, Christians who are members of communions whose "teaching authorities" are effectively separate from the academic world, or for whom liturgy is a primary carrier of tradition, are in a different situation, as may be members of evangelical groups that maintain a powerful, organizationally sustained, ethos. Still, the historical memory of the church is heavily dependent upon generation after generation of scholars. What happens if these scholars are essentially alienated from the communities of faith they nominally serve? What understanding of the church's deposit of faith is conveyed to new generations of seminarians when they receive it chopped into the arbitrary categories of the curriculum and squeezed into the methodological categories of the "guilds"? "Incoherence" and "fragmentation" are words often heard when seminary education is the topic. Even where professors seek to transcend the narrow demands of their scholarly guilds, they find enormous difficulty building curricula in which the different subjects of study meaningfully interact, much less add up to articulated wholes.

The separation of academic theology from the practice of faith may also have something to do with what has been called the "crisis of cognitive claims": the sense inside and outside the academy that we cannot account for the "reality reference" of theological language.

Charles Winquist, another of our contributors, refers to what has happened in the last several decades as "a widening separation between descriptive theological language and the world that it claimed to describe."[22] Winquist goes on to say, "Theology questioned its own possibility. It talked less about God and more about the possibility of talking about God."[23] Hence there has been a move toward acknowledgment that the theological use of language is metaphorical: in no way a mirror or replication of nature. "The question that most theologians had to address was not if their statements were true but if they were meaningful."[24]

This "crisis of cognitive claims," which has really been with us in various forms since the Enlightenment, has led theologians to search for forms of reality reference suitable to the received content of the tradition. The so-called liberal movement sought the needed point of contact in a variety of different, allegedly inherent human capacities, each deemed universal to the species: religious feeling (Schleiermacher), moral experience (Kant, Ritschl), or existential anxiety (Bultmann). For this "liberal" strategy, specific religious traditions were understood to give symbolic expression to one or another of these experiential possibilities. But today we are much less certain of the existence of moral and experiential universals as such and much more aware of the shaping power of particular environments and cultures. We begin to see that the church, or even the particular congregation, functions very much like a culture in its own right and must be studied as such without assuming from the start that the reality categories that apply to one instance also apply to another. The church must be the living, reflecting, social reality inside which the theological task is carried on. If theology is to recover its reality reference, it must be meaningfully resituated in the *ekklesia* as that discipline which grasps the constants of the faith community's thought and action. Theology on this reading ceases to be a discipline that seeks to articulate by intellectual means the nature of reality as such and becomes the ministry of reflection within the community which *is* the historical locus of the reality to which it refers.

Beyond Theory and Practice: Grasping How Faith Takes Form

How, then, may theology become, in Ogden's words, a "fully reflective understanding"[25] of how faith takes form in each place? That, it may be said, is the common object of the articles in this book, different as they are in both outlook and method.

It is clear, as we think about what actually happens in the meeting of tradition with situation, that the relationship is far from what has classically been understood as the movement from "theory" to "practice." A theological enterprise embroiled in such methodological conundrums as have been described cannot be related in such an ordered and intentional way to the lives of diverse, contextually oriented communities of faith. One need only be familiar with the deeply felt gap between learning acquired in our theological schools and the actual needs of congregations to know that the first is not the theory of the second nor is the second the practice of the first! One can, however, put the theory-practice question in another way that reveals a great deal. One can ask of the theological faculty what body of practice its theories imply. And one can ask of the congregation what theories its forms of practice conceal. One can recognize, in fact, that seminary and congregation hardly exhaust the social locations in which theory and practice imply or conceal each other. Multiple contexts—pedagogical, reflective, clerical, action-oriented, liturgical, and so on—can be involved. One can speak of both questions and answers in each context and bring the actual dialogue, such as it is, out of the shadows into the light of analysis.

The essays in this book do this in a variety of ways. Most of the analyses of interaction between tradition and situation to be found here are akin, in the practical realm, to what David Tracy has called a "revised correlational model."[26] Tracy's own writings thus far have applied the model primarily to fundamental and systematic theology, although the forthcoming third volume of his theological trilogy promises to deal with the practical mode of the discipline. Don Browning explains succinctly: "In general terms, a revised correlational program in theology attempts to correlate critically both the questions and answers about human existence derived from an interpretation of the central Christian witness *with* the questions and answers implicit in various interpretations of ordinary human experience."[27] *Some* interpretation of the tradition comes together with *some* interpretation of the situation to create a possibly unprecedented articulation of the faith. The thinking, self-conscious or otherwise, which accompanies this conjunction of tradition with situation is the primary form of practical theology. Such primary thinking may, of course, give rise to secondary thinking, or thinking *about* the primary thinking. The articles in this book are instances of the latter variety of thought.

The words "interpretations" and "critical" are both important. The first because no one has access to either "the raw, uninterpreted Christian fact"[28] or to ordinary experience as a thing in itself. Both tradition and experience will be perceived "as" this or that. The interpretative process will inevitably introduce explanatory categories—philosophical, political, psychological, and so on—which help establish the sense of reality that will preside over the encounter. The word "critical" is also important because interpretations of both tradition and experience need to be viewed with suspicion. Distortions of every kind need to be filtered out. In order to recover our heritage we need to overcome misunderstandings of that heritage. We are constantly being both informed and deformed by the world around us. Even our personal experience needs critical appropriation: we can easily be misled by the apparent content of our consciousness into supposing that we genuinely know our own minds.

Some such correlation takes place wherever the faith becomes concrete in the world. Critical study of these transactions is, perhaps, the heart of practical theology. One is led, in the process of study, to ask questions such as these: What are the different arenas of correlative interaction among tradition, self, and situation? How are these arenas related to each other? What are the elements or factors in each interaction and how may they best be articulated? How free to grow in any conceivable direction is this process? Does it have norms? And so on through many other questions.

It is here, in the lived correlation, that the methodological battle is principally fought. How *free* is the community to combine and recombine in various ways (Whitehead)? Can the process of correlating be taught, and what kind of teaching do the teachers of it need to practice (Groome)? How deeply involved with the whole theological problematic does the correlative process need to be (Winquist and Tracy)? Can the whole process be seen as a "hermeneutic of situations" (Farley)? Does this correlative process in the faith community look to some existing field for primary help, for example, to the field of Christian ethics (Browning)? How can the fields generally thought to be in the practical area relate to this process? Are they discrete intellectual entities or are they genres of a larger whole? Can the method of critical correlation be extended to address global religious pluralism in a threatened world of pain and conflict (Tracy) or is this method itself an artifact of liberal optimism now under devastating fire from liberation and political theologies (Chopp)?

Above all, we must ask whether these different approaches to reflection *about* formation can be translated into styles of reflection genuinely useful *in* formation. Or, to put the same question another way: What will happen if these different ways of reflecting on the encounter of tradition with situation are deliberately brought down into the lassitude, the confusion, the passion (whatever the case may be) of the formation process among actual human beings and tested there for cogency? The practitioners among our contributors (especially White-head and Groome) have done this systematically, but the theorists have not. Will there be an illumination of the contemporary meaning of incarnation? Will there be an uncovering of a "generative grammar" of formation underlying all the manifest differences? Will the different conceptualizations used in such reflection-in-formation prove, in this process, to be tolerable translations of each other? Or will they them-selves begin to look like a new field of irreducible pluralism?

A BRIEF PREVIEW OF THE ESSAYS

The essays employ a variety of terminologies and frame their questions in different ways. This fact is part of the theological situation in which we live. To suppress it editorially would be to do a disservice both to authors and to readers. Each essay, in its own way, recommends a form of reflection on the phenomenon of formation. The essays are arranged in an order which the editors believe significant for our common task.

Edward Farley's essay leads off the collection. Among its virtues is that it sorts out possible meanings of the term "practical theology" in historical perspective. In its most comprehensive contemporary mean-ing, the term embraces the whole field of human and world transforma-tion in and through the gospel. Its domain is human society as such: its injustices, crises, needs, and possibilities. This broad definition gives us a vision of practical theology as concerned both with ecclesial practice and with active Christian presence in every dimension of human exis-tence.

Yet Farley's understanding does not preclude attention to more lim-ited and specialized "regions of praxis" which are inevitable ingredients in the larger scene. Our concern may be the church as an institution. It may be theological education. It may be work of the clergy. It may be the decision making of faith communities such as congregations. It may be the life of the individual believer in the world. And, whatever the region of praxis concerned, practical theology may refer to mental processes occurring *in* the corporate and personal life of faith, or it may be reflection *upon* or *about* these mental processes. If the latter, practical theology may well have a pedagogical form. In that event, it is likely to be organized into departments or fields, programs or courses. It will almost certainly then take on the shape of certain discrete disciplines:

pastoral care, religious education, homiletics, church administration, and so forth. And, if such disciplines take form, they will almost certainly be related to ancillary fields of study such as psychology, education theory, communication theory, theory of organizations, and the like.

Viewing this array of possibilities one is bound to ask whether anything fundamental holds them together. For Farley, the answer is that all these forms of reflection are secondary to *"theology* in its primary form, namely, the activity of reflective wisdom in the believer."[29] This is what Farley, in his recent book, has called "theologia." In the present essay, however, Farley goes a step beyond the well-known book to identify what he sees as the missing element in the whole range of attempts to define "practical theology." Fundamental to this "reflective wisdom in the believer," we need (but do not yet have) "a self-conscious way of thinking," or hermeneutic, for "situations."[30]

What does this mean? Most interpretative activity has been directed toward scripture and tradition. "Situations" have mostly been taken for granted as if they were merely neutral background for the gospel. The inward and environing conditions of life have received attention only when they for some reason became salient or problematic. True, practical pastoral studies have taken "situations" into account through the insights of ancillary disciplines: pastoral care has borrowed psychology and psychiatry, church education has borrowed learning theory, and so on. But what is needed now is a "general theology of being-in-a-situation."[31]

Farley's analysis makes clear that situations exist apart from ourselves but also include us. Our failure to interpret situations systematically, therefore, is not different from the ideological distortion and blindness discussed in the essay by Rebecca Chopp. We may both misinterpret what we see and fail to understand how we ourselves have been shaped by our surroundings. And since to be in a position of ministerial leadership is to be in a very special kind of situation, with its own power relations and forms of imagination, a practical theology of church leadership could and should turn the hermeneutic of situations into a specific pedagogy with a distinctive intellectual form.

Is this a dialectic of "formation" and "reflection"? Yes, of course. Farley prefers different terminology. But he employs the language of hermeneutic precisely to frame a proposal for reaching reflective clarification of all that we otherwise take for granted in and around us: in short, our implicit formation. A more intentional formation—a theological hermeneutic of the world or a hermeneutic for the situation of ministerial leadership—is to supplant the unreflective formation that has made us what we are. We may be formed educationally to be capable of a distinctive kind of reflection within formation and upon it. The pedagogy connected with such formation may be called "practical theology."

Charles Winquist, as we have already seen, is acutely aware of the problem of reality reference in foundational theology. He remarks, "The temptation to separate the concept of ministry from theology is partly a reaction to theology's sense of internal disorder and loss of meaning in a predominantly secular culture."[32] Theology has "questioned its own possibility." It has "talked less about God and more about the possibility of talking about God." But insights into what it means to think theologically in a secular culture are also insights into the possibilities for a relevant ministry. The minister seeks to engender expressions of meaning in the world of the congregation just as the theologian does in the world of the text. Both theology and ministry are ways of making worlds of signification. If theology is an academic hermeneutics, ministry is a practical hermeneutics.

The minister collects experience as it is, and invites people to share in a more satisfying vision of what is real and important in experience. This means challenging all semantic construals of the world—whether philosophical, political, economic, or otherwise—that come to interpretative closure: which would allow us to live our lives on the basis of surface interpretations of experience. Ministry then draws symbols and ideas from the tradition which can function on the levels that have been opened up by prophetic challenge. At this level, ministry is a construction: a making of meaning. In the language of this introductory essay, Winquist gives us a reflection on ministry that is primarily philosophical and hermeneutical in character. This reflection sees ministry as consisting of three movements or moments: first, attending to the ways persons are already formed by language, life experience, and all the rest; second, penetrating the surfaces of these formations to disclose cracks in their depth structures; and finally reforming the experience of life through new "poeisis of the spirit."

Our anthology then turns to two meditations on in-practice styles of inducing reflection in formation. The first is by James D. Whitehead and the second is by Thomas H. Groome. Each of these writers shares Winquist's concern for the integrity and cogency of theological discourse in our time. Each has also worked for many years to lead congregations and other Christian groups to reflect on their traditional-situational formations so that they may be reformed at a higher level of critical awareness.

In Whitehead, Christian life is formed in the interaction of three implicitly interpreted "authorities": Christian tradition, cultural information, and personal experience. This writer sees that these three elements, in any given case, overlap and influence each other. And because each of the elements is plural and ambiguous, we must interpret them as we seek to find the correlation among them. As this interpretative process becomes reflective and critical, we overcome misapprehensions of these gifts as we seek to recover, through them, the gracefulness of God's involvement in our history. The interaction then becomes self-conscious: it becomes imaginative inter*play*.

The crucial moment comes, of course, when what has been conceived in principle is tried out in practice. The strength of Whitehead's proposal lies in the testing and refinement to which it has been subjected in actual use. His critical correlation is seen as a corporate act of a well-led community of faith that moves from insights and clarifications to decisions and actions which help define along the way what this faith community is to be in the midst of the world. Whitehead's article illustrates the method in two forms: one appropriate to decision making in the midst of specific crises, and the other designed for longer-term use as a congregation seeks to explore the meaning of its committed life together.

Whitehead gives a central role in this process to the imagination. Cool, cognitive definitions learned in seminary mask important information about how we are personally and corporately related to, say, the tradition of our particular denomination. "Authority," in fact, is held in being through an exercise of the social imagination that interprets power. The different "authorities" in our situation are then related through an imaginative interplay. Whitehead devotes the latter part of his essay to an exploration of this idea. The interpretative process by which we carry out the correlation of tradition, culture, and experience is inventive, and as such it is a form of play. "The play of interpretation . . . is constitutive of life in the deepest sense. It is what we do and how we do our life."[33] Furthermore, "in such interpretations we imagine the next stage of the Christian tradition."[34]

Thomas Groome begins his essay with a manifesto which, in effect, declares the traditional theory-to-practice paradigm of the relation of theology to ministry bankrupt. He finds reason for hope, however, in the work of Farley, Whitehead, and Browning (both in this volume and

elsewhere). Groome offers his own version of critically reflective inter-
vention in formation seen as lived correlation of interpretations of
tradition, culture, and the situation of the community of faith. For
Groome, however, the issue is not merely one of theological method. It
is one of the social location and purpose of the theological enterprise as
such. He writes, "theology . . . is the right of all in Christian faith who
have the use of reason and an interest in making sense out of their faith
in the context of their history."[35] Furthermore, the locus of theology is
not primarily the academy or the institutional church, but the arena of
the world, its problems, its possibilities. And the purpose of theological
reflection is more than gaining theoretical clarity. It is emancipatory.
"Theology must be for us the way God is for us."[36]

Groome sees irony in the fact that theologians find it much easier to
lecture *about* such new approaches than to practice them. The "shared
praxis approach" he offers is designed to enact in seminary teaching the
process of shared reflection which the future pastor is being trained to
induce in the congregation or parish. Students are taken through the
procedure in which they, in turn, will lead congregations and other
Christian groups. This is a five-step process that suffers from attempts
at summary. It is in essence a proceeding which requires time for
reflection and assimilation and precisely not a definition to be conveyed
in a lecture and learned. As Groome states:

> A shared Christian praxis approach to teaching theology is an intentional
> and dialogical activity (shared) in which the participants reflect critically
> on their own historical situation and lived faith (praxis) in a dialectical
> hermeneutic with the Christian story/vision and reflect critically on the
> Christian story/vision in a dialectical hermeneutic with present historical
> praxis. The purpose of such a teaching process is twofold: formation, by
> God's grace, in personal, ecclesial, and social praxis that is faithful to God's
> reign; and formation in the habitus of theologia, in the ability to do
> theology in the context of one's own history.[37]

There follows an essay by Don S. Browning which picks up several
strands of argument from the authors just considered, considers them
critically, and advances to a position which permits him to repristinate
the early tradition alluded to by Farley in which practical theology and
theological ethics are one and the same. Browning offers an "ethical
refinement" of Groome's method in the form of a "theory of practical
moral rationality" which "can be seen as the formal outline of a practical theology."[38]

Browning provides a fresh version of the five levels of practical moral
judgment for which he is already well known. Critical reflection on the

rules we follow and the roles we play in ordinary life (the nearest-to-hand of Browning's levels) requires us to bring to awareness the other levels as well. Moving from the immediate environs of our moral reasoning toward levels of concern that have broader and broader applicability to the moral life as such, we find the following: the specific *context*—cultural, sociological, ecological—in which we make moral judgments; the general human *tendencies, needs,* and *values* we need to take into account; the general principles of *obligation* we recognize; and, finally, the fundamental *metaphors and symbols* by which we characterize the *ultimate context* of experience. Here, in a different mode from that of our other writers, we find the same concern for grounding practical theology in the basic concerns of fundamental theology, or, otherwise put, to display all theology as having a practical intention. While in one way Browning's five levels constitute a kind of checklist for the dispassionate analysis of moral judgment and action, in another way they unpack what is involved in critical reflection on our situation in the light of the Christian message. Thereby they make contact with the pedagogical visions of Whitehead and Groome.

But in addressing these visions, Browning's analysis introduces an element of theological conceptualization seemingly absent otherwise. A "third point" between our story and the Christian story is needed. To "compare" stories we need some means of grasping the crucial elements in the stories in some common frame of reference. At the level of principles of obligation, for example, we need to try to grasp conceptually the nature of moral seriousness, or the definitions of justice and love, which are embedded in the two stories before we can say whether they are saying the same thing. For this purpose it is vital that the concepts chosen are adequate for the purpose. This is what generates philosophical and theological argument without end. And it can be seen that the relationships between concepts operating at the different levels are also a matter of interest bearing on practical theological reasoning.

Browning closes his essay with a reflection on the task of Christian education as character formation. Faith development, moral development, and emotional development may be seen as related to the more comprehensive and general of Browning's levels. There are, in fact, developmental lines corresponding to each "level of character," each corresponding to a distinct type of learning.

Lewis S. Mudge offers a different sort of reflection on formation. He is interested in the thinking that goes on *within* the community as it moves forward in time, interpreting its tradition and its environment toward the practical decision making that keeps it faithfully in being.

The problem we face in making sense of this today, however, is that all three elements in the practical theology equation are problematic at the same time. Neither tradition, nor context, nor the conceptualization needed to bind them together will hold still for us. The actual formation of any particular Christian faith community is liable to be sui generis, that is, unique—with the consequence that customary ecclesiological generalizations do not wholly apply. We must therefore discover a method that can thematize what is actually going on. This, the writer argues, may begin to be reached by borrowing resources from the field of semiotics: the theory of signs and of the cultural rules that govern their use.

Mudge is anxious to derive his method so far as possible from the practice of the early church itself. The community around Jesus, he argues, takes up and radically transforms the signs of the surrounding culture. This process effects a revisioning of the culture's dialectic of power and imagination. The ministry of Jesus, including his passion and resurrection/ascension, is a vast parable containing many sub-metaphors. Living within this parable, or appropriating it in new situations, the community envisions power in a new way and thereby sees new possibilities for action in a world " 'in front of' the text."[39]

The parabolic image, or metaphor, which best captures Jesus' transformative power may well be that of the Suffering Servant. Mudge uses it as an illustration of the process by which adherence to the Jesus movement itself becomes a lived confession which is then formulated linguistically for application to new situations. One such situation lies behind Paul's Philippian letter. The famous confession of Phil. 2:5–11 becomes a norm for the behavioral formation of the Philippian church, and hence for its contextual signifying or witness.

The essay concludes with reflections on the contemporary church's capacity, following the New Testament pattern, to function in the world as a "sign." Of what? Of the possibility of conceiving a humankind united under the rule of God. "The symbol gives rise to thought."[40] Might not the presence of the church enable humankind to keep thinking *this* thought? Might not the church's presence help its neighbors envision themselves whole?

Our book closes with two challenges. These come from writers who, trained in the "liberal" critical correlation model, move beyond it in different ways. Rebecca Chopp first issues a challenge from the perspective of liberation and political theologies. David Tracy then opens the question of conversation with other religions and the theme of human responsibility in the cosmos.

The method of correlation, Chopp argues, grants privilege to certain experiences and issues, while it ignores others. The project of which the method is a part rests upon assumptions first articulated by Schleiermacher and adopted in general by "liberal" theologies of various kinds. Common human experience is seen as religious. Correlations between interpretations of tradition and interpretations of experience are therefore possible in principle. The tension between loyalty to free autonomous inquiry and loyalty to one's traditional belief structure is thus, in principle, overcome. But the "common experience" here is that of a few, privileged, male persons who conceive "religion" in particular, privatistic ways and ask mainly epistemological questions.

This "liberal" position is today under attack by those who, among other things, question the West's preoccupation with "meaning" and "meaningfulness." Is this not an artifact of a particular sort of culture, a preoccupation that masks what has really been going on in that culture? Liberation and political theologies find themselves joining in the attack. They suggest a rethinking of the very location of religion in the human subject which must lead to a rethinking of the nature and method of theology. It follows that the primary challenge for contemporary theology is no longer the crisis of cognitive claims and the resultant concern with meaning and meaningfulness but now the interruption of events of massive suffering such as the Holocaust and the plight of the Latin American poor.

Any theology that calls itself "practical" today must therefore confront certain new questions. It dare not be only an academic, dispassionate discussion of truth claims. Is not theology itself a political act? Should not theology—above all, theology which claims to be "practical"—work for human realization in history? If so, the word "critical," so often used in its academic sense, must also take on the sense of unmasking the distortions in human situations. It must contain a projection of future transformation of the society in which it operates.

It is important, too, Chopp argues, to unpack the various levels of concern involved in the demand that theology be based in praxis. "Praxis" is easy to invoke, but the impact depends on what is really meant. Not just any arena of intentional action will do. Farley and others, for example, use the word mainly to connote regions of ecclesiastical and ethical activity. This is not enough. Liberation and political theologies reinterpret Christianity as a praxis of global solidarity with those who suffer. In this context, praxis must refer to the whole interconnected life of a community, the life of the polis in the Aristotelian sense. More restricted areas of activity need to be understood in relation to the entire political, cultural, social, and economic systems in which we live and to the questions of justice and human fulfillment in those systems. It follows that the social location of theological work is crucially important, as is the maintenance of a transformative relationship between praxis and theory.

The final essay by David Tracy may be read, in part, as a response. It seeks to show, in effect, that the "liberal" method of critical correlation, which he himself has elaborated in several books, is capable of grounding a practical theology that deals seriously with the challenges of global injustice and suffering as well as confronting a *religious* pluralism transcending that envisioned by the liberation and political perspectives. Practical theology, recognizing that the crisis of cognitive claims continues, must take on the question of the shared praxis of our emerging global community. Tracy offers an instance of the sort of conversation that could emerge at the practical level with other religious traditions. It is dialogue about the issue of nature or cosmos in Christian practical theology itself.

The ecological and nuclear questions challenge the "anthropocentric" character of much Christian theology. Redemption cannot be understood without a reference to creation. History cannot be understood without nature. The categories of "God" and "self" cannot be understood without reference to the category "cosmos" or "world." The relationships between theology and science in the Western world seem simultaneously more promising and more difficult than they have been before. Both theology and science have undergone momentous shifts in self-understanding. And, Tracy asks, has not our preoccupation with political and liberation theologies, however necessary and salutary, blocked the development of our competency in dealing with cosmological concerns? We need an understanding of creation in order to understand fully our own doctrine of redemption. No Christian theology can claim adequacy to the Christian tradition by, in effect, retrieving only God and self (including the social and historical self) while quietly dropping 'world' out of the picture.

But all such reflection is in order to provoke dialogue at the global level concerning praxis. The inescapable fact with which we have to deal is that of massive human suffering under the pressures of deprivation, oppression, and political conflict. In the midst of this suffering, we face the two great issues of ecological crisis and the threat of nuclear holocaust. Both these concerns suggest in graphic terms the meaning of the more theoretical issues just discussed. The question of global justice must include the question of ecology. Likewise the question of nuclear omnicide imposes a need to interpret cosmology anew.

Tracy's article illustrates the manner in which concern for practical theology, once we see the full implications of global pluralism and global praxis in the face of threats to life itself, may generate new programs for both fundamental and systematic theology as well. Just as we cannot understand theology's practical turn without seeing it in relation to the fundamental and systematic tasks, so the practical turn redounds upon theology in its other modes.

NOTES

1. Thomas H. Groome, *Christian Religious Education: Sharing Our Story and Vision* (San Francisco: Harper & Row, 1980).

2. James D. Whitehead and Evelyn Eaton Whitehead, *Method in Ministry: Theological Reflection and Christian Ministry* (New York: Harper & Row, 1981).

3. Charles E. Winquist, *Practical Hermeneutics: A Revised Agenda for the Ministry* (Chico, Calif.: Scholars Press, 1980).

4. Edward Farley, *Theologia: The Fragmentation and Unity of Theological Education* (Philadelphia: Fortress Press, 1983).

5. Don S. Browning, ed., *Practical Theology: The Emerging Field in Theology, Church, and World* (San Francisco: Harper & Row, 1983).

6. Carl S. Dudley, ed., *Building Effective Ministry* (San Francisco: Harper & Row, 1983).

7. James Poling and Donald Miller, *Foundations for a Practical Theology of Ministry* (Nashville: Abingdon Press, 1985).

8. Robert Schreiter, *Constructing Local Theologies* (Maryknoll, N.Y.: Orbis Books, 1985).

9. Joseph C. Hough, Jr., and John B. Cobb, Jr., *Christian Identity and Theological Education* (Chico, Calif.: Scholars Press, 1985).

10. Charles M. Wood, *Vision and Discernment: An Orientation in Theological Study* (Chico, Calif.: Scholars Press, 1985).

11. Paul H. Ballard, ed., *The Foundations of Pastoral Studies and Practical Theology*, Holi 4 (Cardiff: Board of Studies for Pastoral Studies, Faculty of Theology, University College, 1986).

12. Thomas Ogletree, "Dimensions of a Practical Theology: Meaning, Action, Self," in *Practical Theology*, ed. Browning, 84.

13. Ibid.

14. See Schubert M. Ogden, *On Theology* (San Francisco: Harper & Row, 1986), 1 and passim.

15. See Stanley Hauerwas, *A Community of Character: Toward a Constructive*

Christian Social Ethic (Notre Dame, Ind.: University of Notre Dame Press, 1981).

16. William Willimon, "Making Christians in a Secular World," *Christian Century* (October 22, 1986): 914–15.

17. Clifford Geertz, *Islam Observed: Religious Development in Morocco and Indonesia* (New Haven: Yale University Press, 1968).

18. This discussion owes much to the suggestions of Edward C. Hobbs, "Pluralism in the Biblical Context," in *Hermeneutics and Pluralism Reader,* ed. William Wuellner and Marvin Brown (Berkeley: Center for Hermeneutical Studies, 1983), 63–81.

19. See Philip Hefner, "Theology in the Context of Science, Liberation, and Christian Tradition," in *World Views and Warrants* (Lanham, Md.: University Press of America, 1987).

20. Edward Farley, "Interpreting Situations: An Inquiry into the Nature of Practical Theology," in this volume, 8.

21. Ibid.

22. Charles E. Winquist, "Re-visioning Ministry: Postmodern Reflections," in this volume, 29.

23. Ibid.

24. Ibid.

25. Ogden, *On Theology,* 1.

26. David Tracy, *Blessed Rage for Order: The New Pluralism in Theology* (New York: Seabury Press, 1975), passim.

27. Don S. Browning, "Practical Theology and Religious Education," in this volume, 80.

28. Ibid.

29. Farley, "Interpreting Situations," 9.

30. Ibid.

31. Ibid., 11.

32. Winquist, "Re-visioning Ministry," 29.

33. James D. Whitehead, "The Practical Play of Theology," in this volume, 42.

34. Ibid., 44.

35. Thomas H. Groome, "Theology on Our Feet: A Revisionist Pedagogy for Healing the Gap between Academia and Ecclesia," in this volume, 59–60.

36. Ibid., 62.

37. Ibid., 69.

38. Browning, "Practical Theology," 88.

39. Paul Ricoeur, quoted in Lewis S. Mudge, "Thinking in the Community of Faith: Toward an Ecclesial Hermeneutic," in this volume, 116.

40. Ricoeur, in ibid., 117 n.24.

FORMATION AND REFLECTION

1 Interpreting Situations: An Inquiry into the Nature of Practical Theology

EDWARD FARLEY

"Practical theology" may prove not to be a salvageable term. The term is still in use, as a term some seminary faculty members use to locate their teaching in the curriculum of clergy education. As such it functions more as a rubric for self-interpretation and location on the curricular map than a name for a discrete phenomenon. So varied are the approaches and proffered definitions of practical theology in recent literature that it is not even clear what is under discussion. Practical theology may refer to a curricular entity, an area of pastoral studies, a structural aspect of theology itself. In this inquiry I shall provisionally retain the term "practical theology."[1] I cannot, however, presuppose a prevailing consensus about what it refers to; hence, I shall not be formulating the inquiry as if practical theology were an established theological science whose nature and methods call for continued clarification.

I think it is fair to say that the correctives of the recent literature are expansive, concerned to relocate practical theology into a setting broader than clergy education. This inquiry shares in this expansive movement. My focus, however, shall be not so much on what now exists as practical theology as on what does not yet exist. In other words, the concern of the inquiry is with an absence, something not yet developed, not yet thematized for study and education. Since this needed something does fall under a broadened meaning of practical theology, I shall retain the term as a rubric for discussion. What is absent is the thematization of one of the essential components of theology itself, the theological interpretation of situations. In the traditional approach, theology is involved in interpretation but the object of interpretation is the past and the texts of the past. And while believers and church

1

leaders do in fact interpret situations (culture, war, marriage, death, etc.), they do so directly out of the tradition without passing through an inquiry which would uncover what is occurring when we interpret a situation theologically. We do thematize interpretation as it is directed to texts, hence, we are at home in problems of historical method, exegesis, and textual hermeneutics. We have not thematized—become methodically self-conscious about—the interpretation of situations.

The inquiry proceeds in five steps. The first two draw on the history of practical theology to understand why theology has resisted thematizing the interpretation of situations. Briefly, the reason is that the direction of practical theology has proceeded through two steps of narrowing, the outcome being a restriction of practical theology to clergy theology or theology of pastoral leadership. Recent attempts to correct this narrowing by broadening practical theology have produced what looks like an impasse between two exclusive options—practical theology as a science of the church's existence in the world and practical theology as praxis theology. The exploration here suggests that the interpretation of situations is a notion of practical theology that is able to mediate this impasse and get behind it. The third and fourth steps explore a broadened concept of practical theology as a theological interpretation of situations. The final step explores the more specific hermeneutic of the situation of vocation and church leadership.

THE NINETEENTH-CENTURY CONSENSUS: THE CLERICALIZATION OF PRACTICAL THEOLOGY

Present-day theological schools have inherited what we might call the nineteenth-century consensus about practical theology.[2] Pedagogically speaking, this consensus is still largely operative in divinity schools and seminaries. It is this consensus which much recent literature has cast into question. Hence, a few words as to the origin and nature of this consensus, the traditional view of practical theology, are in order. Well known is the fact that practical theology initially named not a separate discipline of theology but a way of describing theology itself.[3] A remnant of this period remains in the almost-universal insistence that "all theology is practical," whatever we say about practical theology.[4] Practical theology's first step toward becoming an area of theology occurred with the distinguishing of moral theology from speculative theology and the occasional use of "practical theology" to designate that. The second step came when the term "practical theology" named an area of studies which included moral theology but was expanded to embrace matters of church polity and pastoral activities.[5] At this stage (the early and mid-eighteenth-century) practical theology is still not called a science but is a parallel term to theoretical theology used to classify certain kinds of theological studies.

The third and decisive step occurred when practical theology was distinguished from moral theology as an area pertaining to the church's fundamental activities.[6] This occurred when late-eighteenth-century German schools organized theological studies into the four standard theological sciences, the fourfold theological encyclopedia. This pattern finds expression in the late-eighteenth-century German writings on the study of theology.[7] This fourfold way of organizing the theological sciences was the framework for the nineteenth-century consensus about practical theology. In this organization practical theology ceases to be a nomenclature inclusive of moral theology and church and pastoral activities. Moral theology (ethics) is assigned along with dogmatics to systematic theology. This narrows the meaning of practical theology to a cluster of studies pertaining to church and ministry.

The eighteenth century is, accordingly, not only the time when practical theology begins to name a distinct set of studies but also when something called "pastoral theology" begins to be the subject and title of written works.[8] In this period pastoral theology like practical theology had both broad and narrow meanings. It named both a comprehensive theology of pastoral activities and also one set of those activities.[9] In the course of the eighteenth and nineteenth centuries both broad and narrow meanings persisted. And although a number of works on the total life and activity of the pastor were entitled "pastoral theology" the nineteenth-century encyclopedia literature tended to restrict the term to one aspect of practical theology, usually pastoral care. Because of the broad meaning of pastoral theology and the now more restricted meaning of practical theology, the two terms frequently meant the same thing, the discipline of clerical activities.[10] In summary, specific eighteenth-century monographs on pastoral theology helped further thematize and synthesize the activities of the minister as a subject of university study, hence this literature was a factor in the narrowing of practical theology to a discipline of churchly and ministerial activities.[11]

A fairly clear consensus was obtained in the nineteenth-century literature on practical theology, Continental and North American. Negatively, it was agreed that practical theology did not include ethics and issues of social and individual moral life. Positively, the consensus consigned to practical theology five subdisciplines: homiletics, catechetics, liturgics, church jurisprudence and polity, and pastoral care.[12] The relation between practical theology, the fourth field, and the other three theological sciences was formulated as the relation of practice to theory. In many cases practical theology was called "applied theology." As to the unifying subject matter, there is a rough consensus that practical theology names the science of the contemporary life and activities of the Christian church.[13] This prominence of the church and church activities in the definition may surprise some contemporary theologians and educators who think of practical theology as a science of the *pastor*. The nineteenth-century consensus did, of course, see practical theology as concerned with regions of pastoral activities, and a few authors explicitly define it that way.[14] But the nineteenth-century consensus viewed the subject of practical theology as the activities of the church as carried out and guided by the activities of the minister.[15] This merging of churchly and clerical activities reflects the view that the church exists, works, endures through activities that are primarily clerical. On the other hand, the consensus resisted the notion that practical theology's sole subject matter is simply ministers and their work separated from a theology of the operations of the church.

The practical theology of modern technological education largely reflects but is not exactly identical with the nineteenth-century consensus. This is because the concept of practical theology underwent a second narrowing. I shall not attempt a historical explanation of this narrowing. I surmise that it took place, in part at least, because of the elusiveness of the proposed subject matter of practical theology, the "churchly operations of Christianity." This language leads one to think that practical theology was a single "scientific" undertaking, focused on a discrete object and using the methods appropriate to that object. In fact a single science of church activities never was forthcoming. What appeared instead were five discrete areas of pedagogy corresponding to the five major activities agreed upon by the consensus, each one with its literatures, methods, and auxiliary disciplines. The context of these enterprises was the university or seminary. And in the university a pedagogical area has existence, status, truth, reality, and value to the degree that that something is a science, an academic discipline. A subject matter may begin as part of another subject matter, but its development tends to be toward independence. Such was the destiny of the five areas of practical theology, to which others have now been added.[16]

The history of practical theology tends to be a history of a number of relatively distinct fields. The single subject matter, the life and operations of the church, did not successfully mature into a single science, but quickly dispersed into the several disciplines pertaining to the activities of ministry. The second narrowing is a narrowing of practical theology as a *church-clergy* science to that of a *clergy* science. This clerical narrowing or exclusive focus on the individuality, career, and office of the minister is not simply the "clerical paradigm." The clerical paradigm is the unifying of theological studies as a whole by means of clergy activities and situations. Even though practical theology had undergone the narrowing to the life and office of the minister, it still did not obtain the status of a single theological science, a science of ministry or church leadership. There were instead the five or more areas of clergy activities, each of which became a relatively independent academic and pedagogical undertaking.

I have expressed this development as a narrowing. This is especially clear if we have in view the nineteenth-century consensus as it occurred in the German literature. But on the North American scene practical theology may never have undergone a narrowing. Although the German theological encyclopedia literature was shaping the American seminary almost from the beginning, there was never an exact transplantation of the German *Wissenschaftlichkeit* into the American seminary fields of study. And the writings in the area of church and clergy activities (practical theology) did not occur for the most part in the form of an encyclopedia proposal about the four theological sciences. Hence, the definitions of practical theology in the German literature are not necessarily expressive of nineteenth-century North America or England. The counterpart literature in both England and America had more the form of the pastor's manual. Its model was Richard Baxter's *The Reformed Pastor,* and the high points of the literature were such offerings as Cotton Mather's *Manuductio ad Ministerium* (1776), Enoch Pond's *Lectures in Pastoral Theology* (1847), and Washington Gladden's *The Christian Pastor and the Working Church* (1898). The focus of this literature is on the person, duties, life, and responsibilities of the pastor.[17] And when a few theological encyclopedic works were written for the American scene toward the end of the nineteenth-century, they tended to reflect the second narrowing and to see practical theology as a science and art of the various functions of the Christian ministry for the preservation and propagation of the Christian religion at home and abroad.[18]

THE CONTEMPORARY CHALLENGE TO THE
NINETEENTH-CENTURY CONSENSUS

In recent years a rather extensive literature of discontent—containing criticisms, correctives, and new proposals—has been directed toward practical theology.[19] These critical responses are, in fact, challenges to the two narrowings of practical theology. The first narrowing left moral theology behind and proposed practical theology as the science of church and pastoral activities. The second narrowing is from pastoral activities in the context of church activities to the discrete activities of the minister. The initial criticism of practical theology was a response to its narrowing to pastoral theology and this occurred in Roman Catholic theological circles in Europe. This corrective advocates a return of practical theology to the church.[20] It accuses the narrowed form of practical theology of being isolated both from theology itself and from ecclesiology, the natural context in which the activities of church leadership should be understood.

The second wave of criticism was a more radical one, questioning the total historical shift of practical theology to ecclesiastical issues. It cast into question both narrowings. These Protestant and Catholic theologians urge a corrective which would restore to theology a comprehensive discipline of praxis as such. Christian praxis in the world is the proposed parameter of practical theology and this is not reducible to a theology of ecclesiastical operations.[21] In this view practical theology is not a theology of the church's self-realization in the world but a theology of human and world transformation. As a post-Marxist critical orientation, it calls for social criticism of the church itself and its function in society. In this approach the realities of contemporary political and social life are the focal point of practical theology.

When practical theology is viewed from the perspective of these contemporary correctives of the nineteenth-century consensus and its clerical narrowing, it seems to have only two forms: the discredited traditional and the viable modern. Hence, the search for practical theology becomes the search for a modern, postclericalized approach.[22] I have pursued this history in order to expose the perils of such an interpretation. This history invites another formulation. Let us acknowledge the force of the modern correctives. Let us also add to this acknowledgment that every moment in the history of practical theology is a corrective, and that the rise of practical theology in the first place was a corrective of what went before. The thematization of moral theology as a particular area of theology distinct from speculative theology corrected a certain understanding of theology. Adding to this studies of the activities of church leadership (pastoral, priestly, "poimenic" or shepherding activities) was a corrective because it extended theological attention to churchly praxis. The focusing of attention on a single theological discipline of church activities, the fourth science, corrects by proposing more refined and specific methods. Even the clerical narrowing of this fourth area correctly argued for the validity of thematizing church leadership as such.

At the same time the history of practical theology is a history of a loss. While each phase of corrective adds a new insight and theme to the history, it does so by supplanting its predecessors. When the step was made from theology as practical to a field—practical theology—and when this was reduced from moral theology to church activities, praxis itself was no longer an immanent moment in theology itself.[23] The advantages present in the rise of independent disciplines of clergy studies were offset by the disadvantages of conducting those studies under comprehensive theological criteria and in relation to other areas of praxis.

This history of practical theology as a history of both correctives and losses provides us with principles of criticism that are, at the same time, possible clues to the nature of practical theology. Each corrective is a valid corrective to the degree that it properly exposes the isolation and abstractness of what it displaces. The principle this founds is that the various phases of the history of practical theology, including modern antitradition correctives, are not necessarily exclusive, but demand serious attention. Thus, practical theology as theology of church and clergy operations need not be abandoned. On the other hand, when we consider the loss that has attended the history of practical theology, especially the major loss involved in the shift from praxis as such (theology as practical) to a specific discipline of theology, we discover another principle. Important as it is to retain different regions of praxis (the different phases of practical theology) in any modern approach, praxis itself as an intrinsic element of theology must be rediscovered. The first principle calls for a practical theology sufficiently comprehensive to embrace various regions of praxis and to treat them in *their relations to each other.* The second principle calls for a practical theology that approaches these regions of praxis from a general thematization and hermeneutic of praxis itself. A modern practical theology is, accordingly, a correction of all approaches that identify the field with only one region of praxis (like clergy activities). It makes the correction by relating various regions of praxis to each other and by an overall hermeneutic of praxis.

We return now to the "problem of practical theology." We have seen practical theology arising out of classical theology viewed as practical and obtaining a nineteenth-century consensus in its German literature. The narrowest form of this consensus makes the activities and person of the minister the subject matter of practical theology. We have also seen two major contemporary alternatives to this view. The one corrects by broadening the field to the church and thus resembles at least the language and intent of the German consensus that practical theology concerns the activities of the church. The other corrects by broadening to praxis and thus resembles the very first stage of practical theology as moral theology. These two major approaches occurring in the modern discussion prompt further questions. First, must the two modern corrections, the church-centered and the praxis-centered, be exclusive of each other or can they be negotiated? Second, are the two modern correctives exclusive of all that went before, or can each of the correctives occurring in the history of practical theology be retained in the total enterprise of practical theology?

The inquiry that follows is guided by the conviction that both the older consensus and its recent challenges attest to valid areas of theological undertakings. The exploration of pastoral activities in the context of the church's situation is surely a valid and necessary discipline and pedagogy. To engage in that exploration as post-theological and "applied," however, is surely a perverse endeavor. Likewise, the exploration of the church's situation as such and the praxis dimension of theology as such are tasks we dare not ignore. All of these explorations however, assume and call for an undertaking which they never quite state. I am calling this undertaking "the interpretation of situations," and I see it as one of five interpretive-reflective activities that constitute the very structure of theology wherever and whenever theology occurs.[24]

INTERPRETING SITUATIONS AS A
DISCIPLINE OF FAITH

Complaints about "theology" are as old as theology itself, especially since the time when theology took the form of a university discipline in twelfth-century Europe. Critics of theology—monastic, Reformation-Protestant, pietist, puritan, activist—contend that theology effects a distanciation from the experientiality and activity of faith. These complaints have contemporary expressions: existentialist, liberationist, deconstructionist, ecclesiastical, clergy-oriented, political. According to these criticisms theology is intrinsically problematic because it fails to address the primacy and integrity of the individual human self, the church's actual situation, the concreteness of living language, the minister's pathos, the world's politics and oppressions. The targets of the complaints are theologians, the theological schools, the churches, the present generation of believers. The complaints resemble each other in one respect. They all have to do with the relation or disrelation of faith and its institutions to actual, problematic, contemporary reality. In other words they have to do with situations; thus, situations of action, church, the individual, the ministry. Frequently these criticisms target each other. Liberation-type criticisms are directed at individualist-existential stances. Political theology aims criticism at ministers and churches whose orientation is social maintenance and legitimation.

All the criticisms together point to an absence, a lacuna in the life, education, and self-understanding of the Christian community. The absence is simply that faith's interpretive response to situations is not identified *as such* among the various interpretive undertakings of the Christian community, for instance in church education, clergy education, preaching, publishing, and so forth. Specific activities like preaching or the relations of men and women are, of course, the subjects of inquiry and discussion. The current literature of criticism and correction is symptomatic of this vacuum. Expressed another way, the disciplines and pedagogies of church and clergy education offer no "practical theology" in the sense of a self-conscious way of thinking toward situations as such.

I have spoken about a vacuum, a lacuna, something not identified and thematized in the church's disciplines and pedagogies. What precisely is this? First, it must be clear that what we are talking about is *theology* in its primary form, namely, the activity of reflective wisdom in the believer.[25] In this form theology is not defined by the context of a school, by clergy education, or by an array of sciences or scholarly endeavors. These are all secondary forms of theology which in its primary form occurs as an adjunct to the life of faith itself. Second, the reflective activity of the believer gathers together several very fundamental activities of interpretation, all evoked by "the situation of the believer." The believer's interpretive activity is not simply in one direction, for instance, toward Scripture. Faith itself is an existence in situations, and that existence involves interpretive acts of everything that structures faith's situation; the transcendent tradition with its paradigm of salvation: thus, the texts of the primary event of the tradition and of its subsequent history, the truth of things, the ever-changing realities that constitute the contemporary situation. All these call forth interpretive acts.

The church's past pedagogical focus has been on one set of these acts, those evoked by the authoritative tradition and its texts. A theory-to-practice paradigm poses the problem of applying the interpreted texts to practice, to culture, the self, the church, piety, and so forth. The problem with this paradigm is that it bypasses most of the structural elements in the situation of the believer and, therefore, many other necessary interpretive acts. One of the bypassed components is that to which the traditional view would "apply" its authorities. This is the situation in a concrete and discrete sense. Human beings tend to exist in situations in an oblivious way. Most of the elements in situations are experienced as background. Situations or their elements get our attention when they become problematic, pose crises, require decision. Here, situations evoke self-conscious interpretive response. For example, the marriage one takes for granted becomes an intensely focused subject matter when it is threatened by disintegration. Situations as problematic can range from very global situations (the crisis in planetary ecology) to "metaphysical" situations (the course and destiny of human history) to very specific situations of the individual (the onset of an illness). That faith responds to and interprets these situations goes without saying. Further, when it does so, certain paradigms are at work, for instance, the theory-to-practice paradigm.

The thesis I am arguing is that the interpretation of situations be self-conscious, self-critical, and disciplined.[26] In other words, similar demands are placed on the believer's interpretation of situations as on the believer's interpretation of ancient texts, or of "heresies" and doctrines. The assumption has often been that if the interpretation of the authoritative texts is done properly, all other interpretations will take care of themselves. It is just at this point that the believer (and the community of believers) falls into uncritical and even idolatrous paradigms of the use of texts. Further, when the interpretation of situations is not itself subjected to critical scrutiny, the believer reads the situation simply out of a kind of obliviousness, an inattention to most of its components. In the theory-to-practice, authoritative-text-(applied)-to-life paradigm, there is high awareness of the text, its meaning and content, and low awareness of the meaning and content of the situation. The ordered learning (education) which creates discipline is aimed at the text. The movement is from disciplined interpretation of the authoritative past to casual and impressionistic grasp of the present.

At this point some of the pedagogical fields of clergy-oriented practical theology might enter a strong protest. They do not simply apply authorities to life in an oblivious way. The very existence of these fields is created by the appropriation of sciences which assist in interpreting the focused situation. Thus, fields of church education, pastoral psychology, homiletics, church and ministry appropriate educational theory, learning theory, psychology of personality, rhetoric, and management theory to assist in interpreting situations of education, counseling, preaching, and so forth. We acknowledge that these appropriations prevent these endeavors from precritical applications of authorities to situations and from mere obliviousness about these situations. On the other hand these appropriations of auxiliary sciences exemplify the lacuna under discussion. These fields have been criticized for permitting their auxiliary disciplines to become central and autonomous, for cutting the connection with theological, ethical, and other dimensions which give them their theological character. In fact, one can discern within these fields responses to such criticisms, and attempts to reappropriate their theological roots. Many are the historical reasons why the disciplines auxiliary to these fields were given such autonomy. One of those reasons is the absence, the lacuna, of what I am calling here practical theology. There was no general theology of being-in-a-situation which provided a method for discerning the major components operative in the special situations of these fields. The absence of this theme and method is not, of course, the "fault" of these fields. Blame is not the game we are playing here. The point, rather, is that the failure to thematize situationality itself has had serious results in the church's educational endeavors at all levels.

INTERPRETING SITUATIONS AS A
THEOLOGICAL HERMENEUTIC

All human beings exist and act in situations and engage in interpretations of situations. This interpretive dimension of human existence does not cease with faith and with life in the community of faith. On the contrary, faith and the world of faith shape the perspective, the "taken-for-granted stock of knowledge," the weighting of what is important, all of which affect the interpretation of situations. In other words interpreting situations from the viewpoint and in the context of faith does create a special hermeneutic task, differentiable from other hermeneutic or interpretive dimensions of theology.[27] This is the reason why interpreting situations can and should be part of a deliberate and self-conscious educational undertaking, part of the church's lay and clergy education. It can be part of an educational undertaking only because it is an identifiable hermeneutics. There is not space here for an extensive exploration of the hermeneutic task of interpreting situations. Instead, I shall describe several features of such a task, items virtually unavoidable when faith engages in the interpretation of situations in a reflective and disciplined way.

EDWARD FARLEY

A situation is the way various items, powers, and events in the environment gather together so as to require responses from participants. In this sense, any living, perhaps any actual, entity exists in situations. Situations like reality itself are never static. Living beings, we might say, live in their environments (contexts) in continuing responses to ever-changing, ever-forming situations. Situations can be very brief in time (such as a thunderstorm or a marital quarrel) or very protracted (such as the Western epoch, the nuclear age). They can also be very local (the situation of a specific family) or very global (the ecological situation of our planet). Hence, local and brief situations can occur within broader and more enduring situations. Participants in situations need not be simply individuals. Groups, communities, collectives, societies all exist in situations. Hence, it is equally proper to explore the situation of a congregation, a denomination, or the church universal. What would make such explorations theological interpretations? The following features constitute at best only an exemplary rather than an exhaustive description of a theological hermeneutic of situations.

The first task interpreting a situation faces is simply identifying the situation and describing its distinctive and constituent features. This task may sound neutral and relatively simple. It is not—for the reason that we human beings filter all situations not only through our world views, the taken-for-granted "knowledge" of our social worlds, but also through our idolatries. We are prone, therefore, to assume that the situation of conflict in Central America is "simply" a battle between Communist totalitarianism and the forces of freedom. Such a grid, needless to say, will remove most of the elements in the situation. In other words the components (powers, events, causalities) of a situation are not simply there on the surface. Discerning the components of a situation is not simply taking a photograph. It is an act of serious and even theological self-criticism. Discerning these components is a difficult task for a second reason. The "components" of a situation are not simply discrete items. A situation is not like a basket of fruit, so that discerning the situation is merely enumerating what fruits occupy the basket. The components of a situation are always different *kinds* of things, things of very different *genre;* human beings as individuals, world views, groups of various sorts, the pressure of the past, futurity, various strata of language (writing, imagery, metaphors, myths, etc.), events, sedimented social power. And we could go on and on. "Reading a situation" is the task of identifying these genres of things and discerning how they together constitute the situation.

12

A second task in the interpretation of situations has to do with the situation's past. Since situations are what occurs in the present, the importance of probing the past of that present may not be self-evident. Human, historical situations do not present to us the whole past. What does persist into situations is the result of repressions in the past of what tradition and its institutions permit to get through. Tradition does hand on the revelatory past—events and narratives that correct, illumine, inspire. At the same time it disguises the origins and even the existence of much of its own content, especially as these contents function to oppress, to establish and maintain power. In pre-Selma America the deep structures of racism operative in American Anglo-Saxon religion and in its churches were virtually invisible. The events and the deep presuppositions that formed and structured the communities of faith in a racist manner were not thematized in the traditioning of the churches. The history of the forming of these structures was "forgotten," repressed in the corporate memory. Certain rationalizations of these deep structures were on the surface and would be appealed to if change were advocated. A similar invisibility and disguise operates now in religious communities with regard to the role and status of women. To grasp the present situation of men and women in the churches calls for more than simply describing present policy. For the present is comprised of and structured by these disguised repressions of the past. And only a certain way of studying the past will uncover these repressions and in so doing will thus uncover something at work in the present.[28]

A third task is to correct the abstraction committed by the focus on a single situation, a situation in its brevity and its specific locality. Situations occur within situations. While it is proper to identify discrete and local situations—for instance, the changing neighborhood of a local congregation—this identification will be distortive if it isolates the situation from more comprehensive and more enduring situations. Larger and longer situations are at work when a neighborhood changes. Such a change may be tied in some way to global economics, to racial migrations, to suburbanization of the middle class. It poses issues of faith's universally human orientation. Hence, a hermeneutic even of a very local situation calls for consideration of intersituational issues, the impingement of other situations on the local situation. It cannot settle for mere internal situational analysis.[29]

A fourth aspect of a hermeneutics of situations may be the most complex of all. We have already seen that theological perspectives and criticism must be operative in all the tasks of discerning the situation. In this fourth task the theological element becomes central. Why is this the case? Let us recall what a situation is, a gathering together of powers and occurrences in the environment as to evoke responses from the participants. A situation is something we have no choice but to respond to in some way. A situation is not, then, a neutral series of objects, something to be noted. It is a concentration of powers which impinge upon us as individual agents or as communities. The situation thus places certain demands on us. This is the case whether it is a situation of being captured and interrogated by a wartime enemy or shopping at the grocery store. The demand of the situation is multidimensional. One kind of demand occurs when the situation is imperiling, dangerous. Another kind occurs when promise and possibility are offered; another when obligation is required. Because of this demand-response feature of situations, the interpretation of situations includes the task of discerning the situation's demand.

A theological version of this task cannot avoid the insights of its own mythos into the corruption and redemption of human beings. Because of that corruption, human beings shape the demand of the situation according to their idolatries, their absolutized self-interests, their ethnocentrisms, their participations in structures of power. Faith then interprets situations and their demands as always containing this element of corruption and redemption. Situations pose to human beings occasions for idolatry and for redemption. The discernment of this dimension of the demand-response is at the very heart of a theological hermeneutic of situations.

PRACTICAL THEOLOGY AS A
HERMENEUTIC OF VOCATION

In the approach being explored here, practical theology as *theology* is one of the dimensions of the believer's reflective life and wisdom. Does this view of its primary location and reality dislocate it from education, from pedagogical undertakings, from the seminary curriculum? Such a consequence would be unfortunate since it would place the believer's (or church leader's) reflective life beyond the reach of the rigorous disciplining that ordered learning (education) at its best can effect. If this is so, then practical theology must be relocated not only in the pedagogies of clergy education but the pedagogies of church education. In other words the church is responsible to conduct an education which thematizes for the believer what it means to interpret, respond to, and live in situations.[30]

Does the notion of a practical theology for the believer as such eliminate the "practical theology" of clergy education, the pedagogies of preaching, education, and the like? The question uncovers a theme we have no time to explore, the theme of another intrinsic dimension of theological reflection. The reason this is a dimension and not an occasional response is that the life and interpretations of faith do not occur in general but in connection with special responsibilities. While this is not limited to the ordained ministry, church education in the past has so emphasized the eduational prerequisites for its ordained leadership that this dimension has virtually been restricted to clergy. The specialized leadership of the church does constitute a situation in itself, a situation that calls for theological interpretation, and whose activities (pastoral care, church administration, and so forth) call for interpretation. Here we have "practical theology" in its more traditional sense. In the framework of this analysis practical theology has a special form because it addresses, thematizes vocation as a situation. Because ministry is itself a situation, it presupposes and needs practical theology in its fundamental sense of a hermeneutic of situations, but moves beyond that to the special requirements of the vocational situation.

What would a practical theology of ministry look like? First, it would teach practical theology as a moment of theological, reflective understanding, not isolated from but connected with the total structure of theological understanding. Second, it would include some attempt to teach practical theology itself, that is, the various hermeneutical components of the interpretation of situations. Third, since church leadership is itself a situation, it would attempt a practical theology of church leadership. Fourth, it would focus on designated areas of the situations of ministry, including preaching, education, pastoral care, and so forth. It would do this *as practical theology*. That is, it would place these activities in relation to other situations so that the theology of practical theology will include the correction of parochial and isolated approaches to these activities. Finally, it would acknowledge the distinctive and peculiar character of these activities as they reflect a double reference to action. First, each one itself is an area of action, thus, for instance, worship and liturgy. Second, each activity is focused beyond itself on areas of churchly and worldly action. It is because of this twofold action referent that the theology of each activity requires practical theology, a hermeneutic that uncovers typical structures in situations of action.

In most past and present literatures it is assumed that practical theology names one of the theological "sciences." If practical theology's fundamental mode is the believer's reflective activity, is it precluded from being a science? I have argued that this basic mode does not

EDWARD FARLEY

preclude but in fact calls for pedagogical modes of practical theology. Does it also call for or permit a scholarly mode, a mode of being a "science"? In this form the question is not very clear. If we are asking whether practical theological reflection can itself take on the character of a science, the answer is negative. The question of practical theology's relation to scholarship arises not in conjunction with its fundamental mode but in conjunction with the pedagogies which may shape and discipline that mode. The question is, accordingly, does the *teaching* of practical theology, including various thematizations of the components of practical theological reflection in interrelated areas of action, require scholarly discipline? I think the answer to this question is affirmative. What this means is that particular interpretive responses to situations can have the character of self-conscious and rigorous inquiry, can appropriate sciences and the product of sciences (linguistic, social-scientific, philosophical, etc.), and the result can be integrated into or related to other such rigorous undertakings.

What are we to say about the status of the specific disciplines of practical theology which still persist in the present form from the nineteenth-century consensus? Are homiletics, liturgics, pastoral care, and the like sciences? They seem to have their scientific status as the result of the impetus toward the independence characteristic of academic fields. Hence, they lay claim to literatures, nomenclatures, methods, professional organizations; in short, the social and formal marks of disciplines of higher education. The cost of this development has been high—clericalization and severation from the basic mode of theological reflection, independence of method from other moments or dimensions of theology, isolation even from other areas of action. My inclination at present is to say that homiletics, pastoral care, and the like name valid areas of clergy education. The problem consists not so much in their existence as pedagogical areas but in their self-understanding as separate sciences. These areas of pedagogy will be more true to themselves if they rediscover how they are rooted in the basic mode of theological reflection and how their own situations should be related to other areas. In other words they need to recover themselves as practical theology. Even if their character as independent theological disciplines is diminished by this recovery, they need not lose their rigor and integrity as areas of pedagogy that make use of scholarly resources. On the contrary, the exercise of practical theological corrective and contextualization may enable new levels of rigor and reality reference.

In conclusion, I have interpreted the problem of practical theology as the problem of correcting the clericalization of the traditional view

16

without a total discreditation of all past correctives. Further, there appears to be a gulf opening up between the two major modern correctives of the traditional view, a gulf between churchly and praxis approaches. This is an unhappy choice because the one finds a way to focus theology on church and clerical life but praxis as such is not in view. The other finds a way to focus theology on praxis but a theology of church situationality and ministry seems to be absent. I have proposed that there is a dimension of theological reflection and understanding itself that is focused directly on situations and calls for a hermeneutics of situations. Situations are its context and object. This does not, however, preclude or discredit a practical theology of church and the activities of church leadership. These are situations in which the believer as (ordained) church leader takes responsible action and as such they are valid areas for the exercise of this hermeneutic. When it is so exercised, however, it should not be the traditional isolated treatment of these activities, but a placing of them in relation to other situations. The following seven theses summarize the argument.

1. Practical theology is a dimension of theological reflection and understanding and therefore is all-pervasive in the faith community and not restricted to a field of clergy education.

2. Practical theology is that dimension of theology in which reflection is directed at a living situation in which the believer or corporate entity is involved.

3. When response to and interpretation of a situation is self-consciously responsible, it can be assisted by a hermeneutic of existing in a situation. Traditional and contemporary hermeneutics have focused primarily on understanding as it is related to and facilitated by texts, with the situation secondary to that. In practical theological hermeneutics the object of interpretation is the situation itself.

4. A hermeneutic of situations will function to uncover the distinctive contents of the situation, will probe its repressed past, will explore its relation to other situations with which it is intertwined, and will also explore the "demand" of the situation through consideration of corruption and redemption.

5. The clergy activities of the traditional version of practical theology are, as situations, valid and important candidates for practical theological interpretation as are the situations of the believer and churchly communities. A practical theology of these activities and environments will correct their traditional pedagogical isolation through a special hermeneutics of these situations.

6. Practical theology like other dimensions of theology can and

should be taught both in the church at large and in schools for clergy education.

7. Practical theology as a dimension of theology and as an educational undertaking can have a rigorous character and should be supported when appropriate by the resources, tools, and disciplines of scholarship.

NOTES

1. Histories of practical theology are located in different types of works. See articles on practical theology and pastoral theology in the standard encyclopedias: the various editions of *Religion in Geschichte und Gegenwart*, the *Realencyklopädie*, the *New Schaff-Herzog Encyclopedia*, and *Sacramentum Mundi*. In addition many of the standard works of theological encyclopedia and histories of theological disciplines contain good accounts of the origin and pre-twentieth-century development of practical theology. See especially Otto Zöckler, ed., *Handbuch der theologischen Wissenschaften*, 4 vols. (Nordingen: Beck, 1883–84), 4:3–15. In English a good example is J. J. van Oosterzee, *Practical Theology* (New York: Charles Scribner's Sons, 1878), 5–17. Two interesting contemporary critical interpretations of the history, especially calling attention to the modern shift from clergy-centered practical theology, are Norbert Mette, *Theorie der Praxis* (Dusseldorf: Patmos-Verlag, 1978), parts I and II, and G. Otto's introductory essay to G. Otto, ed. *Praktisch Theologisches Handbuch* (Hamburg: Furche Verlag, 1970). Seward Hiltner has a brief history of pastoral theology in *Preface to Pastoral Theology* (Nashville and New York: Abingdon Press, 1958). See also Charles Kemp, *Physicians of the Soul: A History of Pastoral Counseling* (New York: Macmillan, 1947), and William A. Clebsch and Charles R. Jackle, *Pastoral Care in Historical Perspective* (Englewood Cliffs, N.J.: Prentice-Hall, 1964).

2. By "nineteenth-century consensus" I mean the view of practical theology as the fourth theological discipline which came to prevail in the German theological encyclopedia works and in the German monographs on practical theology. This consensus is operative in a narrowed form in North American theological seminaries from the nineteenth century to the present day.

3. Theology is understood to be a practical science as early as Duns Scotus. Widespread from the Middle Ages through the seventeenth century is the view that "theology" names a habitus or disposition of the soul. The prevailing view among Protestant Reformed and Lutheran theologians was that this habitus and its knowledge were of the practical not just theoretical kind. Theology is, accordingly, a practical knowledge having the character of wisdom since its object is God and the things of God grasped in the situation of faith and salvation.

4. This introductory insistence that "all theology is practical" is very wide-

spread. We find it in Buddeus: ... tota theologia dogmatica, intuitu finis spectata, practica est (*Isagoge Historica-Theologica* [1727], 434). And it recurs in modern discussions. Thus Tom Ogletree begins his essay with this same insistence: "Dimensions of Practical Theology" in *Practical Theology: The Emerging Field in Theology, Church, and World*, ed. Don Browning (New York: Harper & Row, 1982).

5. The broadening of practical theology to include both moral theology and activities of ministry was proposed as early as Gisbert Voetius, the seventeenth-century Reformed theologian of Holland. His work, *Selectae Disputationes Theologicae* (1648), includes a treatise on practical theology. See John W. Beardslee, ed. and trans., *Reformed Dogmatics* (New York and London: Oxford University Press, 1965), 165ff. This usage is, however, an isolated instance in the seventeenth century. It began to be more frequent in the eighteenth century. Buddeus submits moral theology and church jurisprudence as the two parts of practical theology (*Isagoge Historica-Theologica*, 610). N. H. Gundling (*Die Geschichte der Übrigen Wissenschaften* [1753]) and J. G. Walch (*Einleitung in die theologischen Wissenschaften* [1753]), two midcentury theologians in the pietist tradition, represent this transitional approach. For Gundling practical theology includes pastoral, casuistic, homiletical subjects. For Walch it includes moral theology, church jurisprudence, and pastoral theology.

6. A historical account of what led to this third and decisive stage is not possible here. In part it would be a comprehensive narrative of the origin of the four-fold encyclopedia of theological sciences. See Edward Farley's *Theologia: The Fragmentation and Unity of Theological Education* (Philadelphia: Fortress Press, 1983), chaps. 3 and 4. More specifically, two items in the background play an important role in this development. First, there had existed through many centuries of Christendom a literature written for and about church leaders, priests, ministers. After the Reformation a small but not unimportant Protestant literature of this sort emerged which included Zwingli, *Der Hirt* (1524), E. Sacerius, *Pastorale oder Hirtenbuch* (1550), and Hyperius (Andreas Gerhart), *De Theologo* (1556). These writings addressed the work and education of the Protestant minister and treated specific aspects of that work such as preaching, for instance, Melanchthon's *De Offico Concionatoris* (1535) and Keckermann's *Rheticae ecclesiasticae* (1606). This literature anticipates what later became a field of theological study, poimenics. As the Greek word indicates, the field covered the activities of the shepherd or pastor. The second item in the background was the new attention the German pietist movement gave to the work and person of the minister in the reform of theological education. Incorporated into the education of the minister were such things as instruction of children and ministry to the sick. These items do not themselves add up to a distinct field, practical theology, but they are strands of eighteenth-century German Protestantism which contribute to the third stage.

7. It is difficult to locate the actual beginning of the fourfold encyclopedia in a specific work. The earliest work I have found that clearly speaks of the areas

of study as "theological sciences," and which regards one of them as a science pertaining to the conduct of the office of pastors is J. A. Nösselt, *Anweis zur Bildung angehender Theologen* (1771). He lists homiletics, catechetics, pastoral theology, and church jurisprudence as the "applied" sciences falling within practical theology. Other authors of encyclopedia works at the end of the eighteenth century follow suit. Thus J. F. W. Thum divides theology into theoretical and practical sciences with practical or applied theology embracing homiletics, catechetics, and pastoral care (see his *Theologisch Encyklopädie und Methodologie* [1797]). W. T. Krug likewise divides theological sciences into theoretical and practical areas with practical theology covering homiletics, catechetics, and pastoral theology (see his *Versuch einer systematische Encyklopädie der Wissenschaften* [1796]).

8. The expression "pastoral theology" is anticipated by the sixteenth-century Protestant use of the image "shepherd" to indicate the church leader and minister. It is difficult to determine when this became attached to the word "theology." C. M. Pfaff entitled book 5 of his three-volume *Introduction in historiam Theologiae literarium* (1724) "Pastoral Theology." This included church jurisprudence, casuistics, catechetics, homiletics, and mystical theology. According to J. J. van Oosterzee (*Practical Theology: A Manual for Theological Students* [New York: Charles Scribner's Sons, 1878]), the earliest book entitled "Pastoral Theology" is C. T. Seidel's *Pastoral-Theologie* (1749). In the 1770s pastoral theology became officially established in the reorganization of Roman Catholic theological studies promoted by Maria Theresa as studies giving directives for pastoral practice. For a history of Roman Catholic pastoral theology see Karl Rahner, "Pastoraltheologie," in *Was ist Theologie?* ed. E. Neuhäusler and E. Gössman (Munich: Hüber, 1966).

9. For instance, Krug, *Versuch einer systematische Encyklopädie der Wissenschaften*.

10. The Roman Catholic literature has always preferred the term "pastoral theology," and only recently have Roman Catholic theologians begun to speak of practical theology. Fairly widespread in the Protestant literature is the use of "practical theology" as the comprehensive term for the fourth theological science and "pastoral theology" for one part of this, usually pastoral care or *Seelsorge*, but sometimes also including church polity. Alexander Schweizer's division of practical theology uses pastoral theology in a very narrow sense. After dividing practical theology into church government and church service (cf. Schleiermacher), he sees pastoral theology as one of three areas of church service or clerical activity, namely pastoral care (see his *Über Begriff und Eintheilung der praktischen Theologie* [Leipzig, 1836]).

11. A number of works were published on the Continent in the eighteenth century by both Protestants and Catholics on the ministry or priesthood. As such they continue a genre of writing which in Protestantism had existed since the Reformation. In the eighteenth century a few appear entitled "Pastoral Theology," anticipating the eventual incorporation of treatments of clergy activi-

ties among the theological sciences. Thus we have Seidel's *Pastoral-Theologie* and J. F. von Mosheim's *Pastoral-Theologie* (1766).

12. These five areas of study are included in virtually all of the works on theological study (encyclopedias) in the nineteenth century. There are occasional additions to the five, the most common being missions and evangelistics. A few authors retain apologetics under practical theology, the reason being that they see apologetics as part of the evangelizing activity of the church.

13. We find definitions of practical theology as the science of church activities throughout the literature. Thus, it is "the science of the guidance of ecclesiastical life" (R. König, *Versuch einer Kurzen Anleitung zum Studium der Theologie* [1830]; G. Krause, ed., *Praktische Theologie* [Darmstadt: Wissenschaftliche Buchgesellschaft, 1972], 12). Practical theology focuses on the condition of the church as it evolves out of the past into the present (Philipp K. Marheineke, "Übersichtliche Einleitung in die praktische Theologie" [1837]; see Krause, *Praktische Theologie*, 43). According to Carl Nitzsch, sometimes called the originator of practical theology as a theological discipline, it is the "science of the immediate guidance of Christian-ecclesiastical life" (see Krause, *Praktische Theologie*, 15).

14. König says it concerns the office and duties of the minister (*Versuch einer Kurzen Anleitung zum Studien der Theologie*). Alexandre Vinet describes pastoral theology (which he identifies with practical theology) as "the theory of the Gospel ministry" (*Pastoral Theology* [1824], 4:42). And Philip Schaff calls it the science and art of various functions of the Christian ministry (*Theological Propadeutic* [New York: Charles Scribner's Sons, 1893], 448).

15. Thus "church activities" do not mean something apart from the activities of the church leadership. In fact the two are regarded as virtually the same. Nitzsch's statement is fairly typical. He says that practical and pastoral theology are for the Protestant churches the same because the various kinds of immediate guidance of the church's living functions have their beginning in the office of the pastor (Krause, *Praktische Theologie*, 16). Schweizer, following Schleiermacher's distinction between church government and church service, says that the latter is primarily concerned with the activities of the clergy (Krause, *Praktische Theologie*, 36). What Gerhard Ebeling calls the modern view combines both church and clergy activities. In that view, practical theology is a "sum of disciplines involving ecclesiastical action and instruction preparing a person for the activities involved in church leadership" (Ebeling, *The Study of Theology* [Philadelphia: Fortress Press, 1978], 115).

16. There appears to be a kind of Parkinson's Law at work in the growth and maturation of a subject matter into a science. It is a law of dispersal and it is based on a kind of entelechy which attends the corporate and cognitive enterprises of academia. The law is that any cognitive undertaking that can become independent of the science that gave it birth will do so. We have in this law the story of modern theological education. The life of so-called academic disciplines is not unlike human maturation. In an initial stage the subject matter lives,

perhaps restlessly, in dependence on the parent science. An adolescent stage occurs in which it is anxious to be on its own. Finally, in adulthood, the subject moves out to live as an independent discipline. It may occasionally borrow something from its family, but will do so only when it is sure of its independence. Like most adults the fledgling theological discipline does not like to live alone. Therefore, it looks for a live-in mate, an auxiliary discipline such as rhetoric, psychology, phenomenology, linguistics, and so on. It may eventually become so dependent on this auxiliary discipline that a marriage occurs (as between pastoral care and psychology). On the other hand, the relation may be merely an affair (as theology is now having with deconstruction). The entelechy is clear in direction, namely, that of independence from the original matrix. Once the independence is achieved, the young adult procures all sorts of support to maintain its independence—annual conferences, a professional society, distinctive nomenclature, a refereed journal, sponsored research, and an independent structure in the school.

17. A few of the more important works on the minister and the ministry (pastoral theology) published in the nineteenth century in North America and England are J. H. Blunt, *Directorium Pastorale* (London, 1864); P. Fairbairn, *Pastoral Theology* (Edinburgh, 1875); James M. Hoppin, *Pastoral Theology* (1884); and Thomas Murphy, *Pastoral Theology* (1887). Two of the most influential works on the American scene were translations of Continental works: Vinet (*Pastoral Theology*) and also Oosterzee (*Practical Theology*).

18. Schaff, *Theological Propadeutic*, 448. R. F. Weidner, another American author of a theological encyclopedia, retains the standard definition of practical theology as a theory of the activities of the church, but adds that it is centrally focused on the minister since it is the minister who conducts and leads these activities (*Theological Encyclopedia and Methodology* [1898], 2:177–78).

19. A literature critical of traditional views of practical theology has been especially prominent in Germany since the 1950s when the reform of theological studies was under consideration. Accounts of the German discussion are Martin Doerne's "Zum gegenwärtigen stand der praktischen Theologie," in *Kirche-Theologie Frömmigkeit* (Berlin: Evangelische Verlagsanstalt, 1965), reissued in *Praktische Theologie*, ed. Krause, and Krause's introductory essay to that volume. The German critical literature is both Catholic and Protestant. The Catholic literature, especially stimulated by Rahner's work and carried on by Heinrich Schuster, is exemplified in the massive collection of essays on practical theology originally written for a Vienna conference on practical theology held in 1974. See F. Klostermann and R. Zerfass, eds., *Praktische Theologie Heute* (Munich: Kaiser, 1974). Many of the key Protestant essays written in Germany are collected in the Krause volume. See especially the essays by Wilhelm Jannasch ("Neue Gesamtdarstellungen der Praktischen Theologie") and G. Krause ("Probleme der Praktischen Theologie im Rahmen der Studienreform"). The American discussion appears to be more recent. Indicative of new attempts to formulate practical theology are two recent editions of

Pastoral Psychology: the fall 1980 issue collects papers read at a Princeton conference honoring Seward Hiltner; in winter 1977 Daniel L. Migliore and James N. Lapsley edited a volume which collected essays on pastoral care and practical theology by theologians of differing perspectives. See also Browning, *Practical Theology.*

20. This church-type of diagnosis and prescription for practical theology occurs in both Catholic and Protestant literatures. It may be that Continental Catholic theologians paved the way. The Catholic criticism would expand what has been called "pastoral theology" to practical theology and to a general theological science of church action. Rahner was a key figure in this approach. Highly influential was his *Plan und Aufritz eines Handbuches der Pastoraltheologie* (Freiburg, 1960). But see especially his essay, "Pastoraltheologie," in *Was ist Theologie?* ed. Neuhäusler and Gössmann. There he defines practical theology's object to be the total operation of the church as it exists in its present situation (p. 290). See also F. A. Arnold, K. Rahner, C. Schurr, L. M. Weber, *Handbuch der Pastoraltheologie, Praktische Theologie der Kirche in ihre Gegenwart,* vol. 1 (Freiburg, 1964). H. Schuster has been an important proponent of this view in Continental Roman Catholicism. See his dissertation, "Die Praktische Theologie als wissenschaftlich-theologische Lehre über den jetzt aufgegebenen Vollzug der Kirche" (Innsbruck, 1962). See especially Schuster's essay, "The Nature and Function of Pastoral Theology," in *The Pastoral Mission of the Church,* ed. K. Rahner and H. Schuster, in *Concilium,* vol. 3 (Glen Rock, N.J.: Paulist Press, 1965). A collection of essays indicative of this Continental Catholic approach is R. Zerfass and N. Greinacher, eds., *Einführung in die praktische Theologie* (Munich: Beck, 1976).

A similar church-type broadening of practical theology is also promoted by Continental Protestant theologians. Thus for Ebeling practical theology is oriented toward the event which defines the church and toward the continuation of that event in the context of the concrete reality of life (*Study of Theology,* 120–21). Wolfhart Pannenberg contends that the field of practical theology is the practice of the church in the wider context of society and the life world of Christianity (*Theology and the Philosophy of Science* [London: Darton, Longman & Todd, 1976], 423ff.). Friedrich Mildenberger also takes this approach although he is much more alert to the confusions and complexities involved. Thus he is especially concerned that theology as "science of church action" may be a description of theology as a whole. It also may sacrifice theology's "scientific" status in the university. (See his *Theorie der Theologie: Enzyklopädie als Methodenlehre* [Stuttgart: Calwer Verlag, 1972], 131–41).

There is also an American Protestant correction along the line of a return of practical theology to a church-centered undertaking. See especially the essay by Lewis Mudge, "Thinking in the Community of Faith: Toward an Ecclesial Hermeneutic," in this volume, 103–19.

21. This second and more radical type of criticism of the traditional view is working with or implying a new theological encyclopedia structure. It does not

see practical theology as simply "the fourth science," the discipline of clergy studies or even church action. Instead, practical theology is that part of theology in which theology relates directly to praxis. Clearly, this group is working with the post-Marxist view of praxis and with critical theory. The lacuna it senses in the traditional view is not just a clerical narrowing of a church-oriented science but the failure to thematize praxis as such. In Europe Gerd Otto and Norbert Mette are clear examples. For Mette the reference of practical theology is simply "Christian praxis," or Christian action in the fullest sense of that word. This includes the church's existence in its world situation, but also includes a general theory of action that entails analyses of the situation of humankind in the present (see Mette, *Theorie der Praxis*, 345ff.). Johann Metz likewise poses the question of practical theology from the viewpoint of altering the very nature of theology itself. He looks for a way to incorporate political theology and praxis into theology which at the same time does not violate or ignore the individual human being. For this reason he proffers a "practical fundamental theology" (see *Faith in History and Society: Toward a Practical Fundamental Theology* [New York: Seabury Press, 1980]). In the U.S.A. David Tracy proposes practical theology as the third subdiscipline of theology. It is clearly neither a clergy nor a church discipline but pertains to Christian praxis, to human transformation in its concrete context (see *The Analogical Imagination: Christian Theology and the Culture of Pluralism* [New York: Crossroad, 1981], 69ff., and also Tracy's essay, "The Foundations of Practical Theology," in Browning, *Practical Theology*, 61–82, and "Revisionist Practical Theology and the Meaning of the Public Discourse," *Pastoral Psychology* [Winter 1977]: 83–94).

22. The German discussion in recent decades, Catholic and Protestant, appears united in its criticism of the clericalization of practical theology. Mette's *Theorie der Praxis* contains a good description of the German literature. The Catholic critique is well summarized by Heinrich Schuster in his essay, "Pastoral Theology," *Sacramentum Mundi*, vol. 4. See also his essay, "The Nature and Function of Pastoral Theology," in *Pastoral Mission of the Church*, ed. Rahner and Schuster. A similar discontent with the clerical restriction characterizes recent North American discussions. See the essays in recent editions of *Pastoral Psychology* and in the Browning collection, *Practical Theology*.

23. It could be argued that the church and its theologies never did thematize praxis as such. The discussions from the Middle Ages through the seventeenth century concerning the practical nature of theology come close to this, however, even though they do not offer reflection on how the believer exists interpretively, responsively in a situation of praxis. The important point here is that as long as theology itself is viewed as practical, as concerning praxis, there are grounds for such a development. Once practice is isolated into a special (clergy-oriented) field, the possibility of a hermeneutic of praxis as such seems lost.

24. This analysis of the structure of theology and its study occurs in two chapters in my forthcoming book on the fragility of knowledge. The analysis

argues that theology, the reflective wisdom of the believer, is structured by distinguishable modes of interpretation; namely, interpretation of tradition, truth, action, situation, and vocation. The last three could fall together under the term "practical theology."

25. Farley, *Theologia*, chaps. 2, 7.

26. While this sort of issue does not coincide with any discrete area of study in theological education, it does have a literature. A modern classic of such literature is H. Richard Niebuhr's *Christ and Culture* (New York: Harper Torchbooks, 1956). The literature in question poses the general problem of "faith and culture," and attempts an account of what happens when human beings live in the world (culture, society, subcultures, etc.) in the mode of faith. Compare also Bernard Meland, *Faith and Culture* (New York: Oxford University Press, 1953); Emile Cailliet, *The Christian Approach to Culture* (Nashville: Abingdon Press, 1953); Nels F. S. Ferré, *Christianity and Society* (New York: Harper & Brothers, 1950); Julian Hartt, *A Christian Critique of American Culture* (New York: Harper & Row, 1967); Julian Hartt, ed., *The Critique of Modernity: Theological Reflection on Contemporary Culture* (Charlottesville: University Press of Virginia, 1986); Richard Kroner, *Culture and Faith* (Chicago: University of Chicago Press, 1951). Much of what is now called political theology and liberation theology would be part of this general enterprise. One of the significant features of the liberation theology movement is that it calls for a hermeneutics of present-day situationality.

27. For a beginning attempt to turn the concept of interpretation away from the text to action, although in this case on the model of text interpretation, see Paul Ricoeur, "The Model of Text: Meaningful Action Considered as Text," in *Hermeneutics and the Human Sciences*, ed. and trans. John B. Thompson (Cambridge: Cambridge University Press, 1981). Cf. also Charles Winquist's "practical hermeneutics." While he does not explicitly call for interpretation to address all kinds of situations, his approach could be consistent with that. The reason is that he sees ministry as something that facilitates interpretation in others, the interpretation being something which attends conversion and is sensitive to the depth dimension of occurrences (see *Practical Hermeneutics: A Revised Agenda for the Ministry* [Chico, Calif.: Scholars Press, 1980]).

28. The reader may recognize in these comments on tradition's obliviousness and forgetfulness Martin Heidegger's concept of *Destruktion* (*Being and Time* [London: SCM Press, 1962], 41ff.), Metz's "dangerous memory," Nietzsche's geneological method, and Derrida's deconstruction. While these concepts are not identical, they all refer to an "archaeological" dismantling of tradition for the purpose of exposing what that tradition hides in its very act of transmission. For a clear exposition of this dismantling see Sharon Welch, *Communities of Resistance and Solidarity: A Feminist Theology of Liberation* (Maryknoll, N.Y.: Orbis Books, 1985), chap. 3.

29. One of the problems with the criticisms and corrections of practical theology's parochialism is the generation of new parochialism. A situation is

corrected by appeal to another pressing situation. Thus the corrective takes on the character of an "ism." To limit action to the self's situation is narcissism and privatism. To correct that by appeal to political action minus the self-reference becomes heteronomy and collectivism. To correct by appeal to the church acting in and on itself becomes ecclesiasticism. To correct by sole emphasis on the clergy and its activities becomes clericalism. Perhaps "isms" are intrinsic to serious criticism, the game polemics must play. But analysis of situations in their intersections and interdependence may correct these correctives.

30. This statement assumes a conviction about church education that is anything but universal. The conviction is that church education is theological education. This view repudiates the distribution of subject matter such that theology is assigned to clergy education and something else is done by the church. If theology is in its primary mode a reflective and dialectical understanding evoked by the Christian mythos, then it is not only something which can and should attend the life of the believer as such, but its formation in the educational process should be all-pervasive in the church. This would mean that the church would offer a theological education in ways possible and appropriate to its particular environment, hence would teach all the fundamental dimensions of theological understanding: a hermeneutics of tradition, normative struggles with truth, and hermeneutics of praxis and situationality. In other words, it would teach practical theological understanding. See Edward Farley, "Can Church Education Be Theological Education?" *Theology Today* (Summer 1985).

2 Re-visioning Ministry: Postmodern Reflections

CHARLES E. WINQUIST

Ministry has been so closely allied with the institutional life of the church and the practical problems of institutional management and development that the concept of ministry has become increasingly separated from its grounding in theological understanding. Ministry needs to be conceptualized so that it attends to what is real and important at the heart of religious experience even as it attends to everyday problems in parish life. The budget, building, and governance structures are all part of parish life as are the myriad other details of administrative responsibility that can claim the center of ministerial attention and lead to a forgetfulness of human suffering, aspiration, and possibility. A self-consciousness of ministry that is vital and important is also a consciousness of world in a context of theological understanding.

Practical theology is a theological specialty grounded in theory and practice and it is needed to bring self-consciousness to ministry. Practical theology is not an appendage to ministry nor is it an appendage to foundational or systematic theology. Ministry and the theological specialties are internally related to each other in that the achievements in ministry or in any of the specialties are constitutive elements in the self-definition of the other specialties and of ministry. The theological agenda is reciprocally implicated in the ministerial agenda. A profound concept of ministry cannot be rescued from a shallow concept of theology.

PRACTICE, POLITICS, FOUNDATIONS

As noted by Rebecca Chopp in her essay in this volume, the interruption of events of massive suffering into our historical and immediate

27

consciousness is the primary challenge to contemporary theology. Political and liberation theologians think that theologies that are fixated in crises of cognitive claims concerning meaning and reality fail to address what is real and important for our time and trivialize the agenda for church and ministry. Attention can be too easily averted from the powers of horror at work in history and society if what is reflected in theological discourse is only theological discourse and not the world. Of course, simply issuing a challenge is not a resolution of the problem.

A political theology is still a species of discourse with cognitive foundations and any attendant practical theology is informed by the dominant assumptions that shape that discourse. If the assumptions shift, practical understanding and the politics of ministry also shift. Ideology critique is genealogical and foundational when it seriously criticizes the irrelevance of traditional theology. It is the shifting and shaking of foundations that makes a difference for theology and ministry.

This means that practical theology needs to be foundationally rooted if it is going to contribute to a deepening of our understanding of ministry. A theology that is rooted in what is real and important is the point of access to a ministry that has religious relevance. Although foundational theology may appear to be at the other end of a continuum from practical theology it is itself engaged in a struggle to determine the conditions that make theological thinking possible. Thus, foundational theology is at the heart of practical theology which is at the heart of ministerial self-consciousness. When the foundations of theology shift, the meaning of ministry is altered even when ministry is not self-conscious of its changing conditions. The practice of ministry is primarily a discursive activity and its particular achievements have many connections on multiple levels in the network of meanings and patterns in which it belongs. It cannot withdraw from the domain of its own discursivity and speak a private and simple language. That would be an illusory denial of the world and the attendant false consciousness would be a large step toward irrelevance.

Practical theology has to be aware of the movements in foundational theology and interpret the importance of these movements for the concept of ministry. The practice of theological thinking is not the same as the practice of ministry but, because theology focuses on understanding what is real and important in religious experience and ministry is an interpretation and implementation of the possibilities that mark this understanding, the practice of ministry cannot be constricted into a domain that is smaller than the domain of theological reflection. Interpretation can be praxis as well as theoria and the range of responsible thinking is no less in one than in the other. Foundational theology will continually challenge the artificial constriction of the voice of ministry to the boundaries of institutional church life. Clearly, what is real and important is also social and political.

The temptation to separate the concept of ministry from theology is partly a reaction to theology's sense of internal disorder and loss of meaning in a predominantly secular culture. If we are not able to affirm with Thomas Groome that "we believe in a God who intervenes in the affairs of human history to save humankind and set us free, both personally and politically,"[1] then the radical critique of economic and social oppression in liberation theologies subverts a concept of ministry that aligns itself with the textual strategies of a systematic theology that describes God's action in history. When history is a theater of oppression, a theology of God's presence is a theology of alienation. Here, ministry will sever its theological roots to maintain a practical integrity and work outside of the shadow of an alienated God. A revised and revolutionary concept of ministry can be fully articulated only in alliance with a revised and revolutionary concept of theology. It is not enough to accommodate social and political commitments to liberation within traditional understandings of theological thinking. Ideology critique in its fullest meaning as a voice of liberation requires a foundational revision of theology. To think differently about the world and ministry we need to think differently about thinking. When the tight weaves of language constituting ideological and doctrinal masks are loosened, the body of experience and the experience of the body in its suffering and joy mark the return of repressed forces and must be remarked in the textual strategies of foundational and practical theology.

There are and have been significant tensions and problems in foundational theology. Theology, in the last several decades, has radically questioned the possibilities for remaining in the domain of its own discursivity. This radical reflection has been a response to the experience of a widening separation between descriptive theological language and the world that it claimed to describe. The question that most theologians had to address was not if their statements were true but if they were meaningful. This question is no less significant for ministers. Theology questioned its own possibility. It talked less about God and more about the possibility of talking about God. Its inquiry was of a second order. This second order, theoretical inquiry, has been profoundly influenced by critical philosophical analyses that have shattered the image of language as a replication or mirror of nature. Most foundational theologians have come to acknowledge that the theological use of language is metaphorical and overdetermined in its fundamental structure. Not only is there the use of metaphorical constructions in the theological use of language; but the general use of language connects multiple and diverse patterns of physical, economic, psychological, and political forces so that determinations of meaning are multiple connections (overdetermined) that are complex and naturally ambiguous. Theology has by necessity begun to understand itself as a postcritical hermeneutic of immediate experience, textual traditions, and history.

The scope of the claim that theological discourse is fundamentally metaphorical and overdetermined has application wherever there is the theological use of language. The implications of this claim are immediately apparent for the interpretation of textual traditions but it is not only textual studies that are affected by the second-order critical thinking of foundational theology.

The metaphorical character of theological language that is a problem for interpreting a complex textual tradition is also part of the fundamental problematic for the development of a practical theology. The minister lives in a world that seeks expressions of meaning which can transcend the ordinary meanings of everyday life in their drab regularity. There are many examples in parish life of formulating rites of passage to deepen the significance or complexify the meaning of biological and social transformations. Sacraments of Baptism, confirmation, marriage, eucharistic meals, and last rites access the metaphorical potential of the theological use of language by conjoining diverse patterns of physical, psychological, and cosmological meaning. The rhythm of life from birth through aging to death is played on the stage of a symbolic theater. This intertextual referencing in the pastoral functions of ministry is paralleled in the prophetic function of ministry when historical struggles for human dignity and freedom are conjoined with themes of exile, exodus, redemption, restoration, and apocalypse. The demands on ministry and the achievements of ministry show that representation and the overdetermination of meaning are integral to the achievement of vital ministry just as they are integral to theological thinking.

RECOGNITIONS

When theology reflected itself in seeking understanding of its foundations, it came to a number of recognitions about its work of which at least two impact the concept of ministry.

The first recognition approximates a refusal. We must refuse the temptation to simplify our conception of consciousness by understanding the world of language as a mirror of reality. Literalism is an impoverishment of language and it is also a denial of our experience of language. Although it may not at first be obvious, we experience language as substitutional. For example, in the simple act of naming, substitutions are made that clearly differentiate the semantic world from the perceptual world. With few exceptions, neither written nor phonetic signs materially resemble the perceptual world. The letters d-o-g do not resemble a dog. There is in language usage a gap between what is materially present as a sign in the semantic domain and the referent of the sign which is in a domain of forces and things. This dissimilarity or gap between the semantic domain and what might be designated as the material domain of forces, feelings, and objects of the real world is a fundamental fissure that is a source of ambiguity, polyvalence, and polyvocality in language usage. The gap is a limitation and, surprisingly, a liberation of language functions. Theology is not a literal representation of nature. Theology is instead a display of signs and their dissemination in patterns of connection. This is what we mean by "meaning." Theological thinking is the making of a world of meaning.

Theology does not have to confirm the literal representation of the world. It can display new configurations of meaning that challenge structures of quotidian psychological, economic, and political life. Through parable and proclamation, ministry can fissure sedimented worlds that oppress and mask the vitality of individual and societal forces. Liberation is a work against literalism.

The second recognition that complements this insight and is particularly important for ministry is that a care for persons is implicated in the care for meaning, fantasy, and imagination. The world of meaning which is also the world of persons is a semantic achievement. Ministry knows this world in its textual dissemination. These texts can range from the sacred documents of the tradition collectively celebrated with the community to the fragmented narratives of highly personal stories spoken within the confidentiality of a counseling situation. Most of these texts will have an internal semantic complexity and be overdetermined on several levels of meaning and all of them will be fissured as they mix with and re-present the material realm of forces, feelings, and objects. The complexities of textual topography and textual energetics are so thoroughly a part of even the simplest text that no description of ministry can avoid the task of being a practical hermeneutics without a loss of vitality and significance. The relationship between power and knowledge is foundational but it is also manifested in the surface achievements of language usage although sometimes only symptomatically. The unmasking of this vital relationship is a dimension of the interpretive task.

When ministry understands that it has a responsibility in this interpretive task because its language usage is so highly overdetermined at its foundations and throughout the world of its experience, it will need to fashion tools for overinterpreting experience. That is, it will need ways to attend to the many voices implied by the metaphorical nature of speech acts and ways to attend to the extralinguistic entailments of symbols that reside in the domain of its experience. Single-level interpretation will always constitute a lack or loss of the meanings that are determined on other levels and in other patterns of connectedness. The symbol can only be a sign in one-dimensional thinking so that there would not only be a loss of meaning but also a loss of significance. Ministry cannot be at peace with a literal understanding of the world. Literalism, which is first a repression of the spirit, can easily become in its tight weave of ideology an oppression of the individual and political body.

The actual work of overinterpretation resembles single-level interpretation except that it respects the enigma of symbols and the metaphorical nature of language usage. Instead of trying to close the gaps on any linguistic surface, the gaps become points of access to new levels of interpretation. Overinterpretation is a continual deconstruction of whatever semiotic surface it is interpreting. It is both political and pastoral. It sees the power/knowledge complex in personal and political life and thereby refuses to be satisfied with a shallow understanding of existence. The respect for the enigma of the symbol in a strategy of overinterpretation is an acknowledgment and respect for the realities of power and passion and, in regimes of oppression, the hunger and political disenfranchisement of the individual and social body. Deconstruction of an oppressive surface reveals marginal hopes and a broken connection with significant meaning. Ordinariness is not accepted as normative in strategies of overinterpretation.

HERMENEUTICS

In *Practical Hermeneutics* I described the hermeneutical task of the ministry as threefold and although I would still make the threefold movement an outline of the task, I think that some of the concepts need to be understood more radically. First, ministry has to accept experience as it is given and this process of collection cannot be censored.[2] We must collect experience in its outrageousness, its wonderfulness, its meaninglessness, its meaning, its brokenness, and its wholeness. The metaphoricity and the materiality of life's texts have to be accounted for in this collection. That is, we have to guard against glossing this collection with a tightly woven interpretation that obscures the natural fissures. No cheap grace justifies forgetfulness. The primary act of collection is a care for reality as it shows itself. This gathering includes the ungifted and disenfranchised, the poor and the hungry, as well as the best and the brightest. The first movement situates the work of ministry. This is a movement of primary recognition. It cannot be too polite. It must be uncompromised by doctrinal or ideological expectations or ministry will be an empty calling into a domain of exclusion and shallow privilege. The church of exclusion and privilege risks a semantic and suburban captivity that is ignorant of the body, the body politic, and the body of Christ.

The second movement is to issue an invitation to share in a more satisfying vision of what is real and important in our experience.[3] This is the deconstructive moment in practical hermeneutics. Proclamation challenges understanding with the announcement that something new has entered our lives that cannot be adequately contained within surface interpretations of experience. This is a religious claim against one-dimensional thinking. "We care for the meaning and importance of individual life in the context of the deeper vision of reality that constitutes the significance of calling and conversion."[4] In Christian thought this challenge to the surface of interpretation is readily recognizable in the parabolic teachings of Jesus, the church's extraordinary claim that Jesus is the Christ, or in the many formulations of eschatological expectation.

The religious claim is also a political claim because it attends to the context of life. Here the multiple structures of oppression must be turned upside down so that the downsided voices of the repressed are heard as authentic voices of liberation. These reversals are not easy moves because they challenge dominant modes of thought. Not only must themes of liberation be articulated but the oppressive force of one-dimensional thinking must be deconstructed. It is at this point we can best understand the correspondence between the practice of theological thinking and a liberating political praxis.

The foremost theological claim against one-dimensional thinking is the instantiation of a radical negativity in language by entertaining the concept of God in its discursive reflection.[5] Anselm's "that than which nothing greater can be conceived," Tillich's "ultimate concern" or "what we take seriously without any reservation," and Lonergan's "unrestricted desire to know" are all examples of a radical negativity that challenge the adequacy of any semantic achievement being able to come to interpretive closure.

Ministry in its second hermeneutical movement is prophetic. It is iconoclastic and continually transgresses the surface of the text of experience. It issues the invitation to a deeper and more satisfying experience out of the violence of its reflections. It renders indeterminate the surface of experience and unravels the fabric of whatever interpretation is at hand revealing an underside to meaning which is the passageway to deeper levels of meaning.

This is a work of decentering that reaches into the margins of society and into marginal moments of psychological life. This is a moral commitment but it is in some ways an inversion of Don Browning's claim in this volume that practical theology must center itself in theological ethics. I would more readily align the moral commitment of practical theology and ministerial praxis with a poiesis of the spirit that is marginal and always liminal. I am suggesting that ethical norms and normative images of human fulfillment are at risk in a ministry of parabolic reversals. It is a denial of the closure of human possibilities that is the fundamental moral act in the second hermeneutical movement.

The third movement is a re-collection of experience that draws from tradition and history symbols and ideas that can elaborate interpretation on the deeper levels that have been opened by the deconstruction.[6] The third movement is a construction and the making of meaning. It is an imaginal thinking magnifying the context of life and even the context of our deeply personal stories. Our individual stories are implicated in the stories of God. The instantiation of a radical negativity in the telling of our stories gives a vertical access to the significance of reality that lies outside of the text and at the same time allows for the horizontal deployment and augmentation of meaning within the semantic domain. Meaning is given significance without ceasing to be meaning.

The third movement can be closely tied to the development of narrative theologies. It is here that traditional education in biblical studies, church dogmatics, and the history of religions reveals a symbolic inheritance that sets a stage for a drama of transformation. Individual and collective histories are magnified in an intertextual weave with archetypally significant stories. New possibilities can be envisioned in this enlarged context that can give a forward and downward thrust to vital ministry. In this sense the third movement is an experiment in the approximation of human fulfillment.

The three movements of practical theology and ministerial praxis are not clearly separable from each other and they never come to closure. Construction and deconstruction continually attend to each other's achievement. These movements constitute a dialectical process that is a care for what is real and what is meaningful. The process implicates our life stories into what is real and meaningful and that is surely one of the most significant tasks of ministry.

No matter what other responsibilities are accepted into a contemporary definition of ministry, ministry ceases to be itself unless it attends to the possibilities that are discerned at the heart of religious experience. Theology seeks an understanding of these possibilities and ministry is bound to theology as it implements this vision. Practical hermeneutics is a re-visioning of the ministerial agenda only in the sense that it is a visioning again of what it means to be committed to attend to what is real, meaningful, and important.

NOTES

1. Thomas H. Groome, "Theology on Our Feet: A Revisionist Pedagogy for Healing the Gap between Academia and Ecclesia," in this volume, 62.
2. Charles E. Winquist, *Practical Hermeneutics: A Revised Agenda for the Ministry* (Chico, Calif.: Scholars Press, 1980), 41.
3. Ibid., 41–42.
4. Ibid., 51.
5. Robert Scharlemann, "The Being of God When God Is Not Being God," in *Deconstruction and Theology*, ed. Thomas Altizer et al. (New York: Crossroad, 1982).
6. Winquist, *Practical Hermeneutics*, 42–43.

3 *The Practical Play of Theology*

JAMES D. WHITEHEAD

The search continues for new images and metaphors to describe and guide the practice of theology. We seek models that are at once more lively and more truthful—that better reveal us to ourselves and that energize us for our pursuit and profession. In this essay I will first outline the method of practical, corporate reflection that my colleagues and I have developed over the past decade and have published in *Method in Ministry*. In the second half of the essay, I will illustrate how the central role of the imagination in theological reflection suggests a new and forceful paradigm for doing theology.

From Peter Homans's exploration of theology as "a correlation of images" in *Theology After Freud* to David Tracy's recent *Analogical Imagination*, theologians have been busy recovering the central role of imagination in Christian living. Once considered either a passive abode in which sense perceptions were rearranged, or as a dangerous source of sexual temptations and aggressive fantasies, imagination is being recovered as also a positive, constructive source of religious faith. Faith is being recognized as the surprising ability (and so, seen as gift) to imagine or construe life in a certain fashion. A believer is precisely a person with a certain kind of imagination: one which envisions directions and purposes where the unbeliever sees only random activity or instinctual drives. The image, so popular today, of a "journey of faith" is just that—an image or construct that perceives links between disparate events and finds/establishes a coherent direction among the many surges and reversals which constitute any human life. And we are reminded that when we talk of "models and styles" of practical theology, we are speaking about our imagination. How do we envision what we are about?

36

THE IMAGINATIVE INTERPLAY
OF AUTHORITIES

In *Method in Ministry*, we have imagined the ecclesial reflection that leads to more graceful exercises of faith as the interplay of three authorities, the Christian tradition, cultural information, and personal experience. This is, following Tracy and others, a method of correlation. However, Tracy's correlation of the Christian tradition and "common human experience and language" was found to be too dense for the practical reflection of the ministers we were serving. A bipolar correlation exhibits the economy which is one of the ideals of any model; we sacrificed this economy for what seems a more practicable correlation of the different sources of information and even revelation that influence ministerial reflection. Aware of the considerable overlapping of these three poles (the American culture as influenced by the Christian tradition; the personal experience of the mature Christian as already seasoned by the images and ideals of our religious tradition), we found it educationally very useful to distinguish these three sources of information/revelation.

For those unfamiliar with *Method in Ministry*, it may be useful to recall very briefly several features of this model of reflection. Each pole is recognized as plural and ambiguous in its contribution to reflection and action. Thus the Christian tradition includes insights, images, and convictions given us from Scripture and from the two millennia of pastoral practice. Within this plurality of God's voices (or at least our hermeneutics of what we think we have heard) stands an imposing ambiguity: the tradition is divine and human. This heritage consists of the revelations we have received from God and also the misconceptions, malpractices, and perversions of this revelation of which we are both heirs and collaborators. Thus, the goal of ecclesial reflection on our tradition is always twofold, to recover and overcome. We seek to recover the gracefulness of God's involvement in our heritage, and overcome our repeated misapprehensions of these gifts. The educational aspect of this model becomes clear here: participants are compelled to clarify how different parts of the tradition (e.g., the pastoral epistles, the Old Testament, conciliar decrees) influence their own reflections and decisions. This may be seen as an effort to clarify the participants' "working canon" (to extend Tracy's felicitous phrase from *Analogical Imagination*).

The cultural pole of information in this model enjoys the same pluralism and ambiguity. The theological conviction that we brought to the design of this model is that God abides in cultural life as in individual living—in a highly ambiguous and murky fashion. From the cultural source of information come the biases and convictions that are inscribed in our historical, philosophical, and linguistic past as North Americans. We are shaped, for instance, by contemporary prejudices about sexuality and personal commitment. And we are also gifted by the insights of such cultural forces as developmental psychology and the women's movement. We are continuously being informed and deformed by the cultural forces that surround us; thus the need to clarify and purify this contribution to ministerial reflection and action.

Similarly the pole of personal experience is pluriform and ambiguous. On any practical question of our faith life (e.g., sexuality, authority, justice, celebration), we carry with us deposits of convictions and biases, ambitions and apprehensions. Since these contribute so powerfully to any reflection and decision-making process (however unconsciously), it is important to clarify these and bring them into explicit dialogue with hopes and biases that arise more directly from our religious tradition or our cultural life.

These components of reflection (the model) are moved by a certain dynamic, or method. The method, to put it most simply, is one of listening, assertion, and decision. The danger of such a method is its very simplicity; we are easily distracted from the habits, virtues, and skills that painstakingly constitute the abilities to listen thoroughly even to what frightens us, to sustain the distress and conflict likely to arise in the course of an assertive group discussion, and to generate practical, shared plans for a community's exercise of its faith.

Theology as a practical habitus stands or falls when we arrive at the question of method over against model. A model of theological reflection may exhibit splendid economy or exquisite detail; the question that then arises, at least for the practical theologian, is: how does it work? (Or, as we will explore later, how is it played?) What is the dynamic and what are the skills/virtues necessary to lead us through its stages toward effective, graceful action? What appears in blueprint as a compelling design often turns out to be, *in ambulando*, a mine field. Our method assigns much attention to the listening phase, trying to clarify as much as possible: what *is* the experience or question? Every minister has felt the disaster of proceeding too quickly in an ecclesial reflection, assuming that a common vocabulary meant shared feelings and convictions. In the assertion phase of our method we try to structure honest confrontation, with the expectation of some confusion within both the individual and the group. We suggest that assertiveness is a Christian virtue that leads us into a special intimacy not only with each other, but with our religious tradition. A surprising learning that occurred in the seminars where this method was designed was the ministers' sense of distance from and tentativeness toward their religious heritage. The virtue of this stage developed as the participants found themselves more confident in challenging the tradition and acknowledging the contradictions (in more usual Christian parlance, paradoxes) within the tradition itself.

The conviction of this method was that if sufficient and sufficiently virtuous assertion occurs, insights and possible resolutions will begin to present themselves. On a complex pastoral question no ready-made answer is lying in wait in the tradition or in our experience. But in a truly assertive dialogue a solution—tentative, debatable, reversible—will be generated. This is more than a confidence in educational technique; it is a theological conviction about how the Spirit generates a historical tradition. The inner dynamic of this third stage—the shared planning and decision making that move a group's insights toward performable action—is discussed in chapter 7 of *Method in Ministry.*

Since no method of pastoral reflection enjoys a universal applicability, it may also help to recall the specific groups and pastoral questions with which this model is most concerned. The model was developed during the mid-1970s to assist professional ministers to clarify their own styles of reflection and decision making. Our special interest was the maturing Christian ministers who were both experienced and steeped in the Christian tradition, but were not especially confident about the means and motives for relying on their experience and/or heritage. Our goal in developing the method was to promote both competence and confidence in the exercise of Christian ministry.

This reflective model was also designed for group use. Convinced that theological reflection can be neither theoretical nor private, we tried to develop a corporate style of reflection. Thus we attempted to clarify not only the conceptual relationships of a theological model of reflection, but also its practical components—including the expectable anxieties and conflicts that are a part of any group process. The specific groups that we addressed were leadership teams within particular congregations and ecumenical study groups of ministers.

Theological reflection in ministry always entails an "imaginative interplay of authorities." A method of critical correlation (see Tracy's essay, pp. 139–40) is always a question of *interplay:* this becomes more apparent, perhaps, when there are three players. In this interplay we test the leeway among our religious heritage, our cultural life, and our own experience about some question of concern to the community. Pushing and shoving should be expected here, as in any practical interplay. This aspect of theological reflection, with both its danger and delight, will be elaborated in the next section of this essay.

This is an interplay of *authorities*. Each pole of information/revelation has a certain different force in our lives. Various denominations and communities attribute differing weights to their religious heritage and their own experience on any question of their faith life. The model assumes both the presence and the difference of these authorities. It argues that effective and enjoyable interplay (that is, graceful correlation) happens only if these authorities really engage one another. If the tradition overwhelms an individual's personal experience with its interpretation (e.g., of the person's homosexuality), no correlation or interplay occurs; likewise, if one's experience is so absorbing that it ignores or rejects any information from the religious tradition, no exchange happens. A critical correlation is easily and often aborted by a severe imbalance of these authorities. An imbalance always prevails (for we weight our religious tradition, culture, and experience differently), but this must remain within limits for the interplay, the enlivening engagement and correlation, to occur. Critical correlation happens only as we gain some explicit awareness of what kind of, and how much, authority each pole contributes to any practical question of our Christian life.

The third feature of note here, after those of interplay and authority, is imagination. As we developed this model of reflection in ministry we were persuaded of the importance of imagination as an alternate source of religious information. We were convinced (who is not?) that our deepest convictions and biases abide not in clear and available intellectual concepts, but in the images and fantasies often hidden somewhere within us. How to gain access to these? A common strategy employed in our reflective method was a brief, guided fantasy around some question of religious value. For example, with professional ministers and educators we would begin a workshop on method in ministry with an imaginative exercise around the notion of "tradition." This image carries for each of us different connotations—of safety, of resentment, of weightiness. These feelings about our religious tradition are easily lost beneath "cool" cognitive definitions learned in theology. This educational strategy appeals to the imagination for this alternative and more important information. Workshop participants are often startled by the feelings that are triggered by their own imaginings about "tradition." Intriguingly, theological educators who commonly exhibit intellectual impatience and even truculence about their religious tradition, often find emerging from their imaginations much friendlier feelings. As every practitioner knows, surprise is often a sign that the imagination is really engaged and that we are not merely routing our ideas through the imagination to cloak them with "useful symbols."

As this method of ministerial reflection was critiqued and fine-tuned by a variety of groups over the past ten years, we have become aware that imagination is involved here in ways more profound than we had suspected. As we better understand the model as an interplay of three authorities, we also begin to recognize, helped by Richard Sennett's discussions in *Authority*, how authority is itself an exercise of the social imagination. Authority is not only an interpretation of power, but an interpretation executed by the social imagination. We recognize power in individuals and in society and in this recognition we both acknowledge and authorize this power. This interpretation of where power is, how strong it is, and what it is for, is, in an important way, a constructive and collective exercise of the imagination. Without further defending this interpretation of interpretation, we may say that it has persuaded us to see (imagine) our model somewhat differently. Once this contribution of imagination to authority was joined to the earlier notion of correlation as interplay, one begins to appreciate the imaginative interplay which characterizes both a vital group reflection and a maturing individual. A paradigm, both for practical theology and for Christian maturing, begins to emerge.

THE PLAY OF PRACTICAL THEOLOGY

When we ask about "the fundamental metaphors that guide practical theology," we are inquiring about the master images by which we describe and authorize our activity. The specific activity in this context is a corporate reflection on some significant question for Christian life, a reflection which intends to move through clarification and purification toward some practical, graceful action. When we engage in such activity, whether with a group of ministerial students or a parish council, what are we doing?

Blown by the winds of recent reading and my own imagination, I would suggest that what we are doing is playing. The paradigm of play has been gaining increasing attention and favor in philosophy, psychology, and theology as we better recognize the role of imagination in interpretation and the play involved in any correlation. Theologian John Dominic Crossan, in *Cliffs of Fall*, suggests that play is more than a metaphor; it is, in fact, a "metaphor of metaphors" (p. 67), a comprehensive image of human living. Literary critic Jacques Ehrmann, in

"Homo Ludens Revisited," summarizes the radical nature of the paradigm for deconstructionists: "The chief characteristic of reality is that it is played" (p. 56).

French philosopher Jacques Derrida and his cohorts deconstruct Johann Huizinga's classic approach to play in *Homo Ludens* by refusing the dichotomy between reality and play, and between serious work and frivolous play. In so doing, they also reject—and this will be important for practical theology—the distinction between theory and practice. This approach also denies that play is essentially mimetic or imitative. Buoyed by contemporary hermeneutical currents, they assert the inventive aspect of interpretation—interpretation as the symbolic construction of meaning, the essential activity of human life. In interpretation we do not merely find already existing patterns in life, we invent them. (Derrida might insist that we do not trace out preexistent patterns, but from traces we conjecture and play out new meanings.) The play of interpretation is thus understood as neither frivolous (opposed to work) nor mimetic (opposed to reality). Instead, it is inventive and comprehensive; it is constitutive of life in the deepest sense. It is what we do and how we do our life.

The paradigm of play is dramatically ambitious: every paradigm is by nature ambitious, and the drama of this paradigm is accentuated by the verbal tics and eccentricities of the deconstructionists. My reading of Erik Erikson in *Toys and Reasons* and the British psychologist D. W. Winnicott in *Playing and Reality* allows a considerable taming of the deconstructionist hyperbole about this paradigm and brings it more directly into touch with methods of practical theology. Specifically, Erikson exploits play as "testing the leeway" in a manner that resonates with the theological exercise of correlation: both in personal maturing and ecclesial reflection, we test the leeway, the "limited mobility" that pertains between our religious tradition and our own experience. Winnicott's discussion of the child's first testing of the space between self and other, between dependence and independence, adds further sophistication to this aspect of the paradigm. Erikson also fruitfully expands the suggestion in Crossan that play involves us in "disciplined failure" (p. 77). Such an incorporation of failure, extending even to a theology of error, is crucial both to group reflection and to personal religious growth. In a variety of ways, then, play suggests itself as a paradigm of human living that has special relevance to practical, ecclesial reflection. I would like to trace this relevance, beginning at the beginning—that is, with connections between methodological notions of play and theologies of creation.

The Practical Play of Theology

Paradigms of Creation

In one of our imaginations we Christians have envisioned creation as something we *inhabit*. Creation is acknowledged here as God's accomplished production. We find ourselves within a finished creation. In such a stable environment the challenge is to understand and obey the rules (the natural law) which govern the creatures of this world. In such a picture of reality we expect to find little "play" or leeway. Such play would infer a wobbly creation, a faulty design—an insult to its crafter. In such a creation our most creative acts are re-creative, re-productive; we re-do in mimesis what has been fully and perfectly modeled for us in the original creation. This vision of life imparts a sacred privilege to origins and will likely elicit nostalgia as we seek to emulate God's original plans for us. Adam and Eve's naming of the animals, a playful interpretation left to them in an unfinished creation, hints at this model's insufficiency.

Creation has also been envisioned by Christians as something to be *worked*. This industrial metaphor grows out of a specific interpretation of the original creation in a six-day (work) week. There is more room for human creativity in this model of creation since we are co-creators, taking up where God left off (after a rest day on the Sabbath). How fully accomplished creation was during that first fateful week is debatable; thus some play appears between our work and God's. But the chief characteristic of this paradigm may be its seriousness. A sober model, this paradigm has had great influence in the industrial West. It combines creativity with a lack of playfulness (the mis-imagination of adult maturity?). Implications of such a purposeful paradigm are that creation (and our creative works) is not for its own sake but for something else (e.g., heaven), and that it need not involve delight or pleasure.

A third paradigm of creation envisions reality as something being *played*. The chief characteristics of this model are the incompletion of reality, waiting to be further imagined and played, and the delight and risk of such ongoing invention.

Although the Crossan/Derrida interpretation of this paradigm has some novel features, the imagination of creation as play is an ancient one. "All the world's a stage" is a cherished vision of reality, but one which we have most often interpreted as an invitation to play out already fully scripted roles. The delight and inventiveness of play in this traditional interpretation (even an explicit script leaves some room or play for different intonations and gestures) is that of mimesis, rather than any radical creativity. The eternal author and temporal performers are sharply and clearly distinguished.

Plato would combine the image of play with a conviction about a fully accomplished reality: "All of us, then, men and women alike, must fall in with our role and spend life making our play [*paidiàs*] as perfect as possible" (*Laws* 7, 803c). The clues to Plato's deepest conviction about reality lie, of course, in the words "fall in with" and "as perfect as possible." Human life is here understood as role-playing a part already perfectly scripted in the ideal of each vocation. This interpretation of reality as mimesis is reinforced by Plato in the sentence which precedes the above: "Humans . . . have been constructed as a plaything [*paignion*] of god and this is, in fact, the finest thing about them." Here creation (for the Platonic Christian) is interpreted as God's play, with humans being passive, fully fated objects in this divine delight.

Crossan and Derrida twist the paradigm of reality/creation as play in a different direction. For them play is seized in its most inventive aspect. In play we imagine reality, and our place in it, anew. We more than imitate or reproduce; we invent. In the continuing play of creation we introduce new motifs—whether these be about nuclear warfare, homosexual holiness, or women priests. If these are variations on old motifs (ancient questions of a just war, sexuality, and community leadership), they are also new. It is precisely in the leeway between the old and the new, the traditional and contemporary experience, that we play our lives. And in this interpretive play we make our lives: we *identify* ourselves. As this is true for personal development, it is the case for ecclesial reflection. The correlation we find among our tradition, our culture, and our personal experience is a more-than-mimetic play; in such interpretations we imagine the next stage of the Christian tradition. We write a chapter never before existing in this literary classic.

Another aspect of play stressed by Crossan and Derrida is its universality and ubiquity. We play our lives not just in movements of diversion and recreation; play is not merely a "time out." And we play our lives not just in reworking unresolved problems (a therapeutic model of play); play is not simply remedial, not "over time." We play our lives everywhere and all the time. It is what we do. I will examine other facets of play that illustrate its relationship to practical theology after first recalling some of the obstacles that stand like scandals against this paradigm.

Provocative with Pitfalls

As positively provocative and heuristic as this paradigm is, it also carries with it numerous pitfalls. We carry with us several culturally rooted biases about play. The praxis of play requires an unencumbering of ourselves from these theories.

As one might expect, these biases are inscribed in our language. One such bias is that play is childish. The Greek word for "play," seen in the quote from Plato, is *paidià*, the word for children is *paidiá*, different only in accent. More than linguistically, we have emphasized childhood as the proper domain of play. Whether this is the free play of responsibility-less childhood, or the earnest play of a child practicing for life (as, for example, in parts of Piaget and Bettelheim), children and play seem made for one another. An implication of such a nexus is that adults are expected to set aside play. Artists and athletes are, of course, exceptions: these pretenders and "adults playing a child's game" distract us and console us (and forgive us?) during the serious exercise of our adult responsibilities.

Some of the therapeutic interpretations of play alluded to above may also be a fruit of our limiting of play to childhood. A remedial view of play interprets such activity as an effort to rework problems left unresolved from an earlier period of life. In free association, role-playing, and other playful exercises we return to these questions, seeking resolutions and healing.

Ernst Kris's wonderful phrase "regression in the service of ego" may be recalled in this context. We often interpret adult play (for example, baby talk between lovers) as a playful regression. The suggestion may be that we play *by* returning to childhood, the true home of play. Such approaches to play exhibit a reductionism that is at least at odds with Crossan's, Derrida's, and my interpretation of play. One might argue that forging such an exclusive link between the child and play tends not only to infantilize play, but contributes to an idolatry of infancy. If human maturing is an *ongoing* interplay of attachment/separation and dependence/independence, it is a critical correlation in which childhood functions as neither unique nor privileged playground. An idolatry of childhood deprives adult life of its integrity, reducing it instead to the function of playground for endless remedial games of hide and seek. Perhaps the baby talk between many lovers, despite its immediate appearance, is not regressive (even taking "regressive" in its most conscious, intentional senses), but another mode of the adult play of intimacy. By refusing dichotomies of child/adult and play/serious, we may rediscover modes of healthy adult play that make more attractive to us this emerging paradigm of human living and ecclesial reflection.

A second bias about play is inscribed in the other language that lies at the root of Western culture. The Latin word for "play," *ludere*, has given us such words as "ludicrous" and "illusory." Such words argue the frivolous and insubstantial nature of human play. Our language trains us daily to understand play as inconsequential. "He didn't mean it; he was just playing around." When we speak about playing a role we most often mean stepping out of reality in order to impersonate, to be something unreal.

If play is unreal, it is ultimately frivolous and nonserious. This frivolous character of play may take us in the direction of illusion and deceit; it may also lead us into sin. A famous passage in our Scriptures suggests connections between play, immorality, and even idolatry. The Israelites, unfaithful to Yahweh in Moses' absence, build a golden calf; then, "the people sat down to eat and drink, and rose up to play" (Exod. 32:6). Saint Paul quotes this passage (the only use of the verb *paízein* in the New Testament) in warning the community in Corinth to abstain from sexual immorality (1 Cor. 10:7). In both texts the "rising up to play" is a sojourn not to the tennis court or the video arcade, but to an old-fashioned debauch. Play is not only childish and unreal; it is often immoral.

With such biases, cultural and religious, surrounding play, can it be rescued? Where might we find the authorization to imagine the power of play in another light? One clue is found in chapter 8 of the Book of Proverbs. This book, borrowing heavily from Israel's neighbors, provides a strikingly non-Israelite story of creation. Wisdom or Sophia, the feminine form of God, speaks:

> I was by his side, a master crafter,
> delighting him day after day,
> ever at play in his presence,
> at play everywhere in his world,
> delighting to be with the children of humanity.
> (vv. 30–31, Jerusalem Bible)

Innumerable questions, linguistic and theological, surround this text. Who is this "Sophia," companion and player with the Creator? Hebrew texts differ, some suggesting "child," others "master crafter." (See the *Jerome Biblical Commentary* 29:23; p. 500). The choice of "child" settles a number of questions: the Creator's play is with a child, not with an adult who could be construed as a consort. But apart from the non-Jewish suggestion of a female player in the creation (more appealing today than in recent millennia), the passage asserts connections among creation, play, and delight. Creation here is neither the serious production of an industrious God, nor the solitary play of a bachelor Creator. Rather it is in companionship and with delight that creation is first played.

THE LEAP OF PRACTICAL THEOLOGY

Play, as a paradigm both of reality and of doing practical theology, meets its first challenge in escaping the cultural biases which beset it. It encounters its second challenge in becoming more than a rhetorical flourish, in taking on specific detail and force which rescue it from the realm of pious and pastoral jargon. Let me suggest one path to such a "toughening" of play.

Erik Erikson, in *Toys and Reasons*, takes up Plato's suggestion that play originates in the random leap of the child (*Laws* 2, 672c). Erikson points to three distinct elements in such gratuitous, energetic bounds. The child leaps out of delight. For no good purpose (such as later learned ambitions of winning prizes or making money), the child simply leaps. Performed out of delight, the leap is for its own sake.

Second, such a leap is a move against gravity. The child, in Erikson's phrase, "tests the leeway," challenging the gravity and givenness of life. If play is, in part, delight, it is also assertion and contest.

Third, to leap is to fall; to launch oneself upward is also to come back down to earth. Following Erikson in interpreting play as consisting in these elements of a leap, we may test the adequacy of the play paradigm in the context of practical theology.

We are understanding practical theology as that process by which Christians reflect on some significant question of life and through clarification and purification move toward some graceful action. Such reflection happens individually, of course, in personal exercises of discernment and conscience. Here we are especially interested in its communal exercise, whether that be a reflection and action process pursued by a group of pastoral theologians, the ministerial team of a parish, or the larger congregation itself. What insight can we gain by examining the corporate reflection process of Christians as a religious leap of play?

Play as Delight

The first of the three elements of a playful leap may be the most difficult to link to practical theology. A leap is, in the present context, a purposeless exercise. It is an activity of delight undertaken for its own sake. How distant this seems from most of our efforts of communal reflection and action. Yet it may be useful to examine the leap of reflection more closely.

JAMES D. WHITEHEAD

In an effort of reflection and decision we do, like the child, leave the status quo. We leap without knowing exactly where we will come down—at least in a genuine reflection. To experience our efforts of collective reflection as delightful and for their own sake, we need to see them as the *stuff* of our Christian life, rather than simply as tools for achieving goals. Often we tell ourselves: if we can just resolve this debate about nuclear warfare, then we can get back to our usual life and duties; if we could just settle the questions and emotions evoked by this gay couple wanting to be more thoroughly included in the community, then we could get on with life. The paradigm of play—and play as an endless number of invigorating, exhausting leaps—reminds us that such challenging exercises of reflection and decision *are* our Christian life. Doing practical theology is neither an emergency maneuver nor a temporary burden in Christian life; it *is* our life, how we do, who we are. It is in such activities that we identify ourselves and imagine our religious tradition's future. It may become more of a delight as we learn to savor the leaping itself and become more comfortable with and skilled at the accompanying falls.

If the delight aspect of our theological leap is challenging, so is the leap being for its own sake. Our Christian heritage has a deep-running and powerful tradition about our actions being for something else: life on this earth is *for* heaven; sexual intercourse is *for* children; acts of charity are performed *for* the purpose of saving souls. As we examine the theories that underpin and undercut our practice of faith, we become more aware of the "awful purposefulness" of much Christian behavior. Here, perhaps, our liturgies may minister to us. Liturgy, we believe, is a corporate exercise of worship that is, ultimately, for its own sake. Huizinga recalls Romano Guardini's definition of liturgy as "Zwecklos aber doch sinnvoll—pointless, but full of significance" (p. 19). Frequently Christian purposefulness has turned even the play of liturgy to other ends—whether filling Sunday coffers or saving souls. And yet we recognize that the liturgy is, as celebration, for its own sake. In gratitude, reconciliation, and mourning, we celebrate the presence and power of God. We know that such celebrations effect community, but this comes as a grace of the liturgy rather than its goal.

To stress our corporate reflections as playful—exercises of delight and for their own sake—may drive us to despair. Or it may encourage us to get better at such play. If these efforts of reflection are seen not as stopgap measures to be gotten through, but as the very exercise of our faith, as how Christian life continues to be interpreted, created, and played, then we may gain more energy and wit to improve our play. Reimagining how and why we interact can be the beginning of a more delightful and virtuous interplay in a community.

Finally, and most practically, we bring the paradigm of playful leaps into touch with our own vocations as practical theologians by asking this question: where, in my efforts of communal reflection (of practical theology), do I experience delight? Where is my own career, in this regard, more than a burden or a duty? Where does the delight of these difficult, often wounding efforts remind me that practical theology is itself a celebration, something worth doing for its own sake?

Testing the Leeway

The second element of our playful leap is more obviously a part of practical theology: in leaping we test the limits and explore the limited mobility of our Christian lives. If the child's leap is purposeless, it does have an inner economy: to find how high, how often it can leap. Erikson finds in this aspect of the leap a model for human maturing. We always find ourselves in a context of limited mobility. Gravity restricts our leap, but not totally. The choices that craft our identity, life style, and career all occur within the limits of our personal abilities, our race and gender, and our economic environment. It is precisely in the interplay of possibility and limits that we play out our lives. With no sense of limit (most dramatically concretized in adult commitments of love and work) our lives bounce irresponsibly along. With no sense of mobility—of possibility, of change, of newness—our lives grow stagnant, losing their flexibility and play.

Practical theology happens in the interplay between the Christian tradition and contemporary experience, between theory and practice, between law and compassion. The critical correlation of theology, from Tillich to Ogden to Tracy, operates in this flexible interplay. The central questions facing practical theology today contest the leeway between our religious inheritance and the demands of contemporary life. Will our theories of a just war flex enough to contain or deny nuclear war? Is there enough flexibility in Christian understandings of human sexuality to respond to the hopes of homosexual Christians? What leeway is there in the historical Catholic vision of priesthood that allows for an inclusion of women in this form of official ministry? In each instance we, as practical theologians, are testing the limited mobility that prevails between our heritage and present-day life. When we judge there to be no leeway in the tradition ("Christianity is hopelessly out of date"), we tend to leave the church. And we may carry with us a theology of creation that denies leeway: such flexibility may be judged an insult to the Creator, an imperfection that cannot be admitted. Instead of envisioning creation as an ongoing interpretation of who we are, we may elect a fundamentalistic view of a finished creation into which contemporary experience must obediently fit.

The assertion and contesting implied in this element of play reminds us it is not a simple delight. But if we are persuaded that creation is still being played and that our group reflections and community planning are parts of that play, we may be encouraged to get better at playing. Only by playing more gracefully will we recover its delight. Some delight returns as we recall that these "contests" between tradition and experience are affairs of intimacy. We engage our religious tradition when we wrestle Jacoblike with some part of Scripture or our denominational history.

We are embracing something that we love, even if at times this is a complex love/hate relationship. Such encounters, as exercises of intimacy, are meant to be exhausting and invigorating.

Roger Caillois, in *Man, Play and Games,* explores the aspect of risk in a way that illumines this invigorating part of play. In the risk and chance of play we commit ourselves to something that we cannot fully control. Caillois's name for this aspect of play is *alea,* the dice of the gambler. This name may evoke for the classics-educated theologian not visions of Las Vegas but rather Julius Caesar at the Rubicon saying "alea iacta est." In turn, this memory may describe the commitment of the pastor initiating a reflective process in the parish: "We have committed ourselves to something we cannot control. God help us!" In this discussion Caillois combines the leap of play and its commitment to test the leeway without knowing the outcome. He also adumbrates the third element of such playful leaps—failure.

Falling

The third aspect of the leap of faith and of practical theology is the most poignant and painful part of play: in leaping we must be prepared to fall. The child learns that leaping includes falling; to fall is not a disastrous, disgracing facet of play, but an integral part of the exercise. In each leap, childlike or theological, we risk falling and failure. Both the jumping child and the reflective Christian community are challenged to incorporate falling into their play. How do we learn to fall gracefully?

The challenge here concerns a theology of failure. And again it might be instructive to revisit parts of our religious tradition that imperil such a theology. In a finished creation, as we have seen, there is little room for error; movement tends to appear as infidelity and sin. A strain of perfectionism in Christian spirituality has contributed mightily to a crippling of play: maturity in such a spirituality is translated as *teleios, perfectus,* finished. No leeway survives, no space or playground in which to leap and test and fall.

There does survive, however, within our religious heritage a few hints or clues to a theology of failure. In our Easter liturgy we recall the original Fall as a *felix culpa.* What could this mean? How can a fault, a failure of such tragic proportions, be construed as happy? Might this suggest, in the paradigm being explored here, that the Fall was a part, an integral part of creation? What if creation is imagined as God's leap of delight? What if in creation God tests the leeway between God and non-God, pushing the limit until something non-God breaks off, existing separately now as creature? Then Adam and Eve's fall can be imagined as a subsequent but necessary part of that divine play—as creation coming down to earth.

Apart from such extravagancies, the Christian confession of *felix culpa* asserts that the Fall had a profound benefit: it brought the Son of God into human life. The Fall was not simply a failure, for it was fruitful. It was graceful in an ironic way, perhaps even integral to some larger design.

And again, as practical theologians like to do, we can push these reflections to a more immediate, practical focus. At both the personal and ecclesial levels we experience failure as an integral part of religious maturing. By midlife we gain the perspective (at least if we are graced enough) to see the important role of the failures of our own loving and working. Our life is scarred by certain fallings; but in the graceful light of retrospection these are not all incidental or shameful. Some of these wounds have contributed in strange but tangible ways to who we now are. They seem integral to our lives: we would not be who we are (a vocational insight) without these identifying marks.

Our own maturing almost seems to demand certain "falls from grace." Some of these falls have been personal, sinful fallings, and others seem to be more developmental losses—such as the letting go of adolescent dreams of achievement and narrow expectations of God and others. Such "de-illusionments" (in Daniel Levinson's vocabulary) are happy failures, fallings necessary for our growth.

These developmental losses occur also in an ecclesial context. The first leapings of our childlike faith include for many of us visions of a perfect church, of an all-satisfying religious heritage. As we grow we are often felled by the failures, narrowness, and even sinfulness of our own religious tradition. These developmental fallings parallel our learning that our parents are not perfect. Our religious maturing demands that our parents and our church fail us in this way, so that we may enter into an adult relationship with them. The fruit of this maturing is a tolerance for error and failure, a virtue crucial for effective reflection and decision making in a community.

The paradigm of play as leap urges a healthy view of falling. It suggests that a mature player is not one who never errs, but one who has learned how to fall gracefully. An example would be the acrobat or gymnast (images not too distant from the career of the practical theologian or minister) who must learn to fall well. Even when such persons come down "wrong" (turning an ankle, landing on their head, etc.), they learn to bounce up with a flourish and smile—as though the fall were part of the act (as, in our larger sense, it is).

A growing comfort with failure makes us more graceful players. Psychologist George Vaillant, in his *Adaptation to Life*, summarizes connections between play, failure, and psychological maturity:

> It is hard to separate capacity to trust from capacity to play, for play is dangerous until we can trust both ourselves and our opponents to harness rage. In play, we must trust enough and love enough to risk losing without despair, to bear winning without guilt, and to laugh at error without mockery. (P. 309)

The trust that becomes the environment of mature play develops only as we learn to tame losing and error.

The importance of failure has a special significance in practical theology because this part of the theological enterprise is committed to practical decision making. An ungraceful gain for theology, as it moved from its status as habitus to faculty, was that it would forestall and avoid practical decisions—and the embarrassing errors necessarily concomitant to such practical activities. Academic theology today can still avoid many falls by refusing to play in the practical arena. Practical theology does not enjoy that privilege. As such it has no choice except to learn to fall as gracefully as possible. And in its commitment to the maturing of faith communities through group reflection, practical theology can help groups of believers learn to fail well. In the contact sport of a community reflection, we must expect to fail and, at times, be wounded. For ourselves and our communities we demythologize failure and falling when we re-imagine it as an integral and unavoidable part of the play of our vocations.

Practicing theology is hard work and serious business. But it is much more than that: it is our play with God's creation. In the corporate reflection that shapes and defends our life of shared faith, we not only hold onto past truths; we re-imagine them. And we test the leeway between gospel and experience, between our high ideals and a doable life. In the midst of this invigorating play, we fall again and again—not such an unlikely fate in a religious tradition developed under the shadow of a cross. Doing the theology of our daily lives, we play out a drama that is both ancient and novel: it has been done before, but never in quite this way.

The paradigm of play, celebrated in such diverse players as Crossan, Erikson, and Winnicott, encourages us to re-imagine the seriousness and delight of what we are about. If we can overleap our inherited biases about play, we may employ this metaphor to clarify and enliven the practice of theology.

BIBLIOGRAPHY: PLAY, IMAGINATION, AND PRACTICING THEOLOGY

Caillois, Roger. *Man, Play, and Games.* Translated by Meyer Barash. New York: Shocken Books, 1979.

Crossan, John Dominic. *Cliffs of Fall: Paradox and Polyvalence in the Parables of Jesus.* New York: Seabury Press, 1980. In chap. 3 of this collection of essays on parables and metaphors, Crossan suggests play as the metaphor of metaphors.

Derrida, Jacques. "Structure, Sign and Play in the Discourse of the Human Sciences." In *Writing and Difference,* trans. Alan Bass, 278–93. Chicago: University of Chicago Press, 1978.

Ehrmann, Jacques. "Homo Ludens Revisited." *Yale French Studies* 41 (1968): 31–57.

Erikson, Erik. *Toys and Reasons: Stages in the Ritualization of Experience.* New York: W. W. Norton, 1977.

Homans, Peter. *Theology After Freud: An Interpretive Inquiry.* New York: Irvington, 1970.

Huizinga, Johann. *Homo Ludens: A Study of the Play Element in Culture.* Boston: Beacon Press, 1955. First published in 1944, Huizinga's analysis of play has become the starting point for all recent reflections.

Levinson, Daniel. *The Seasons of a Man's Life.* New York: Alfred A. Knopf, 1978.

Sennett, Richard. *Authority.* New York: Random House, 1981.

Tracy, David. *The Analogical Imagination: Christian Theology and the Culture of Pluralism.* New York: Crossroad, 1981.

Vaillant, George. *Adaptation to Life.* Boston: Little, Brown, 1977.

Whitehead, James D., and Evelyn Eaton Whitehead. *Method in Ministry:*

JAMES D. WHITEHEAD

Theological Reflection and Christian Ministry. San Francisco: Harper & Row, 1981.

————. "The Religious Imagination." *Liturgy* 5, no. 1 (Summer 1985): 54–59.

————. "The Virtue of Imagination." Chap. 7 in *Seasons of Strength: New Visions of Adult Christian Maturing.* New York: Doubleday, 1986.

Winnicott, D. W. *Playing and Reality.* New York: Basic Books, 1971.

4 Theology on Our Feet: A Revisionist Pedagogy for Healing the Gap between Academia and Ecclesia

THOMAS H. GROOME

A WIDENING GAP?

There is a profound problem with how theology is typically taught, and if theology is ever to be "practical" it will have to be taught differently. That is the basic thesis of this essay. My way into this issue will be through the existential fact of the widening gap between academia (university, seminary, or wherever theology is taught) and ecclesia. Instead of a mutually supportive and dialectical unity between academia and ecclesia, there is a dichotomous gap that seems to be growing even wider. The growing gap has the impact of making theology even less "practical" than it has ever been. That loss of "practicality" has many expressions but it is experienced especially by people being prepared for ministry through the traditional mode of theological education who find themselves largely unprepared to *do* theology in the ecclesia.

At first glance the solution would seem to be obvious—provide stronger academic training for our pastoral ministers in theology and scripture, deepen their pastoral skills in preaching, teaching, counseling, and so on, and then they will be effective mediators between the research of the scholars and the faith life of the people. Would that the solution could be so simple! I contend that such a solution betrays a "from theory-to-practice" mind-set that is itself part of the problem. Speaking from my own experience of the local church as a Roman Catholic, I submit that one (but only one) litmus test for the width of the gap between academia and ecclesia is the typical Sunday sermon. Only in rare instances does one hear a sermon that reflects the contemporary state of theological consciousness or biblical research for the pastoral context. An account of a recent Sunday experience may help to indicate my point.

THOMAS H. GROOME

The celebrant was a young, newly ordained priest. I know the seminary in which he had been trained to be a very fine one "academically." That he had read widely in church history, contemporary theology, and critical biblical scholarship, I had no doubt. I waited with anticipation for a fine sermon. I was thoroughly disappointed. The sermon would be charitably described as a collection of pious platitudes that bore no relation to the struggles, joys, and life realities of the congregation.

A later analysis of the experience led me to conclude that the young man may have "known about theology" but he did not know "how *to do* theology" in the social context in which he found himself. He may have learned what the scholars think, but he had not learned how to think like a theologian in a pastoral context. The young man had been poorly trained, not so much in "content" as in "process." He had not been formed in the "habitus" of doing theology. In consequence he did little that Sunday by way of bringing the congregation to the habit of reflecting on their lives in faith either. Whatever our response to the problem, it will not be solved by simply increasing the academic rigor of ministerial training in its present form.

Let me acknowledge here that there are many pieces to the puzzle at hand. I will focus on only one part of it, namely, the theological formation of people for church ministry. But my focus is not arbitrary. Part of the agenda of this collection is the relationship between academia and ecclesia. But beyond that, I am convinced that if there is to be a more effective mediation between academia and ecclesia (and thus if theology is to be historically practical), the primary agents of that must be our pastoral ministers. My proposal for an alternative approach to ministerial preparation, however, is grounded in a particular analysis of our present educational practice and in some strong convictions about the foundational issues that undergird the whole theological enterprise. If my proposal is to get a hearing, I believe I must begin with those convictions because they constitute its rationale.

SOME STRONG CONVICTIONS

The standard paradigm presently in operation for preparing future ministers is to give them heavy doses of what are presumed to be theoretical sciences in divinity (systematics, church history, scripture, or whatever) and then to tag on, almost as an afterthought, some training in pastoral skills to help them apply that theory to practice. It may seem tautological to say it, but such a paradigm obviously presumes a one-way relationship between theory and practice with theory always the point of departure; that theory is something from "outside" to be applied and practice something to receive it; that one is always to move from theory to practice in what Edward Farley calls a "source-to-application"[1] process. I am convinced that for ministerial preparation at least, that paradigm is bankrupt. Within it, we will never narrow the gap between academia and ecclesia because the dichotomy is built into the very paradigm itself. A brief analysis of how the standard paradigm understands the purpose, locus, and agents of theology will make this clear.

To begin with, the theory-to-practice paradigm presumes, at least implicitly, that the primary purpose of theology is theoretical investigation and clarity of a very ahistorical and metaphysical kind. Quite obviously the best locus for such a scholarly enterprise is academia and not the context of a Christian faith community in the world. In fact one can do theoretical and scholarly research best in a library since the data for attention are the scriptural, historical, and doctrinal documents of the Christian tradition. The primary agents of such an enterprise are scholars trained in the sciences and tools for interpreting those documents and coming to logical and systematic clarity about them.

Insofar as the scholars have an explicitly practical interest at all, they presume a "trickle-down" process, much akin to our nation's present approach to economics. The people at the top have the knowledge wealth that is to spill over on the baptized but non–theologically trained Christians below. In the theory-to-practice paradigm, theology is done either for the people or to the people. While lip service can be paid on occasion to the *sensus fidelium,* the fact that theology is also to be done by the people seems to be forgotten. Neither the lived faith of the community, with all of its struggles, joys, pains, and praxis in the world, nor the historical context with its social, cultural, and political realities is taken seriously in the theological enterprise as other than points of application for the theory already assembled. If that paradigm continues, then theology will be practical only by accident rather than by design.

The most obvious implication for people being trained for ministry by such a mode of theological education is that they are more likely to end up knowing about theology in a theoretical sense than being able to do theology in the context of a pastoral situation. If the praxis of history is not a partner in the theological enterprise by which they are trained, we cannot expect them to develop the disposition and consciousness to think theologically in a pastoral context. If they have been formed to do theology in their heads, they are not prepared to do it on their feet. In short, the theory-to-practice paradigm of theological education does not prepare people in what Farley calls the "habitus" of doing theology. While it is not easy to nail down exactly what Farley means by "habitus," he obviously intends an enculturated disposition that leads to theological wisdom and understanding when faith is made conscious and reflective in an existential and historical situation.

There are, of course, some hopeful signs that an alternative paradigm for theological education is emerging. To understand those signs of hope it will help, first, to place the still-dominant paradigm in a historical perspective. Farley's fine work *Theologia* will help us here. He is convinced that there is a subversive memory in the history of theology itself that can subvert the theory-to-practice paradigm. To begin with, Farley points to two premodern meanings of the word "theology."

> First, theology is a term for an actual, individual cognition of God and things related to God, a cognition which in most treatments attends faith and has eternal happiness as its final goal. Second, theology is a term for a discipline, a self-conscious scholarly enterprise of understanding. In the former sense theology is a habit *(habitus)* of the human soul. In the latter it is a discipline, usually occurring in some sort of pedagogical setting.[2]

Here Farley is pointing to both the disposition of soul and the science of mind dimensions that he claims were constitutive of theology from its beginnings. He contends that theological training called for the formation of people in the art and disposition (habitus) of bringing both faith and reason to interpret the meaning of the Christian tradition in the context of historical reality. That is what he means by *theologia*— theology as both habitus and scientia, in which practice is present by definition,[3] and to that, he contends, we must return.

As Farley unfolds the story of *theologia* he details the various shifts that resulted in a loss of theology as a practical habitus to seeing it instead as a fragmented collection of subdisciplines that are pursued only with theoretical and scientific interests. "In brief, this shift is from theology viewed as a *habitus*, or act of practical knowledge having the primary character of wisdom, to theology used as a generic term for a cluster of disciplines."[4]

The cluster of academic disciplines took various formulations. In Protestant seminary education it typically followed the division laid out by Schleiermacher in his *Brief Outline of Theological Study* (1811),[5] namely Bible, church history, systematic theology, and practical theology (also sometimes called applied or pastoral theology). In my own Catholic seminary experience the division was Bible; church history;

fundamental, moral, and dogmatic theology; and then applied theology, which typically included homiletics, catechetics, and liturgy. Regardless of the division of subdisciplines in this encyclopedia understanding of theology, the reality emerged that the first ones named were seen as serious theoretical disciplines of research and learning, while practical theology came to be recognized as a kind of delivery system.[6] Instead of being engaged as a constitutive dimension of all theology, the practical interest was considered less serious (in the academic sense), something that could be tagged on to a cluster of scientific theological disciplines under the aegis of practical theology. In time, practical theology became reduced to a search for useful techniques and technologies that were more influenced by the social sciences than by its own theological foundations.[7]

Quite clearly, we need a new understanding of the theological enterprise and a different approach to doing theological education for ministry. But the new paradigm cannot emerge if we simply tackle it as a "how-to" question. (Like many others, I am growing weary of *the* foundational issue in theology being treated as simply one of method.) We must also challenge the assumptions of the theory-to-practice paradigm concerning the who (scholars), where (academia), and why (theoretical clarity) of theology. Here I can do no more than indicate briefly my own response to those foundational questions. But indicate them I must if the approach I propose later is to be appreciated as contributing to an alternative mode for doing theological education.

The "Who" of Theology

Who should do theology? Who are the rightful subjects of this enterprise and its historical agents? Certainly the assumption of the theory-to-practice paradigm that theology belongs to either an academic or a church oligarchy is a usurpation of the enterprise.

Anselm's definition of theology "as faith seeking understanding" has been challenged as incomplete and with good reason. But there is still a basic truth in what it does say. I believe it contains a subversive memory that challenges our present operating assumptions about ownership of theology.

To begin with, Anselm's definition presupposes Christian faith, which itself presupposes a Christian community. It also presupposes that would-be theologians have the ability to reason and an interest in coming to understand their faith. But note well that that is all "faith seeking understanding" presupposes. In other words, theology, at least by Anselm's definition, is the right of all in Christian faith who have the use of reason and an interest in making sense out of their faith in the context of their history.

That right must be honored if people are to become subjects of their own faith history rather than objects for whom or to whom theology is done by specialists. That we democratize theology is demanded, I believe, not simply by Anselm's definition of theology but by our very understanding of the human person. We need to recognize the fact that people have a natural tendency and capacity to speak their own "word about God" (*theos logia*) and stop seeing it as something very difficult that only specialists can do. With Karl Rahner I agree that embedded in the heart of human existence is a "supernatural existential,"[8] an a priori mediation of God's grace that gives the human a natural capacity for the divine. By nature we are lured to the transcendent, to reach out in freedom toward self-conscious and expressed relationship with the divine.

When that capacity for God is made explicit in the context of a Christian community and its meaning interpreted and lived through the symbols and mythos of the Christian tradition, then the theological word of all members of the community needs expression if they are to be subjects of their own faith and full subjects within the Christian community. In short, all baptized Christians should be enabled to think theologically for themselves and for each other. That is why it is essential to form pastoral ministers in the habitus of theologia. They themselves must know how to do theology on their feet if they are to sponsor their people in how to think theologically toward "a sapiential (existential, personal) and praxis-oriented understanding"[9] of their lives in faith.

As I make clear elsewhere in this essay, the claim for inclusiveness of theology's subjects and agents does not deny the essential and invaluable service that the trained theological and scriptural specialists render to the rest of the community. I am only insisting that retaining the theological enterprise exclusively in the hands of either an academic or a church oligarchy is a form of "knowledge control"[10] that promotes dependency among ordinary Christians.[11]

The "Where" of Theology

By the "where" question here I am raising the issue of the locus for doing theology and thus, by implication, the resources to be consulted (the fontes) for theological wisdom. I mentioned above that under the theory-to-practice paradigm the locus of theology is academia and the fontes to be attended to are the scriptural, historical, and doctrinal documents of the Christian tradition. Such a limited view will not be adequate for a new paradigm.

The *primary* locus for theology is not academia, nor even ecclesia, but human history as it unfolds in the world. Why? Because human history is the locus of God's activity in time and thus always the first source of God's self-disclosure at any time. Echoing the sentiment of Anselm, Gordon Kaufman contends that "with the word 'God' we are attempting to indicate the last or ultimate point of reference to which all action, consciousness and reflection can lead."[12] Out of my own self-consciously Christian faith, I contend that the reverse of Kaufman's definition is equally true. God is not only the ultimate telos but also the primary source from which all historical action, consciousness, and reflection arise. God is not merely beyond or at the end of or outside of human history. The whole Hebrew and Christian dispensations insist that our God is a God present within history, a God who pitches God's tent and dwells among us (see Lev. 26:11–13; John 1:14). Unlike the Removed and Unmoved Mover of Greek philosophy, the God of Abraham and Sarah, the God of Moses and Miriam, the God of Jesus and Mary is indeed God of the heavens but is also God of the earth, an Incarnate God who enters into human history with saving power.

Because the world is the arena of God's saving activity, human history must be the primary locus, the point of both departure and arrival for rational discourse about God. This means that the praxis of God in history as it is co-constituted through human praxis is our primary text and context for doing theology. And because the whole created order and the activity that constitute human history are potential disclosures of God to us, then all the human sciences, disciplines of learning, and ways of knowing are potential resources for our theologizing. To say less than this is to propose something less than a radical monotheism. Because God is the only God, all history is salvation history and there is no dimension of history or no authentic human insight of which God is not God. Theology must arise from and return to the locus of God's universal activity—the world.

Lest I be misunderstood, I am not arguing here that contemporary praxis is the only locus of God's self-disclosure as if each generation of people in faith should start over to create their own theology *ex nihilo*. No! Negatively, I am pushing back against the locus presumed by the dominant paradigm which tends to reflect upon God apart from historical reality in order to assemble the truth about God in an ideational form to then bring it to history, as it were, "from the outside in." That *modus operandi* forgets the universality of God's grace and presence within history, long before we begin to theologize.

Put positively, I am claiming that present human praxis, on personal, interpersonal, and social levels, is an essential starting point and locus for doing theology. Even academic investigation of sacred texts that reflect God's primordial revelation to our community must be carried on consciously in the context of and in dialogue with our historical reality. As those primary texts arose from God's self-disclosure in history, so if we are to appropriate their revelatory possibility for our time, they must not be treated as reified revelations from outside of time. We must come, instead, to appropriate them as reflections or mirrors of the truth already present in our present reality.[13] Quite obviously, training people to take their historical reality seriously in doing theology requires a training process that itself reflects that value.

The "Why" of Theology

Why do we do theology at all? What is the purpose of trying to bring our faith to understanding? In Jurgen Habermas's term, what is "the knowledge constitutive interest" that shapes the enterprise? Quite obviously, we do not do theology for God's sake. We can presume that God knows who God is without our theologizing. Thus, we are left with the inevitable conclusion that we attempt rational discourse about God for our own sakes and for the sake of the world.

In the dominant paradigm the purpose of theology would seem to be the task of coming to systematized clarity about divine truths, the search for orthodoxa—a true word about matters of faith. Gustavo Gutierrez calls that purpose "rational knowledge about God"[14] and recognizes it as one permanent task of theology. But it cannot be the only nor even the dominant task of the enterprise. If theology is to be for us, it must be for more than our heads. To leave its purpose at theoretical clarity alone would be to imply that the God of Hebrew and Christian revelation is no more than an Idea. That would be contrary to the whole thrust of the God revealed in the Jewish and Christian scriptures. As Johann Baptist Metz claims, correctly I believe, the Christian notion of God is both practical[15] and political.[16] We believe in a God who intervenes in the affairs of human history to save humankind and set us free, both personally and politically. If our rational discourse about God is to be faithful to that God, then theology must be for us the way God is for us.

The primary symbol of God's intentions for us in both the Hebrew and Christian scriptures is the reign of God, the reign of peace and justice, love and freedom for all humankind and all creation. That is how God is for us. God is working out God's reign within human history, and never without the human activity that constitutes our history. And as God wills shalom for all, so, in our covenant with God, we are called to live according to God's will for all people. Rational discourse about God's activity in history must dispose us to engage the praxis of history in faithfulness to God's intent.

To paraphrase Marx's *Eleventh Thesis on Feuerbach*, the task of Christian theology is not simply to interpret the world but to empower Christians to participate in changing it. The direction of such change and conversion must be humanization and liberation for all of God's people and creation. If Christian theology is to be for us the way God is for us, it must help to make and keep life human. Otherwise it is not Christian theology at all. Far from being a secondary interest or subdiscipline within theology, all theology must be "practical" in the sense of bringing us to a renewed praxis of Christian faith in the world.

Even when scholars are attending to the classic documents of the tradition, their hermeneutical stance must not be one of feigned neutrality in the value-free sense. Their interest must be an emancipatory one (à la Habermas)[17] and a passion for the peace and justice of God's reign. With hermeneutics of suspicion and retrieval they must be alert to what Metz calls the dangerous and subversive memories that will call the oppressive structures of reality into question and pose emancipatory possibilities for us. This means that every theologian, even the most specialized and scholarly researcher, must be as concerned for orthopraxis as he or she is for orthodoxy.

SIGNS OF HOPE IN NOETIC PRAXIS FOR A NEW PARADIGM

While the theory-to-practice paradigm is still reigning (especially in how we teach theology), there are significant signs that we are in the twilight days of its rule. A whole new paradigm for doing theology and thus theological education is emerging. Instead of seeing theory in an idealistic and ahistorical sense as one's starting point, this new paradigm insists that the praxis of people in history must be either one's point of departure (as with political and liberation theologians) or an equal interlocutor with theory (as with theologians who favor a critical correlative approach) when one does theology. In summary, this new paradigm is a retrieval of historical praxis as an authentic partner in knowing and understanding God's self-disclosure to us and the meaning of that disclosure for our lives in the world. This new paradigm promises to broaden the locus of theology beyond academia to the church in the world; to expand its participants to include all of God's people in faith; and to widen its interlocutors to include other sciences of human investigation. In essence, it does this by a new *modus operandi* that maintains a dialectical unity between praxis and theory instead of the "from theory-to-practice" mode.

Matthew Lamb offers what may well be the most helpful schema to date for understanding this paradigmatic shift toward a dialectical unity between praxis and theory in doing theology. Lamb outlines five types or models of the relationship between theory and praxis that are reflected in theological method. My summary of the first three types will be brief since it is the emerging paradigm represented by models 4 and 5 that are of most interest to us here.

Lamb names the first type "the primacy of theory"[18] model. He notes that in this model "theory was supreme as the knowledge of necessary and eternal truths or first principles."[19] In this arrangement "moral and pastoral theology are basically prudential applications of dogmatic theory and hierarchical authority, which latter remains essentially the same despite variations in prudential application."[20] We have sufficiently critiqued this model already.

The second model gives total primacy to praxis as if theoretical formulations about the Christian tradition have nothing normative to contribute to theological understanding. Here "theory is understood primarily as a more or less extrinsic reflection on . . . praxis"[21] and "doctrinal theory is at best extrinsic and secondary."[22] Lamb lists three variants of this model but all of them have in common "a rejection of classical-traditionalist metaphysics. Theory is not given a necessary domain of eternal truths but is seen as no more than ever revisable approximations to the flux of contingent events in history."[23] I find this second model unacceptable because it forgets the revelatory possibilities for us in the story of God's self-disclosure to our people over time, and refuses to recognize the theory that has arisen from the praxis in faith of the people before us. In that sense it is historically naive.

The third, Lamb calls "the primacy of Faith-Love" model, and names the early Barth as its prototype. In this model, both theory and practice count for naught; it "emphasizes the non identity of Christian faith-love vis-a-vis theory-praxis."[24] Here the subject and only source of theological understanding is the God revealed in Jesus Christ. It is God's Word in revelation that grounds both theory and praxis. God's Word and the ability to know its meaning for our lives are pure gifts of God's grace. The theologian's task is, by grace, to appropriate the basic attitudes of Christian faith, trust, and love in order to find judgment and consolation in God's Word. As Lamb notes wryly, "a charge of theological fideism would be a compliment to Barth."[25] I reject this model as inadequate because it robs us of our historical agency and reduces human history to "basketweaving."

Lamb calls the fourth type "critical theoretic correlations" and says that "this type of reflection on the theory-praxis relationship seeks to establish a critical theoretic correlation between Christian tradition and the exigencies of theory and praxis."[26] In maintaining a correlation between theory and praxis, it sees both as essential to and yet neither one as synonymous with God's self-disclosure in history. The theologians of this type "seek through their correlations to articulate a union of identity and non identity between Christianity and the categories of theory-praxis."[27] Lamb cites a number of variations to this model and lists many leading theologians within it. He points, however, to the method of critical correlation developed by David Tracy as the most obvious and contemporary expression of the model. The difference between this type and the fifth one that follows is that while both take praxis and theory seriously as essential partners in doing theology, here the critical correlation is a theoretical one.

Lamb calls the fifth type "critical praxis correlation." Here the point of critical correlation between theory and praxis is primarily in praxis; historical praxis grounds the activity of theorizing. "Praxis is not only the goal but also the foundation of theory. This applies to any theorizing, including theology."[28] Authentic Christian praxis demands engagement in the historical struggles for conversion and transformation, both personal and social. Such emancipatory praxis is the locus for authenticating and reformulating theory which must be held in a dialectical unity, or critical correlation with praxis. While Lamb identifies three variants of this type also, within it he lists the work of Bernard Lonergan, as well as the whole corpus of political and liberation theologies.

Lamb's description may suffer from the limitations of any typology. For our interest in an emerging theological paradigm that takes praxis seriously in the theological enterprise, however, his typology helps to make a number of significant points.

To begin with, Lamb's typology represents approximately a historical evolution, with the theologies under types 4 and 5 being the most contemporary. In other words, a broad-based consensus is emerging around theological method that (1) attempts to take historical praxis as either its starting point or as an essential and equal partner with theory in the interpretation of the Christian tradition; and (2) calls for a critical correlation between theory and praxis, however that correlative moment is to be mediated.

It follows that for theology to hold theory and praxis in critical correlation, a critical analysis of both contemporary praxis and of the theoretical formulations and sources of the Christian tradition is required. Critique of present praxis must engage theologians with a whole new set of interlocutors. Lamb lists some of them as critical sociologists, psychologists, economists, environmentalists, political scientists, historians, and educators. And critique of theory demands an approach that activates a hermeneutic of both suspicion and retrieval toward the "faith handed down" in either scriptural, symbolic, or doctrinal formulations.

In light of these conclusions, and the evidence that a new praxis paradigm for doing theology is emerging, the question might well be posed—well, then, is the problem not almost solved? Have we not exaggerated the dominance of the theory-to-practice paradigm when in fact it is now generally out of vogue and in its twilight days? Have we not created a "straw person" here to be easily refuted? I say no and here I come to what may be the most central point in this whole essay.

The new paradigm has been clarified only on the level of what Lamb refers to as "noetic praxis," at the level of critical understanding. In the actual teaching/learning moment that typically constitutes theological education (at least in our North American context), the theory-to-practice paradigm still reigns in the very praxis of teaching itself. Put succinctly, to form people in a way of doing theology that holds theory and praxis in a critical correlation demands a teaching/learning process that itself holds theory and praxis in a critical correlation. Even professors committed to the new praxis paradigm will often not teach it through a praxis process of pedagogy. But one cannot simply lecture to people in a theory-to-practice mode and expect them to be formed in a habit of mind, heart, and style that integrates theological research and faith commitment in the world. The fact of the matter is that we have yet to learn how to teach theology in a mode that honors the convictions inherent in the new paradigm. The most crucial task facing theological education now is the development of approaches to the art of teaching that reflect our convictions about the role of historical praxis in theological method. Otherwise, the old paradigm will be maintained by the very way we teach about the new one.[29]

SIGNS OF HOPE IN TEACHING PRAXIS

As we found signs of hope for a praxis paradigm in theological method, so too, although more incipient, are there signs that a more adequate pedagogical praxis is emerging that will be capable of forming people in the *habitus* of doing theology. I think immediately of the process for doing pastoral theology developed by James and Evelyn Whitehead (summarized at the beginning of his chapter in this collection). Their approach attempts to correlate critically the three variables of the Christian tradition, cultural sources, and personal experience to move participants from insight through decision to concrete pastoral action.[30] The "pastoral circle" approach developed by Joseph Holland and Peter Henriot that includes the moments of insertion, social analysis, theological reflection, and pastoral planning has shown itself to be a powerful way of bringing people to do theology toward the end of social consciousness–raising and action for peace and justice.[31] The five levels for practical moral thinking developed by Don Browning could also be a significant contribution to a teaching process that holds theory and praxis in a critical correlation.[32] In the latter part of *Theologia*, Farley makes an interesting proposal that I find incomplete but promising in that he delineates what I consider to be the appropriate components for a new teaching praxis in theological education. While he says nothing by way of describing the actual teaching praxis that would effect his proposal, I will overview his suggestion in more detail here because his precise interest is in theological education that can form the *habitus* of *theologia*.

Farley outlines four pedagogical steps that he deems necessary to form people in the *habitus* of *theologia* as a sapiential and dialectical discipline. The first step is to attend to the concrete historical situation of the people attempting to come to theological understanding. Farley argues for "the primacy of the situation" because "there is simply no way of conducting theology above the grid of life itself."[33] As I interpret him here, Farley intends that the participants analyze their historical situation both from the perspective of faith (albeit at this first step "prereflexive") and from the perspective of the relevant social science disciplines.[34]

The second movement is when the faith tradition intervenes to bring a hermeneutic of suspicion to the situation. Farley describes the faith tradition as "the total mythos of Christian faith, i.e., the essence of Christianity, the primary symbols, the themes of proclamation, the dogmas of tradition."[35] In this second movement he intends tradition to critique the life situation, to raise consciousness on both personal and social/political levels.

In the third movement Farley argues that a similar hermeneutic of suspicion must be brought to the expression of the tradition itself. Without this our present understanding of the tradition would become

THOMAS H. GROOME

an object of idolatry. Only by such a hermeneutic of suspicion toward the tradition "are the elements in the tradition which serve oppression, ideology and the legitimation of privilege unmasked."[36]

At this stage, the participants are ready for a fourth movement in which they discern "the persisting imagery, symbols, and doctrines of that mythos [i.e., the Christian tradition] which expresses enduring truth."[37] They do so in order to return to the situation with a more theonomous interpretation of the historical reality from the perspective of the central themes of the Christian tradition. At that point of re-engaging the situation, the central symbol for Farley is the kingdom of God which he describes as "*the situation* as God undergirds it, pervades it, disposes it, lures it to its best possibilities."[38]

This is what Farley's outline helps to clarify for me. First, theology at its very heart is a pastoral activity. Within that pastoral activity, the various theological subdisciplines that are academic and research-oriented specializations and forms of expertise (Scripture exegesis, church history, systematics, etc.) and indeed the social sciences that enable us to critically understand the pastoral reality are valued and essential partners. Without those specializations a critical hermeneutic of both suspicion and retrieval cannot be brought to either the tradition or to the historical reality. In such a configuration, the exegetes, historians, and systematicians all play significant roles in the theological drama. But none of them nor the sum total of their subdisciplines apart from the pastoral reality constitutes the primary plot. If they did we would be back to doing theology in our heads instead of on our feet.

But Farley's construct, while it has potential, still requires a great deal of development before it can be readily appropriated by others as a usable approach to the concrete praxis of teaching theology. This is the point perhaps at which my own work may have something to contribute to the task of forging such a pedagogy. For some years now, I have been attempting to develop in myself and others a habitus of approaching Christian religious education by a process I have called shared Christian praxis. I have written about it in some detail elsewhere.[39] I offer it in brief outline here, not to pose it as the sole solution to our search but to contribute the little I have come to know from my own praxis to the search for an adequate pedagogy for theological education. I share it too because, while it first developed as an approach to religious education, at its heart it is a process of bringing people to do theology in a mode that might be faithful to all I have outlined thus far in this essay. I have used the shared praxis process in my own teaching with undergraduate theology students and with graduate students in religious education and pastoral ministry. I offer it here as a modest proposal.

A MODEST PROPOSAL

Shared Christian praxis as an approach to teaching theology attempts to honor three basic imperatives that must be honored if our teaching is to form people in the habitus of doing theology through any kind of critically correlative mode.

1. Because God is active in the world through the activity that constitutes human history, the participants must attend to their own historical praxis in faith (even if prereflexive) and to the intentional human activity of the world around them. This praxis must be named and brought to systematic analysis and critical consciousness.

2. The participants must attend with hermeneutics of suspicion and retrieval to the story and vision that have arisen from the praxis of the Christian faith community over time (what Tracy might call the "Christian fact")[40] and attempt a critical appropriation thereof.

3. These two sources, present historical praxis and the story/vision (in whatever form), must be placed in a dialectical hermeneutic with each other so that people may come to a lived response within history that is transforming for self, for church, and for society toward the coming of God's reign.

Gathering these three imperatives together, we are ready for a working description of this way of teaching theology.

> A shared Christian praxis approach to teaching theology is an intentional and dialogical activity (shared) in which the participants reflect critically on their own historical situation and lived faith (praxis) in a dialectical hermeneutic with the Christian story/vision and reflect critically on the Christian story/vision in a dialectical hermeneutic with present historical praxis. The purpose of such a teaching process is twofold: formation, by God's grace, in personal, ecclesial, and social praxis that is faithful to God's reign; and formation in the habitus of theologia, in the ability to do theology in the context of one's own history.

Perhaps the most effective way to unpack that description is to describe how I try to use the approach in my own teaching. I typically organize a shared praxis approach around a focusing activity and then five pedagogical movements. Each of the movements can be done in a myriad of different ways and with many different teaching styles and methods. I can only briefly describe the essence of each movement here. At the end of each one I will outline a recent experience with the process and what we did at each particular movement. The example is taken from an undergraduate theology course. The course was built around three major themes, namely, a theological understanding of ourselves, of God, and of Jesus Christ. I will describe what took place around the first theme which we called "A Search for a Christian Understanding of Ourselves." Basically this was an introductory-level statement to a Christian anthropology. (The unit was spaced over the first month of the semester meeting for two and one-half hours each week.)

Focusing Activity

The purpose of the focusing activity is to bring the attention of the participants to bear upon the overarching theme of this particular part of the curriculum in a way that helps them to identify the theme in their own life praxis. The focusing act should be a kind of icon through which people can look to recognize what Paulo Freire would call the "generative theme" of the learning unit, i.e., the key historical or faith life issue as it is reflected in their own life praxis.

For example, I did the focusing activity on Christian anthropology by an opening parable-type story and a brief lecture that did no more than establish the question of "who are we" as crucial to how we live our lives and relate to each other and to the world. In order to get the students thinking about their own operative anthropology, I offered some possible models that are suggested by contemporary society (consumer, climber, rugged individual, etc.)—all the time asking the question, "But who do you think we are?" The first class session did little more than encourage them to think about their own operating understanding of who they are; in other words, not so much their theory about themselves and others as their praxis.

Movement 1: Expressing/Naming Present Praxis

The purpose of this first movement is to bring the participants to an expression/naming of their own praxis of the theme or focus as they recognize it in their historical experience. Thus, depending on the topic and context, the first movement invites participants to express their own understanding, feeling, reaction, sentiment, overt activity, valuing, meaning making, truth, belief, and the like (thus praxis, broadly defined), around the particular theme.

Returning to our example, I prepared the students for movement 1 by giving an assignment at the end of the previous class that they were to complete and bring with them to the second meeting. Their task was to give a good deal of thought to the question and write a one-page reflection on "My everyday (i.e., operative) understanding of myself as a person." In the class session I invited the participants to share their reflections first in small groups and then with the whole group, always leaving people free not to share their reflections but to enter into the dialogue by simply listening to other people's statements and comparing them to their own. I made some observations and probing-type questions during this time that were directed at eliciting more complete statements of their present praxis. We spent the latter part of movement 1 attempting to construct together "the typical understanding of the human person that is operative in our society."

Movement 2: Critical Reflection on Present Praxis

The purpose of the second movement is to bring the participants to reflect critically on their own and on society's praxis as expressed in the first movement. I understand critical reflection as engaging people in the activities of critical reason, analytical memory, and creative imagination.

Through critical reason people are invited to "decode" (Freire's word) their present reality that typically comes to us "coded" as the way things are and ought to be. Critical reason calls present praxis into question and asks "why" of it with a hermeneutic of suspicion which never presumes that "that's the way it is" or "ought to be."

Analytical memory invites people to uncover the personal and social genesis of present praxis to see the constitutive interests, assumptions, and ideologies which undergird that praxis as they have named it. As it attends to the genesis of one's own praxis, analytical memory can be biographical and psychological. As it attends to the social genesis of present praxis, analytical memory must also be contextual and sociological. It is a re-*membering* in the sense of coming to see how one's membership in certain social, political, economic, and cultural environments has shaped present praxis. Insofar as the participants (the facilitator included) have access to the insights of the social sciences (sociology, anthropology, psychology, political science, economics, etc.), they will bring the insights of those sciences to bear on the issue at hand. While those sciences have their own internal criteria and methodological norms, I will say something below about the primary criterion for evaluating their insights for theology as a pastoral activity.

Creative imagination invites the participants to image and create new possibilities beyond present praxis instead of simply accepting it fatalistically as a "given." The purpose of attending to the present with reason and memory is that we may intend the future. Such intentionality requires an envisioning of the consequences of present praxis and an imagining of what is not yet but might be. By bringing reason, memory, and imagination to reflect critically on their own present praxis, the participants come to express and critique what we can call metaphorically their own "stories" and "visions."

With our theology class, this movement took place over a number of sessions. I opened it by explaining briefly some insights from psychology and sociology on how one's self-identity is always socially and culturally mediated. The thrust of the reflective questioning here was to get the participants to do their own social analysis of what they had expressed in movement 1 and the possible consequences of their understanding for themselves and for their relationships with others. In subsequent classes we reviewed and critiqued "A Spectrum of Answers"[41] that outlines some responses to the anthropological question by the natural sciences, social sciences, literature, and philosophy. The constant questions throughout this movement were: Who or what has influenced our understanding of ourselves? What are its consequences? Is there anything we would want to change about that understanding?

Movement 3: Encounter with the Christian Story and Vision

The purpose of the third movement is to make accessible to the participants the story and vision of the broader Christian faith community and tradition as it pertains to the topic at hand. "Story" here means much more than narrative although I favor a historical/narrative presentation of the Christian story.[42] I use story as a metaphor for the whole faith tradition of the Christian community, however that is expressed or embodied. Our story is congealed in written scriptures and interpretations, doctrines and dogmas, symbols and rituals, artifacts and structures, spiritualities, visual images, and so on. In a sense, the story is our *theoria*, but instead of being expressed only as a metaphysical system of ideas, it is encountered as the historical and practical wisdom that our faith community has come to over time. "Vision" is used as a metaphor for the truth claims that the story makes upon us, the response it invites, and the promise it has for our lives.

Let me make an important point here. The contributions of the experts in the various subdisciplines of theology are essential and vital in this third movement if the story made present and the vision proposed are themselves to reflect a critical appropriation of the historical faith of the Christian community and its implications for the present and future. This does not mean that the theologian must be personally trained in all of those disciplines (impossible) but he/she must have access to their scholarly findings. The resources drawn upon must reflect the scholarship of the exegetes, historians, systematicians, ethicists, and so on. Guided by the scholarly criteria and methodological checks of their own disciplines, and bringing hermeneutics of suspicion and retrieval to the tradition, the work of the scholars is most crucial to this third movement in the process.

As the teacher selects from the story what to make accessible (and we always make "selections"), she/he must be critically conscious of one's own principle of selectivity. In the enterprise of Christian theology, whether we are drawing from the insights of the social sciences or from the theological subdisciplines, our overall principle of selectivity must always be an emancipatory one—that peace and justice, love and freedom may be advanced within human history. This implies criteria of appropriateness (as Tracy insists) to the story of the kingdom already and faithfulness to the vision of the kingdom not yet.

The third movement too can be done in a myriad of ways and different teaching methods can be used. In the context of our class, my style at this movement was basically a lecture approach. Here I can only hint at the outline of my presentations. We traced some of the theological anthropologies that have emerged over the history of the Christian tradition, beginning with the Hebrew scriptures and coming down to the present day with its variety of positions. We incorporated reflections on nature, grace, original sin, and human freedom. Around each one of those topics there was a good deal of dialogue and the fourth movement (critical appropriation) constantly dovetailed into the presentations.

The vision was interspersed throughout the story as I attempted to explicate the personal and social/political implications of the various insights and positions. The third movement concluded with an overall statement of who our Christian faith calls us to become together, at least in the view of this professor.[43]

Movement 4: A Dialectical Hermeneutic between
Praxis and Story/Vision

The purpose of the fourth movement is to promote among the participants a two-way dialectical hermeneutic between their critical reflection on present praxis (movements 1 and 2) and what was made accessible by the teacher in the third movement. Thus, the basic intention of the fourth movement is twofold: (1) to bring the participants to a dialectical critique of present praxis in light of the story/vision; and (2) to invite the participants to critique the theological understanding made accessible at the third movement in light of present praxis. As the theologian brought a hermeneutic of suspicion and retrieval to make present the story/vision, so now the participants, in light of their own praxis, are invited to bring a similar hermeneutic to what was presented to them by the teacher in the third movement.[44] In one sense, the fourth movement does to the third what the second movement did to the first. In essence, movement 4 is a critical appropriation of the story/vision to present praxis.

Returning to our example, at the end of the third movement I gave the students an assignment to write a statement of what from my presentations and their own reading they would *agree* with and affirm, what they would *disagree* with or question, and an *insight of their own* that they would add to all that had been said. (Note that the dialectical style of this fourth movement is Hegelian.) Again we worked through their statements in class. My role was to facilitate the dialogue, asking probing questions that might promote their own appropriation of the material and continuing to act as a resource person when there were misunderstandings or questions for further clarity.

Movement 5: Invitation to a New or Renewed Praxis

One way of describing the intent of the fifth movement is to say that it is a dialectical hermeneutic between the vision that arose from the story and their own visions of present praxis that were expressed in movement 2. In essence, this fifth movement is an invitation to decision/ response that is a new or renewed praxis. The historical or noetic praxis that arises from this fifth movement will vary a great deal, depending on the topic of attention, the participants, and the context. The fifth movement could lead to the articulation of a new and practical understanding or to a decision for overt action, or to a variety of responses in between.

With the class, the fifth movement basically brought the participants back to the question posed at the opening movement a month before. After a good deal of dialogue, their assignment was to write an essay (this one to be graded) on "My theological understanding of the person, the challenges it poses in our society, and the decisions it invites from my life."

SOME AFTERTHOUGHTS

Returning to the constant underlying issue of this paper—the gap between theology as typically taught in academia and the faith life of the ecclesia—I opined that at least part of the problem is caused by a dichotomy between theory and praxis within the science of theology itself, both in the dominant paradigm of theological method and in the typical paradigm for teaching theology. I contended that there are signs of hope for a new theological paradigm that holds theoria and praxis in a dialectical unity with each other. We are equally in need, however, of approaches to teaching theology that hold theoria and praxis in a fruitful tension and dialectical unity in the very teaching act itself. Without such teaching processes, future pastoral ministers, and indeed theologians of any kind, will not be formed in the habitus of doing theology and the gap between academia and ecclesia will grow even wider. Or, to state that another way, theology will continue to be done in some heads instead of on all our feet. It will not be "practical."

I believe shared praxis has some potential for healing the theory/praxis gap in how we do and teach theology. It begins with an expressing of (movement 1) and critical reflection upon present praxis (movement 2), moves to encounter a critical appropriation of the theoria that comes from the "faith handed down" (movement 3), attempts to place those two sources of knowing (praxis and theoria) in a dialectical hermeneutic with each other (movement 4) to come to a decision/response of ongoing praxis (movement 5).

Tracy has defined theology as "the discipline that articulates mutually critical correlations between the meaning and truth of an interpretation of the Christian fact and the meaning and truth of an interpretation of the contemporary situation."[45] Perhaps what I have outlined above as a shared praxis approach is no more than a description of one possible way of operationalizing that definition of theology in the actual praxis of teaching. I would settle for doing as much.[46]

NOTES

1. Edward Farley, *Theologia: The Fragmentation and Unity of Theological Education* (Philadelphia: Fortress Press, 1983), 135.

2. Ibid., 31.

3. Farley writes, "Prior to the theological encyclopedia movement and in the time when the genre of theology was a *habitus*, a sapiential knowledge, practice was built into theology by definition" (ibid., 132).

4. Ibid., 81.

5. See Friedrich Schleiermacher, *Brief Outline on the Study of Theology*, ed. and trans. Terrence T. Tice (Richmond: John Knox Press, 1966).

6. Don Browning describes this outcome well when he writes: "At its best, practical theology in this model simply applied the results of exegetical, church historical and systematic theology to the concrete operations of church life or, more narrowly, to the activities of the clergy" ("The Revival of Practical Theology," *The Christian Century* 101, no. 4 [Feb. 1–8, 1984]: 135).

7. It is important to note, I believe, that the triumph in theology of a "from-

theory-to-practice" paradigm was a reflection of the triumph in Western philosophy of a from-theory-to-practice epistemological assumption with theory understood in a very scientized and ideational sense. For a scholarly treatment of how this epistemology came to prevail in the West, see Nicholas Lobkowicz, *Theory and Practice: The History of a Marxist Concept, from Aristotle to Marx* (Notre Dame, Ind.: University of Notre Dame Press, 1967). For a more detailed statement on the educational implications of this epistemological shift, see Thomas H. Groome, *Christian Religious Education: Sharing Our Story and Vision* (San Francisco: Harper & Row, 1980), chap. 8.

8. For a detailed treatment of Rahner's notion of the "supernatural existential," see Karl Rahner, *Foundations of Christian Faith* (New York: Seabury Press, 1978), especially the opening chapters.

9. Farley, *Theologia*, 170.

10. For a most insightful analysis of "knowledge control," see the work of Michel Foucault, for example, *Power/Knowledge: Selected Interviews and Other Writings, 1972–1977* (New York: Pantheon Books, 1981).

11. A confronting and contemporary instance of ordinary people doing theology is the *comunidades de base* movement so prevalent throughout Latin America. See Sergio Torres and John Eagleson, eds., *The Challenge of Basic Christian Communities* (Maryknoll, N.Y.: Orbis Books, 1981).

12. Gordon D. Kaufman, *An Essay on Theological Method* (Missoula, Mont.: Scholars Press, 1979), 11.

13. Gutierrez makes a similar point when he writes: "History is the locus where God reveals the mystery of His person. His word reaches us insofar as we are inserted into the historical becoming of (human) kind" (Gustavo Gutierrez, "The Praxis of Liberation and the Christian Faith," *Lumen Vitae*, 29 [Sept. 1974]: 386).

14. Gustavo Gutierrez, *A Theology of Liberation* (Maryknoll, N.Y.: Orbis Books, 1973), 4.

15. Johann Baptist Metz, *Faith in History and Society: Toward a Practical Fundamental Theology* (New York: Seabury Press, 1980), 51.

16. Ibid., 67.

17. For Habermas's understanding of cognitive interest and emancipation, see Jurgen Habermas, *Knowledge and Human Interest* (Boston: Beacon Press, 1971).

18. Matthew L. Lamb, *Solidarity with Victims: Toward a Theology of Social Transformation* (New York: Crossroad, 1982), 66.

19. Ibid.

20. Ibid., 66–67.

21. Ibid., 68.

22. Ibid., 73.

23. Ibid., 68–69.

24. Ibid.

25. Ibid., 74.

26. Ibid., 75.

27. Ibid., 76.

28. Ibid., 86.

29. I am convinced that the question of how we teach theology is a political issue. Lamb calls all those who take praxis as their starting point "political theologians." What such political theologians must realize, at least those predominantly occupied with teaching, is that their primary political praxis is the very act of teaching itself. Since the earliest attempts to understand the nature of educational activity, both Plato and Aristotle understood it as a political act. The political nature of education has been re-presented most forcefully in our own day by the work of Paulo Freire. See especially his *Pedagogy of the Oppressed* (New York: Seabury Press, 1970). Theological education is as political as any other form of education. The politics of praxis theologians, or critical correlative ones, must be reflected in the political choices they make about how to teach.

30. For a more detailed account, see James D. Whitehead and Evelyn Eaton Whitehead, *Method in Ministry: Theological Reflection and Christian Ministry* (New York: Seabury Press, 1980).

31. Joe Holland and Peter Henriot, *Social Analysis: Linking Faith and Justice* (Maryknoll, N.Y.: Orbis Books, 1983).

32. See Don Browning, *Religious Ethics and Pastoral Care* (Philadelphia: Fortress Press, 1983).

33. Farley, *Theologia*, 165.

34. Here I am depending somewhat on Browning's interpretation, since he is more familiar with Farley's work than I. From my own reading, however, I could not find such an obvious attention to the social sciences in Farley's work. See Browning, "Revival," 138.

35. Farley, *Theologia*, 166.

36. Ibid., 167.

37. Ibid., 168.

38. Ibid. (Farley's italics).

39. See Groome, *Christian Religious Education*, especially chaps. 7–10.

40. When I first came across David Tracy's notion of the "Christian fact" in *Blessed Rage for Order: The New Pluralism in Theology* (New York: Seabury Press, 1975), it seemed to capture exactly what I intend by the metaphor of Christian story. I resist using Tracy's phrase, however, because in a teaching context, at least, it sounds too final and complete. Tracy certainly intends the Christian fact to be critically appropriated. But I prefer the term "story," because it connotes something that is more open-ended. Good stories can be told and retold and improved with the telling. In an empirically minded culture we tend to simply accept "the facts."

41. This is found in Richard P. McBrien, *Catholicism* (Minneapolis: Winston Press, 1980), 104–21. We were using vol. 1 of McBrien's two-volume series as one of the required readings for the course.

77

42. Metz writes, "I make a plea for a narrative and practical structure of Christianity" (*Faith*, 164).

43. It is imperative that the lecturer at this third movement have a style of "making accessible" rather than "imposing upon" as he/she presents the story. Even occasional comments throughout the presentation can make it clear that this is one teacher's interpretation and invite the participants to come to their own positions. That is when even a lecture becomes "dialogical" in style. This is necessary if the fourth movement is to be effective.

44. This movement presupposes that the participants are capable of bringing criteria of adequacy, appropriateness, and coherence (see Tracy, *Rage*, 64–87) to what was made accessible at the third movement. That may seem like a large assumption. My experience is that students new to the approach are usually hesitant to critically appropriate anything that the teacher presents. With the right prompting and encouragement, however, I have found this hesitancy to disappear. The key I believe is not to underrate the "common-sense" knowing of even the neophytes to theology. For a very insightful analysis of the relationship between "common sense" and "scientific expertise," see E. V. Sullivan, "Common Sense from a Critical Historical Perspective," in *Common Sense*, ed. David Olson (Toronto: Routledge & Kegan Paul, 1980).

45. David Tracy, "The Foundations of Practical Theology," in *Practical Theology: The Emerging Field in Theology, Church, and World*, ed. Don S. Browning (New York: Harper & Row, 1982), 62.

46. While my own genesis in this approach was not initially influenced by Tracy's work (Freire, Habermas, and Dwayne Huebner were among my dominant influences), I certainly found it affirming and clarifying when I encountered it.

5 *Practical Theology and Religious Education*

DON S. BROWNING*

Christian religious education should be ordered as an aspect of practical theology. Doing this will not only clarify the place of Christian religious education within the curriculum of theological education, it will also illuminate the very process, dynamics, and aims of Christian religious education itself. Christian religious education should be understood as a process of practical theology aimed at creating individuals capable of entering into a community of practical theological reflection and participating in the action that would follow from it.

But this raises the initial question as to what model of practical theology we should use to guide Christian religious education. It is my conviction that for our time it should be a revised correlational model of practical theology. The phrase "revised correlational model" refers to a distinctive approach to theology associated with the name of David Tracy. Tracy's sources are multiple, but as applied to practical theology, something like Tracy's methodology was developed in the writings of Seward Hiltner and Daniel Day Williams, although there is no evidence that Tracy himself has in any way relied on these two thinkers.[1]

In a variety of recent writings I have outlined my own views as to what this method would look like when applied to practical theology. Tracy's writings have applied the method primarily to fundamental and systematic theology, although he has indeed said some very important things about practical theology, and this promises to be the next subject of his major three-volume work on theology.[2]

In what follows, I somewhat loosely follow Tracy while developing

*The thoughts in this article were first formulated in the early phases of the National Faculty Seminar on Religious Education (1983–1986) sponsored by the Center for Congregational Studies of Christian Theological Seminary and The Lilly Endowment.

some of his insights in directions suitable to my own purposes as recently set forth in my *Religious Ethics and Pastoral Care*.[3] In general terms, a revised correlational program in theology attempts to correlate critically both the questions and answers about human existence derived from an interpretation of the central Christian witness *with* the questions and answers implicit in various interpretations of ordinary human experience. The same method applied to practical theology means a critical correlation between the norms for human action and fulfillment revealed in interpretations of the Christian witness *and* the norms for action and fulfillment implicit in various interpretations of ordinary human experience. At the outset, it should be noticed that the method of critical correlation deals with *interpretations*—interpretations of the norms of action and fulfillment to be found in the Christian witness and interpretations of the norms of action and fulfillment found in ordinary experience. I emphasize interpretations because the practical theologian never has access to either the raw, uninterpreted Christian fact or the unbiased and uninterpreted reality of ordinary experience. This is why practical theology must be seen, as should Christian religious education, as first of all an interpretative or hermeneutical task.

A revised correlational practical theology should be critical, public, and centered in theological ethics. By critical, I mean to suggest that although practical theology must begin with faith as formed by a community of believers, it must go beyond an unreflective attitude and seek understanding and reasons, especially for its practical action. It must be public in the sense that it should attempt to relate the Christian message not only to the inner life of the church but to the public world in all its pluralistic, secular, and rapidly changing character. To do this, of course, it must all the more respond to the challenge of expressing itself in both an evocative *and* a critical language. But finally, practical theology should center itself in theological ethics. It is my position that theological ethics is the center of the practical theological disciplines. It is the discipline that most self-consciously concerns itself with both the norms of human action and the norms of human fulfillment. Not only is it the case on logical grounds that theological ethics should be the center of practical theology but, in addition, theological ethics has made significant gains in our day and can be seen as the premiere region of practical theology, partially due to its dialogue with and use of the powerful tools of moral philosophy.

To elect theological ethics as the center of the practical theological enterprise requires amplification. First, the phrase "practical theology" was first used within the decision of the Lateran Council of 1215 that each metropolitan church should appoint a magister who was to have the responsibility for penitential practice and the moral discipline of the church. This established a close relation between practical theology and moral theology.[4] This is a relation that lasted several centuries within the Catholic Church, but fell upon hard times within Protestantism.

Second, to give theological ethics such a prominent place in practical theology is to state its centrality for all the other more specialized regions of practical theology such as worship, religious education, and pastoral care. For instance, although there is a certain sense in which worship or liturgics is the most fundamental of the regions of practical theology, as it is basic to the Christian life, it is uniquely dependent upon theological ethics to receive its content. Worship can perform a variety of functions: it both legitimates and renews our normative visions of everyday life. It provides a foundation to our views of how life should be lived. It renews that view and frequently helps to restructure it when our everyday world seems to break down. Hence, there is a strong structural component in any act of worship, as Victor Turner, Anthony Wallace, and Claude Levi-Strauss have shown.[5] By structural component I mean to refer to the wide range of both implicit and explicit understandings about how the social world should be. Questions about the structure of the social world are basically ethical questions. Hence, to answer the question about the kind of social world that worship should confirm, revitalize, or create, one must resort to an implicit or explicit theological ethic.

Theological ethics is even more crucial for religious education (catechetics) and pastoral care (poimenics). Ethics involves two questions that are both of key importance for a proper orientation to those specific regions of practical theology. The disciplines of ethics, whether secular or theological, must establish the principles, methods, and procedures necessary to undergird our social praxis. In addition, the disciplines of ethics must help us answer the question of the nature of human fulfillment. According to standard distinctions made in moral theology, the first set of questions are "deontic" questions which try to answer the question of what we are obligated to do.[6] The second set of questions are "aretaic" questions which try to identify the nature of the good person and the nature of morally proper character, motivation, and virtue.[7] Since both religious education and pastoral care are types of social praxis, they are full of questions requiring objective (deontic) ethical decision making. Questions in pastoral care such as who should be cared for, how, when, and how often are basically ethical questions.

Similarly, in the area of religious education, questions about who should be taught, when, how much, and how often are basically moral questions. But even more important for both pastoral care and religious education are the aretaic ethical decisions about the nature of the good person and the nature of good character and virtue. If a central goal of Christian religious education is to help create a Christian person, then clearly a Christian ethic dealing with aretaic questions is fundamental. It is similarly fundamental to pastoral care. If pastoral care help. heal, guide, reconcile, and sustain broken or perplexed people, both Christian and non-Christian, it must have various normative images of human fulfillment (the aretaic question) against which to measure brokenness and to understand health and wholeness.

The failure to anchor Christian religious education in the more fundamental discipline of practical theology and its key subdiscipline of theological ethics explains much of the confusion that has beset the educational task of the church. It has led us to fail to see Christian education within its proper disciplinary context, and it has blinded us to the truth that a central goal of Christian education is to help create people who are themselves practical theological thinkers and actors.

RELIGIOUS EDUCATION AS PRACTICAL THEOLOGY: SOME CONTEMPORARY STATEMENTS

Practical Theology in Westerhoff

Within the recent past there have been several efforts to state the nature of Christian religious education as an expression of practical theology. I will review some of these statements and evaluate them from the perspective of my initial remarks about a revised correlational approach to practical theology that gives a central place to theological ethics.

John H. Westerhoff in his recent *Building God's People in a Materialistic Society*[8] has presented a vigorous call to envision Christian education as a practical theological enterprise. "Education to be Christian," he tells us, "assumes an awareness of the process by which we make rational sense of ourselves and the world."[9] After making the standard distinction between fundamental, systematic, and practical theology, he divides practical theology into five dimensions—the liturgical, the moral, the spiritual, the pastoral, and the catechetical.[10] The usefulness of his proposal is found in his claim that each of these dimensions of practical theology is related to and includes all the others. For instance, it is possible to speak of the Christian education potential of each of the other dimensions of practical theology—the liturgical, spiritual, moral, and pastoral. I am especially interested in his understanding of the place of the moral dimension within practical theology as a whole and Christian education in particular. Following the work of the Christian ethicist Stanley Hauerwas and the Christian educator Craig Dykstra,[11] Westerhoff sees theological ethics as primarily an aretaic discipline. Hence, the practical theological discipline of Christian ethics has to do with understanding the implications of the Christian story for the kind of character Christians are supposed to have, and the moral dimension of the practical theological discipline of Christian education deals with forming the character of individuals by helping them appropriate, within the context of a Christian community, the full significance of the Christian story.[12] Christian ethics and religious education are not primarily a matter of moral decision making although, of course, they entail this eventually. They have the job first of comprehending and internalizing the characterological implications of the Christian story. Once this occurs, it is assumed that good decisions will more or less automatically follow.

In taking this position, Westerhoff is both pointing to the centrality of the practical theological discipline of Christian ethics for the practical theological task of Christian education and, at the same time, taking a very particular, and I believe somewhat one-sided, approach to theological ethics. In repudiating all ethics of principle in the name of ethics of character, it is not clear that he has given Christian education its full range of resources. For it is not certain that we must choose between principle and character in either theological ethics or Christian education. In fact, I will argue below that an adequate practical theology of either theological ethics or Christian education requires both. And this will be all the more clear when we fully understand the centrality of theological ethics for all the other regions of practical theology, including that of Christian religious education.

Practical Theology in Fowler

In an essay entitled "Practical Theology and the Shaping of Christian Lives," James Fowler also has placed Christian education within the context of practical theology and has taken a position strongly resembling Westerhoff's. Fowler defines practical theology as "critical and constructive reflection on the praxis of the Christian community's life and work in its various dimensions."[13] Although practical theology is understood by Fowler as critical reflection and in this sense seen as philosophical in character, it is both animated by and primarily addressed to the living reality of the faith community.

A practical theology of Christian education is seen by Fowler as critical reflection on the church's task in the "*formation and transforma-tion of persons*."[14] It has its foundation in what the great metaphors of God the Creator, Governor, and Redeemer suggest for Christian char-acter. In addition, it requires a theory of general faith development, a more specific theory of Christian faith development, and finally a theory of the methods and strategies guiding formation in faith. Fowler is similar to Westerhoff in emphasizing the interest of Christian education in the formation of Christian character in contrast to more objective principles and methods constitutive of moral decision making. In addi-tion to the formative influences of H. R. Niebuhr, he too more recently has been profoundly influenced by Hauerwas[15] as well as work on a theology of virtue by Bernard Haring and Don Saliers.[16] In taking such a position he is emphasizing the importance for Christian education of the aretaic approach to theological ethics. Hence, although close to the position I will advocate, I will emphasize the importance to Christian education of both deontic and aretaic approaches to theological ethics and moral theology. Furthermore, in addition to affirming the impor-tance of the confessing ecclesia as both inspiring context and primary concern of Christian education, I will emphasize the critical and public character of Christian education as well.

Practical Theology in the Christian
Religious Education of Groome

In his widely appreciated *Christian Religious Education*,[17] Thomas Groome has not set out intentionally to construct a practical theology of Christian education, but as a matter of fact this is precisely what he has done. The excellence of this book, in my opinion, comes from the seriousness of his effort in writing a theology of praxis that addresses the particular region of Christian education. It is also the case that in the essay written for this volume he has more directly addressed the question of the relation of practical theology to education.[18]

Groome's practical theology of Christian religious education parallels to a considerable degree the details of my own approach briefly outlined at the beginning of this essay. He follows in a general way a revised correlational approach and, in addition, his practical theology is criti-cal, public, and centered in theological ethics. It is, however, his reluc-tance to recognize the full weight of the role of theological ethics in his practical theology that points to whatever difficulties exist in this out-standing work. For Groome, more than any other contemporary con-tributor to Christian education, has in effect anchored his educational theories in the practical theological region of theological ethics. But he has not adequately realized what he has done and therefore has not developed the fully worked-out ethical position that his perspective requires.

But before embarking on a discussion of this point, I will summarize briefly the ways his practical theology of education can be understood as revised, correlational, critical, and public. First, Groome conceives of his educational method as entailing a dialectical conversation between, on the one hand, our own present praxis and personal story, and, on the other, the implication for our praxis of the story and vision of the Christian faith. This should be seen as a hermeneutical conversation not unlike Hans-Georg Gadamer's interpretative conversation between differing horizons of consciousness.[19] In one place in *Christian Religious Education* Groome explicitly, although briefly, acknowledges the similarity of his position with the revised correlational method. He writes,

> What I intend here is very close to what I understand David Tracy to mean by "critical correlation." Tracy sees that there are "two main sources" of "fundamental theological reflection" (*Blessed Rage for Order*, p. 64), namely "the Christian fact" and common human experience and language. Both sources must themselves be critiqued and then critically correlated with each other.[20]

Second, as can be readily seen from the above quote, Groome intends his practical theology of education to be critical. By critical, I take it, he means to affirm yet go beyond both a confessional stance in theology and a socialization stance in educational methodology. He is fully aware that faith first emerges out of the confessional stance of worshiping, believing, and practicing religious community,[21] but he also believes that Christian maturity within the conflicting perspectives of a pluralistic society requires submitting our confessional beginning points to critical philosophical reflection. But Groome never speaks about the role of rational and philosophical reflection quite that explicitly. Instead, he does speak of such things as critiquing the Christian "story" in light of our personal story and critiquing our personal stories in light of the Christian story.[22] Such points suggest a critical, philosophical approach and do indeed raise the question of how it is actually controlled and made responsible. This consideration becomes somewhat acute when Groome admits that a practical result of this process of mutual criticism might involve going beyond the Christian story, especially at what he calls in one place its "lower echelon of the hierarchy of truths."[23]

And finally, Groome should be seen as doing a practical theology of

Christian religious education that attempts to address the diverse publics of a pluralistic society. This can be seen, first of all, in his interest in a mutual critique between the Christian story and common human experience. The result of this would be to present reasons for one's faith, especially for the practical and ethical implications of one's faith. But in addition it means addressing the educational problems not only of the local congregation but being concerned as well from a Christian perspective about education wherever it occurs in our pluralistic and secular society.

But the final success of Groome's attempt to be revised, correlational, critical, and public depends more on an adequate theological ethic than he seems prepared to face. Groome fully acknowledges that his "shared praxis" approach to education is, as all praxis, a kind of political activity. But he does not provide an ethical methodology to guide this shared political and community-forming activity. Groome's five movements in the shared praxis approach constitute a valid outline, in my judgment, for a practical theological methodology of a critical correlational kind. It is both a pedagogical procedure and a practical theological method. It makes teaching an exercise in faithful practical theological thinking and acting. Yet these five movements—(1) naming the group's present activity, (2) critically reflecting on its consequences, (3) presenting the Christian story and vision as it applies to the topic at hand, (4) dialectically relating this story and vision to the group's stories and visions, and finally (5) choosing a personal faith response for the future[24]—cannot become controllable, especially on more complex praxis issues, unless they are infused with a more discernible ethic.

Groome is partially aware of this and does present some guidelines on ethical decision making in his *Christian Religious Education*. They are suggestive but probably not sufficient. For instance, there are long and insightful discussions of the symbol of the kingdom of God and how both love and justice are seen to be dimensions of it.[25] But his discussions of love and justice are not fine-tuned enough. Groome seems to have little awareness of the large number of different definitions of both love and justice functioning in contemporary theological ethics. It would be difficult to unpack what he has said on either of these principles in terms of some of the standard distinctions used in moral philosophy and widely employed in present-day religious ethics—distinctions that are important because they truly make a practical difference in how a principle actually functions. Would more deontic approaches to ethics be the model he has in mind? This seems clearly to be the case in contrast to the more aretaic models functioning in Westerhoff and Fowler. Groome, in contrast to Westerhoff and Fowler, is not just interested in forming good people, although he is certainly interested in that. He is also interested in forming people who can think and act according to the objective requirements of the kingdom. But if his approach is more deontic, would rule or act deontology be more appropriate? Is act or rule utilitarianism closer to what he believes is required by the kingdom of God? Or is there some alternative that he has in mind?

He does, in *Christian Religious Education*, give us three principles to guide the ethical dimensions of a shared praxis dialogue—"consequences, continuity, and community/church."[26] But what do these principles mean and how far do they carry us forward? By "consequences" he means whether a particular praxis contributes to the coming of the kingdom. But this, it must be admitted, would be difficult to answer unless one has a more precise definition than that given by Groome about just what kind of love and justice the kingdom entails. For instance, if justice were defined like the utilitarians and some situation ethicists (who are generally utilitarians), then whatever action produces more overall good for the largest number of people would be seen to have the best consequences.[27] But this definition of justice would be seen by some deontologists, such as a John Rawls or a Ronald Green,[28] as decisively unjust. An increase of good for most people, they would argue, could still result in a significant number of people at the lower levels of society not participating in this overall increase.[29] So, without more being said about the criteria for judging consequences, this principle would not go far in enhancing decision making in a shared praxis situation.

By "continuity" Groome means that decisions "made by people in a shared praxis group must be in continuity with the story of the Christian community before them."[30] But without more discussion about the content of the central ethical principles of the kingdom, one would lack the criteria to determine continuity. In addition, there would be no critical way to determine whether that which was continuous with the essence of tradition was also humanly and ethically justifiable.

And finally, by "community/church," Groome means to suggest that decisions subject to the guidance of the Holy Spirit both within the immediate community and the larger ecumenical church will be sounder than those made without this communally shared guidance.[31] But we must ask, just how would Groome know that such decisions are wiser unless they are consistent with some prior understanding of the basic ethical principles implicit within the kingdom? The point is that these three criteria cannot themselves guide praxis: rather, they assume principles and distinctions that Groome has not given us but which we sooner or later would need.

AN ETHICAL REFINEMENT OF GROOME'S
SHARED PRAXIS APPROACH

My high regard for Groome's practical theology of Christian religious education stimulates me to try to refine his five movements with a more explicit theological ethic. To do this, I will present my theory of the five levels of practical moral thinking, relate them to Groome's method, and then conclude with some notes about the different pedagogical requirements that each of the five levels entails.

In a series of articles, and especially in my *Religious Ethics and Pastoral Care*,[32] I have been gradually evolving a theory of practical moral rationality. Because I understand ethical thinking as always in some way assuming a larger world view that it arrives at partially on faith, this theory also can be seen as the formal outline of a practical theology.

This theory has both a deontic and an aretaic side. In this it agrees somewhat more with Groome than it does with either Westerhoff or Fowler. It begins with the conviction that our aretaic images of good character are decisively influenced by prior images, which we regard as objective, about how the world really is and about what right moral thinking actually entails. This is why I begin with a presentation of the five levels of practical moral thinking stated in an objective mode and, after this is done, move to a more aretaic statement of the five levels. What follows must be compressed because of the limitation of space, but I hope it helps illustrate, with special reference to the work of Groome, the ways the practical theological region of theological ethics can help place Christian education on a more solid footing.

Over the last few years, I have developed the conviction that there are five levels to practical moral thinking. Although there is some merit in referring to these levels with the term "dimensions," in this essay I will continue to use the language of "levels." There is (1) a visional or metaphorical level, (2) an obligational level, (3) a tendency-need level, (4) a contextual level, and (5) a rule-role level. These five levels are hierarchically organized in that the higher levels have more extensive influence over the total process of moral thinking than the lower. But, at the same time, each of the levels has a partial independence from all the other levels, including those levels above. By this I mean that fresh judgments are made at each of the five levels which are never simply logically derived from the higher levels. Nonetheless, each of the five levels is required for purposes of making actual, concrete moral decisions: the five levels complete each other and, at least to some degree, depend on each other.

The five levels arise from five fundamental questions which I believe we implicitly or explicitly ask ourselves when we think freshly about praxis issues. The most fundamental question is, What kind of world do we live in? To answer that question we must necessarily resort to metaphors and narratives which symbolically and dramatically represent the ultimate context of our experience. The second most basic question is, What should we do? To answer this, we resort to some general principle which tells us rather abstractly but comprehensively what we are morally justified in doing. We find such general principles in the Golden Rule and the principles of neighbor love found in the Second Great Commandment. We also find them in utilitarian and Kantian principles of obligation or in maxims of punitive reciprocity such as "an eye for an eye and a tooth for a tooth." The third question asks, What are the basic tendencies, needs, and values which humans, because of their nature, seek to satisfy? Such information is crucial for answering the question of what nonmoral goods and values are the important ones for our principles of obligation to properly mediate or adjudicate. Fourth, there is the question, What is the present cultural, sociological, or ecological *context,* and what constraints does it place on our actions? And finally, after gaining answers to the four questions above, we ask, What should be the concrete rules and roles that we should follow?

In suggesting that these five questions are always in some way present in all instances of free and autonomous moral thinking, I do not mean that they are consciously so, nor do I mean that we always start with the higher or more basic questions and systematically go down from there. In fact, we probably generally back into the higher questions as we gradually move from the problem we are confronting to a more theoretical analysis of how we *are presently* thinking, and then how we *should in the future* think, about the issue that we are facing. In fact, we generally start out, as Groome suggests, with an analysis of our present action (what I call the rules and roles that govern our present praxis) and then move backward in an effort to uncover our grounding assumptions to a fuller analysis of the higher levels of moral thinking. This, of course, would be something analogous to the critical reflection on our story and vision that Groome refers to in his second movement.

My proposal is to differentiate what Groome has in mind by the

Christian story and our more personal stories in light of these five levels. When this is done, the dialectical conversation that Groome envisions between the Christian story and our individual stories can be more truly critical, and we can have a much clearer picture about what this conversation will consist of. For instance, to compare my story or that of my group to the Christian story entails comparing my deep metaphors to the deep metaphors of the Christian faith. It means critically correlating my actual principle or principles of obligation to the principles of the Christian story. It means comparing the tendencies and needs which I or my society value as fundamental to human existence with those deemed important by the Christian message. It would entail comparing contrasting perceptions of context and rules and roles. It would be at these lower levels of practical moral thinking that we can expect, and rightfully, the greatest room for variation between people who sometimes allegedly orient themselves to the same religious stories.

But critical reflection assumes that we can find a third perspective that somehow transcends both our own stories and the Christian story from which to test both, and that will provide a vantage point from which to inject a philosophical note into our Christian religious education. Let me share some of the fruits of my own critical reflection about the Christian story.

The narrative line of the Christian story is grounded in three basic metaphors which are used to represent the character of God's nature and action. H. R. Niebuhr has suggested with good reason that the metaphors of Creator, Governor, and Redeemer applied to God are a useful summary of the deep metaphors of the Christian faith. These metaphors have communicated to Christians that they live in a world that is basically good, that is morally serious, and that is open to change and redeemable.

But to say that God is Governor and morally serious does not say much until we advance some kind of proposition defining the nature of that moral seriousness. We do this when we advance a definition of justice or a position about the nature of love that gives content to the Christian story's claims about moral seriousness. Here we find great variation between different theologians and different strands of the Christian tradition as to how to articulate the principles of obligation implicit within the Christian story. It is my opinion that the most satisfactory answers to this question come from those who give more Kantian interpretations to the Christian concepts of love and justice. I find the theological application by Ronald Green in his *Religious Reason* of John Rawls's neo-Kantian principle of justice as fairness to be especially satisfying.[33] Justice as fairness is a deontological principle in that it does not arrive at an understanding of either love or justice by asking which action will bring about the largest amount of nonmoral good, as do the teleologists.[34] Rather it asks what is just or fair when the parties involved in a decision are impartial or blind to the particular benefits a decision might yield to them and try to envision instead what would be fair no matter where one might stand in the social system. Green has argued persuasively that it is possible to unpack both the principle of neighbor love and the justice of the kingdom of God in light of this understanding of impartiality.

Whether Green is correct is not an issue that I can settle within the confines of this paper. My goal instead is to illustrate a range of issues in the practical theological region of theological ethics for the practical theological region of religious education. To think critically about the dialectical relation between the principles of obligation of the Christian story and the principles of obligation within my own story is to raise questions of just this kind. This is especially true if a practical theology of education is to take part in a public dialogue in a pluralistic society. The flexible relation between our visions and metaphors of ultimacy (level 1) and our principles of obligation (level 2) can be seen by the fact that similar principles of obligation can be found within the context of considerably different metaphorical visions. For instance, it is widely known that something like the Golden Rule can be found in different religious faiths with vastly different metaphors of ultimacy. Cooperation between diverse religious traditions can be achieved precisely because such flexibility exists between the five levels of practical moral thinking.

With regard to the lower three levels of practical moral thinking, a few things need to be said to complete my illustrative remarks. If I am correct in arguing for a more deontological understanding of the Christian principles of obligation, one would still need some theory of the basic human tendencies and needs which must be fairly and impartially actualized (love) and mediated (justice). One would need knowledge of one's social and ecological context, but not because this contextual knowledge can justifiably determine either our metaphors of ultimacy or our principles of obligation. The empirical disciplines that give us such knowledge should not influence the content of the higher levels of practical moral thinking, but they can give us information about which of our sometimes conflicting tendencies and needs can be fairly actualized and justly adjudicated within the constraints of our present context.

And finally, when judgments at these higher four levels are made, then we should have new critical perspectives from which to test and possibly transform the rules and roles of our present praxis. This is what a revised correlational approach to shared praxis in Christian education is really about. It is a complex process. We should enter into it with our eyes wide open. Even if the details of my own position on the content of these five levels is open to question, that should not obscure the validity of my main point, i.e., that a critical dialogue between our stories and the Christian story would eventually necessitate a critical conversation on these five levels.

THE ARETAIC PERSPECTIVE ON THE
FIVE LEVELS

In spite of my concern to state first the more objective side of practical moral reason, I believe there is a characterological counterpart to the five levels I have discussed. And I am fully aware that to the Christian educator, the characterological analogues to the five levels are the subject matter of greater interest. It would be precisely the task of Christian religious education, in contrast to religious or theological ethics, to form people who have the kind of character, inclinations, readiness, and knowledge necessary to approach the five levels of practical moral thinking from a Christian perspective. The formation and transformation of humans into acting Christians is precisely the task of Christian religious education. But it has been my argument that just what it means to be an acting Christian cannot be known to Christian education without assistance from the practical theological region of theological ethics.

The objective and aretaic perspectives on the five levels are represented thus:

Objective	*Aretaic*
1. Visional or Metaphoric	1. Faith Development
2. Obligational	2. Moral Development
3. Tendency-Need	3. Emotional Development
4. Contextual	4. Perceptual or Ego Development
5. Rule-Role	5. Rule-Role Development

This representation suggests that not only a characterological counterpart to each of the five levels of practical moral thinking can be specified, but that, in addition, each of these five aretaic dimensions has a developmental line. Not only is faith development the aretaic analogue

92

to the visional or metaphoric level of practical moral reason but also faith, as Fowler has tried to argue, has a developmental line. Similarly, the obligational level of practical moral reason has a characterological counterpart in our capacity for moral reasoning and this too has a developmental line as Kohlberg, Carol Gilligan, and others have suggested. The tendency-need level of moral reasoning has a developmental counterpart in our emotional line of development as psychoanalysis in general and especially the work of Erikson has shown. I believe that we can also trace developmental lines in our ego's capacity to perceive, interpret, and test the empirical realities of our environment and, finally, even a developmental line in our capacity to occupy and devise appropriate roles and establish appropriate rules. To suggest that there are identifiable developmental lines for these five levels of character is not to suggest that the lines are totally separate and distinct. But it is my point, following recent developments in psychoanalytic theory, especially the work of John Gedo and Arnold Goldberg,[35] to point out that our development has different lines entailing slightly different psychobiological infrastructures that are themselves shaped and activated by different types of learnings.

Types of Learning and the Five Levels of Character

It is a complex task to shape people who have the characterological readiness to critically participate in shared praxis guided by a Christian approach to the five levels. Of course, when it is artfully done it does not seem complex. But when analyzed and reflected upon, we see clearly how complex it truly is.

The learning entailed in faith development doubtless is of two kinds. If one were to look at faith development from the perspective of Hauerwas and Westerhoff, learning as socialization would be the model employed.[36] Hauerwas's contribution has been to show how a community such as the church is the bearer of a vision which itself forms character for those who participate in that community. This character is the framework for how the individuals of that community discern the world. This discernment is their faith.[37]

Fowler adds a structuralist point of view to this process. Following Piaget's structuralist theory of development, he demonstrates what the natural differentiation and complexification of our cognitive structures do to our faith development. He has shown that faith development is not totally the result of socializing forces of a community, although he has recently acknowledged the importance and maybe even the predominance of these forces for the shaping of faith. But within these larger socializing influences, structuralism helps us to see how our own faith is also shaped by the transformation of our intellectual operations as these operations function on our inherited communal relations and the kind of world view that they imply. Fowler has shown that there must be sufficient freedom, pluralism, and diversity in our social experience for the cognitive tensions to occur which stimulate higher-level intellectual transformations.[38] But in making this valuable point, he sometimes fails to say strongly enough that unless our intellectual operations are working on significant visions mediated by trusted communities, this natural transformational process is not likely to occur or *at least* not occur in the direction he believes is normative. There is no need to make a fundamental choice between the more dynamic and historical model of Hauerwas and the structuralism of Fowler to comprehend the nature of the formation of faith, although it is best to see Fowler's structural model as increasing our understanding of certain structural transformations that can occur within, yet sometimes transcend, these initial socializing forces.

Moral development also has both a psychodynamic and a structuralist dimension. There is little doubt that at its more rudimentary levels, moral development requires some of the dynamics of superego formation as Freud first conceptualized this process. Attachments are formed and the internalization of the cherished values of loved ones occurs in an effort to ward off the threat of object loss.[39] This is one of the reasons we so readily internalize the values and narratives of our communities of socialization; they are objects of our affections and we fear to lose them. But in addition, the differentiation and transformation of our intellectual operations working on the ordering of our interpersonal relations and conflicts must also be, as Kohlberg argues, an important part of acquiring more autonomous moral judgment. There is no need to make a choice between Freud and Kohlberg; they simply describe different although overlapping phases of the moral development process.

Nor is there a need to make a choice between Kohlberg and the recent challenge to his position by Craig Dykstra.[40] It is my conviction that in virtually repudiating Kohlberg, and thereby repudiating the role of principles in Christian ethics, Dykstra has in effect collapsed my level 2 (principles of obligation and the development of our capacity to use them) into level 1 (metaphors of ultimacy, stories, and faith). My interest in distinguishing those two levels also functions to resist the idea that simple socialization into the Christian story is itself sufficient to stimulate the differentiations and structural transformations necessary for our moral development in a pluralistic society.

A discussion of the kind of learning involved in emotional development raises the question of the relation of emotional development and faith development. It is clear that both of them entail dynamics of affectional attachment, identification with meaningful relations, and the development of typical patterns and modalities for coping with desire and anxiety. Neither emotional development nor faith development can occur without the development of intense interpersonal relations that are, at the same time, afflicted with the common tensions, losses, constraints, and delays of gratification typical of all life processes. Both emotional development and faith development involve learning how to cope with these strains and threats to our object relations. The difference between faith development and emotional development is primarily one of perspective. When we speak of emotional development, we have in mind the psychobiological needs that we bring to the world; when we speak of faith development, we have in mind our developing picture or sense of the world and its deep possibilities that our psychobiological needs learn to expect. Hence, emotional development is the subjective pole and faith development the objective pole of the self-world interaction or dialectic that marks the nature of experience. Fowler's contribution, once again, has been to show that we bring intellectual operations to this interaction and that these operations are at least a factor in the way our interpersonal relations witness to the deeper possibilities of the world.

Emotional development is crucial for the more objective process of practical moral thinking and action. Emotional maturity means in part having experiential access to one's own generic tendencies and needs. Although certain kinds of moral problems require that this experiential knowledge must be supplemented by more objective knowledge of human nature, it is still the case that there is no substitute for this experiential knowledge of our own needs. It is the presupposition of our empathy into the needs of others. It provides the empathic element in the command to "Love your neighbor as yourself." It protects our practical moral decision making from becoming too mechanical, rationalistic, and detached. Yet, as I indicated above, intuitive knowledge of our own tendencies and needs does not necessarily lead to right moral action. It is only when this inner knowledge is guided by genuinely moral mediating principles that true moral action can emerge.

At level 4, knowledge of a sociological, ecological, or economic kind about our contexts is more properly informational than the kinds of knowledge required at the higher three levels of character formation. The learning involved is more directly cognitive. Although there is doubtless, in some way, a role for instruction at each of the five aretaic levels, it is most relevant at this level.

And finally, at the last level, we learn roles and concrete rules most easily when we actually enact them. Every educational process must have this more concrete level of participation when we learn by doing. This is the great wisdom behind the renewal of catechumenate models of education which Regis Duffy has so effectively pointed to in his *Real Presence* and *A Roman Catholic Theology of Pastoral Care*.[41] But a revised correlational approach to a practical theology of Christian education requires not only actual enactment of roles and rules but critical reflection on them as well. To do this involves the learnings connected with a self-conscious practical moral theological method of the kind proposed in this paper. It entails referring back to the more objective appropriation of the five levels presented earlier in this paper. It is precisely my proposal that Christian religious education in the future be built on such a method and, at the same time, help teach such a method as a part of intentional Christian living in a complex, modern, and pluralistic society.

IMPLICATIONS FOR THEOLOGICAL EDUCATION

Two propositions relevant to theological education follow from the account set forth above on the nature of education for practical theological thinking and acting. These are that (1) learning for practical theological thinking and acting entails making appeals to several different lines of development, and (2) addressing these different lines of development entails multiple experiences that are themselves mediated by individuals and communities playing different yet overlapping roles.

It is the presupposition of these remarks that it should be the primary goal of theological education within the seminary to educate practical theological thinkers and actors. This should be more fundamental to the task of the seminary than the education of ordained ministers. Not all seminary students need become professional ministers, but all ordained ministers also should be practical theological thinkers and actors. But such is also the case for those students who will use their theological education in a ministry of the laity.

It is helpful to understand the divinity school or seminary as the center of an interlocking group of communities and persons involved in the practical theological education of its seminary students. The seminary provides the core of the academic courses. Through its field education, it also provides the professional directors who orchestrate the educational contributions of the other relevant communities and persons, i.e., field education in local congregations, supervisory relations with senior pastors, close relations with lay people, and the like. In light of this network of relations, it is possible to specify where the various components of education in practical theological thinking are most likely to take place.

First, the key element that makes education for practical theological thinking truly educational is the critical appropriation of a self-conscious model for practical theological reflection. It is the seminary itself in its academic instruction that should provide the student with such a model or models. Hence, it is the explicit task of the seminary to enable the student to master a practical theological methodology. It is my position that the most satisfactory methodology will be built around a revised correlational model of the kind outlined earlier in the paper. Such a model, to be truly rigorous, should be built around a critical correlation of the five levels of practical moral thinking. The revised correlational method makes it possible to critically correlate (1) the gospel witness at each of the five levels, (2) significant cultural options in terms of their implications for each of the five levels, and (3) one's own personal experience in terms of its implications for the levels. This three-way critical dialogue should run throughout the student's theological education and provide the structure that will bridge the existential and theoretical aspects of the student's learning.

It is possible to use this three-way dialogue as a model around which the action-reflection components of ministerial education can be organized. This would be true of clinical pastoral education. It would also be true for other action-reflection models. In *Religious Ethics and Pastoral Care*, I have identified four steps of practical theological thinking that portray the time sequence of such thinking. I have argued that there is (1) a step of experiencing and defining the problem, (2) a step of deeper attention, listening, and understanding, (3) a step of critical analysis and critical comparison of the relevant options, including one's Christian commitments, and (4) a final step of decision and strategy. [42] Although the five levels of practical moral thinking can help analyze, in various ways, each of these steps, they are most relevant to the task of critical comparison and decision which occurs at the last two steps.

What I envision is a coming together of explicit practical theological methodology and a program of action and reflection. A critical correlational approach to practical theology, buttressed by the tools of the five levels, provides a model to guide clinical pastoral education, seminary-based practicums, and action-reflection within the context of the parish.

Let me set forth some examples of how it would work. At appropriate times, individuals would not only attempt to retrieve the basic vision and metaphors of the Christian story, but they would look at their own action for what it reveals about their visions and deep metaphors. Not only should this be a matter of students sharing with one another, but it also should be a matter of professors, supervisors, teaching ministers sharing as well. They would not share just their own intellectual understanding of the "normative" metaphors of the Christian religion, but what their actions and daily praxis suggest about their own actual operative metaphors of ultimacy or, as said from the aretaic perspective, their own operative faith. This is consistent with what I said above when I argued that faith is developed by sharing personal perceptions and deep attitudes within the context of a community of faith which itself has particular narratives and metaphors of ultimacy that project a certain view of the world. This is often spoken of as a matter of telling our personal stories in the context of being addressed by the Christian story. Although this is an important part of learning at this first level, I also have argued that it is not in contradiction to the kind of differentiation and transformation of the more structural aspects of faith spoken of by Fowler. Confronting diverse views of faith differentiates and transforms the more cognitive aspects of our faith, as Fowler has argued. Sharing our personal stories and metaphors within the context of a community which is itself in a hermeneutic conversation with the stories and deep metaphors of the Christian faith is also likely to shape and transform our personal faith.

Such a dialogue should proceed in the context of situations of praxis, i.e., within the context of situations where people are asking, What is it that we should do? Such situations call forth even more prominently the second level of practical theological thinking, i.e., the obligational level. I have already argued that the obligational implications of the Christian story can be abstracted from the Christian story and stand as general principles which themselves can be philosophically tested for their adequacy. Action-reflection within the context of seminary education must use both that kind of moral learning that Freud spoke about and that which Kohlberg writes about. At times the affection and respect of the student for professor, supervisor, and minister will lead the student to identify with the moral commitments and principles of obligation of the beloved authority. In addition, and gradually, the interaction between student, peers, and supervisors around moral issues will further transform and make more inclusive those cognitive structures most pertinent to moral thinking. But without exposure to action-reflection in a group setting that is itself located within a worshiping community, these kinds of learning are not likely to take place.

But the action-reflection process around the first two levels of practical moral thinking can also involve reflection of the third or cultural pole of the context of praxis. In addition to narrative-metaphor structure and ethical principles of the Christian story and that of one's own personal experience, attention should be given to these aspects of the various cultures that impinge upon our experience. For instance, the metaphors in Western industrial culture of endless material and scientific expansion and the principle of ethical egoism and enlightened self-interest pervade much of our immediate cultural life and should be brought into conversation with the Christian story. Our more personal experience, standing in the middle between the Christian witness and culture, must be reflected on to determine to what, in the end, our practice is finally committed. Now that I have illustrated how culture enters into this three-way conversation at the visional and obligational levels, in order to economize space I will confine my remaining illustrations to the interaction of the Christian story and our personal experience.

Action-reflection models must also attend to the third level of practical theological thinking—the tendency-need or emotional level. Above I argued that this entails helping people develop an awareness and acceptance of their own most basic emotional needs. This not only has a humanizing effect on the theological student, but it is also doubtless a presupposition of the possibility of empathic relating to the emotional needs of others. Hence, such reflection is ethically relevant, but it is not ethically sufficient. Empathically relating to one's own and to others' needs does not guarantee that one will discover a moral way of addressing those needs. Hence, action-reflection must not become arrested at this level, as it frequently does in clinical pastoral education, but must bring this heightened awareness of needs, one's own and others', back to reflection on the appropriate principles of obligation required to justly order those needs and, as well, to reflection on the visions and deep metaphors that give them final significance.

Learnings at the fourth level can also occur in the action-reflection situation. Here learning about situations can be both cognitive and experiential. There is a real place for sociological, economic, and cultural information about the various contexts of action. But there is also a place for experiential participation in the situations of action. This is the wisdom of the phrase "identification with the oppressed" and other such exhortations to learn about situations through direct involvement. It is clear that the full complexity of any situation can never be captured by any science or by any system of conceptuality whatsoever, including a theological one. Therefore, there is no substitute for direct experiential contact with situations for the purpose of action-reflection. Yet, at the same time, such experiential learning must be balanced by more abstract analyses from a variety of disciplines and it must be disciplined with a methodological understanding of where such knowledge belongs within the total context of practical theological thinking. Exposure alone does not go far.

Finally, action-reflection must have a fifth level—a rule-role level. This is to suggest that not only must action-reflection in its various contexts think about action, it must also enact action. It must develop various concrete rules for action and various roles that order action. And as it does so, it must further reflection by opening itself to the whole theoretical moment implicit in critical correlational thinking. Of course, I do not mean to suggest that there is no role for simulation and games in the enacting of action. It would be tedious, exhausting, and probably impulsive if all action-reflection actually entailed real action. There is a great place for the imaginative projecting of action and the imaginative assessment of the consequences of action. But it probably means that probes into the enactment of real action and the concrete roles and rules that should guide it must also be a part of action-reflection in its various contexts.

The seminary and divinity school should provide the critical theory to guide this process. Action-reflection must be based upon a theory of practical theological thinking or it will disintegrate into formless thought and impulsive action. But guided by such a theory, it can be indispensable to the growth in the Christian life necessary for ministry in both its professional and lay expressions.

NOTES

1. Seward Hiltner, *Preface to Pastoral Theology* (Nashville and New York: Abingdon Press, 1958); Daniel Day Williams, "Truth in a Theological Perspective," *Journal of Religion* (October 1948), and *The Minister and the Care of Souls* (New York: Harper & Row, 1961).

2. David Tracy, *Blessed Rage for Order: The New Pluralism in Theology* (New

York: Seabury Press, 1975), and *The Analogical Imagination: Christian Theology and the Culture of Pluralism* (New York: Crossroad, 1981).

3. Don Browning, *Religious Ethics and Pastoral Care* (Philadelphia: Fortress Press, 1983).

4. Wolfhart Pannenberg, *Theology and the Philosophy of Science,* trans. Francis McDonagh (Philadelphia: Westminster Press, 1976), 426.

5. Victor Turner, *The Ritual Process: Structure and Anti-Structure* (Chicago: Aldine Publishing, 1969); Anthony Wallace, *Religion: An Anthropological View* (New York: Random House, 1966); Claude Levi-Strauss, *Structural Anthropology,* trans. Claire Jacobson and Brooke G. Schoepf (New York: Basic Books, 1963).

6. William Frankena, *Ethics* (Englewood Cliffs, N.J.: Prentice-Hall, 1973), 9.

7. Ibid.

8. John H. Westerhoff III, *Building God's People in a Materialistic Society* (New York: Seabury Press, 1983).

9. Ibid., 6.

10. Ibid., 9.

11. Stanley Hauerwas, *A Community of Character: Toward a Constructive Christian Social Ethic* (Notre Dame, Ind.: Notre Dame University Press, 1981); Craig Dykstra, *Vision and Character: A Christian Educator's Alternative to Kohlberg* (New York: Paulist Press, 1981).

12. Westerhoff, *Building God's People,* 80–84, 93.

13. James Fowler, "Practical Theology and the Shaping of Christian Lives," in *Practical Theology: The Emerging Field in Theology, Church, and World,* ed. Don Browning (New York: Harper & Row, 1982), 154.

14. Ibid., 155 (Browning's italics).

15. James Fowler, *Becoming Adult, Becoming Christian: Adult Development and Christian Faith* (San Francisco: Harper & Row, 1984), 42.

16. Fowler, "Practical Theology," 161.

17. Thomas H. Groome, *Christian Religious Education: Sharing Our Story and Vision* (New York: Harper & Row, 1980).

18. Thomas H. Groome, "Theology on Our Feet: A Revisionist Pedagogy for Healing the Gap between Academia and Ecclesia," in this volume, 55–78.

19. Hans-Georg Gadamer, *Truth and Method* (New York: Seabury Press, 1975).

20. Groome, *Christian Religious Education,* 232. He acknowledges the same point on pp. 69–74 in his article for this volume. Earlier in this article Groome seems to associate Tracy with a correlation of *theory* position, but this overlooks the praxis-oriented expressions of his correlational position as I summarized on pp. 80–82 of this essay. See David Tracy, "The Foundations of Practical Theology," in *Practical Theology,* ed. Browning, 76.

21. C. Ellis Nelson, *Where Faith Begins* (Richmond: John Knox Press, 1971).

22. Groome, *Christian Religious Education,* 217.

23. Ibid., 199.

24. Ibid., 207–31.

25. Ibid., 35–51.

26. Ibid., 198.

27. Frankena, *Ethics*, 14–16, 34–43.

28. John Rawls, *A Theory of Justice* (Cambridge: Harvard University Press, 1971); Ronald Green, *Religious Reason: The Rational and Moral Basis of Religious Belief* (New York: Oxford University Press, 1978).

29. For a succinct statement of the deontologist's argument against utilitarian theories of justice see Frankena, *Ethics*, 41.

30. Groome, *Christian Religious Education*, 198.

31. Ibid., 199.

32. Browning, *Religious Ethics*.

33. Green, *Religious Reason*, 131–32; Browning, *Religious Ethics*, 64–68.

34. Frankena, *Ethics*, 34.

35. John Gedo and Arnold Goldberg, *Models of the Mind: A Psychoanalytic Theory* (Chicago: University of Chicago Press, 1973).

36. For a founding statement of this point of view, see Nelson, *Where Faith Begins*, esp. 35–66.

37. Hauerwas, *Community of Character*, 130–34.

38. James Fowler, *Stages of Faith: The Psychology of Human Development and the Quest for Meaning* (San Francisco: Harper & Row, 1981), 151–211.

39. Sigmund Freud, *New Introductory Lectures on Psycho-Analysis*, trans. W. J. H. Sprott (New York: W. W. Norton, 1933), 86–88.

40. Dykstra, *Vision and Character*, 33–62.

41. Regis Duffy, *Real Presence: Worship, Sacraments, and Commitment* (San Francisco: Harper & Row, 1982), and *A Roman Catholic Theology of Pastoral Care* (Philadelphia: Fortress Press, 1983).

42. Browning, *Religious Ethics*, 99.

6 Thinking in the Community of Faith: Toward an Ecclesial Hermeneutic

LEWIS S. MUDGE

Practical theologians, whatever their viewpoint or approach, need ways of thinking *about* the thinking that goes on *in* the shared life of faith. Faith communities both grow out of and generate symbolic interactions, and therefore involve thinking processes. Those who seek to reflect upon these processes, perhaps to bring them into relation with norms or to assess their faithfulness, need categories that permit the reasoning intrinsic to shared faith to speak for itself, while encouraging critical judgments concerning it to be made.

What is the nature of the thinking that underlies, accompanies, and sustains faithful life-together? Several writers have recently sought to describe it. Edward Farley's notion of "theologia," of theology as "habitus,"[1] despite its elusiveness and tendency to individualism, surely moves in the right direction. Robert Bellah and his associates perhaps come closer to the lay mind and to the actual phenomena of collective awareness with their Tocquevillian term "habits of the heart."[2] But Saint Paul long ago identified and addressed the same notion of community-embedded thought. "Have this mind among yourselves," he wrote to the Philippian church, "which is yours in Christ Jesus . . ." (Phil. 2:5). And to the Romans, ". . . be transformed by the renewal of your mind . . ." (Rom. 12:2). What is this way of thinking, this making of a common mind, but the deliberation that contextually forms and carries forward the life of shared discipleship? It is certainly not what we now call "systematic theology." It is, rather, that which systematic theology needs to thematize and study if it wishes to recover its ecclesial vocation.

If the truth be told, academic theologians have typically set little store by the symbolic exchanges, linguistic and otherwise, that actually constitute the fabric of the faith community. Best, we think, to give a wide berth to all such regions of intellectual chaos. Yet here lie the primary thought movements that actually shape the community's decisions, and therefore its social form. Here lie the mostly unspoken patterns of signification that account for the way some things "make sense" to us in congregational meetings or in daily life, while other things do not. To the extent that the theologian is rooted in a faith community, these sign sets will influence his or her more explicit intellectual inclinations—the sorts of things that "make sense" in his or her academic theological discourse—as well.

This essay seeks a fresh approach to the description and analysis of the faith community's primary thinking processes. The approach sought is hermeneutical in genre, but follows the lead of those who have extended the scope of hermeneutic from the world of texts and textlike products to the human life-world as such, seen as an arena of activated, interrelated, signs. It argues furthermore that there is such a thing as lived, and not merely discursive, exegesis. A community of faith may be understood as such an exegesis, following certain rules or norms, of the signs of the world around it. And by being such a lived exegesis of the world, the community becomes a signifying element *in* that world. The embodied and normed exegesis of signs itself becomes a new sign. Because this process is practical and communal, and not merely academic, it is itself a process of symbolic interaction. Hence it involves a kind of thinking in action which is precisely that which we are trying to understand. To the extent that this thinking *is* exegetical in nature, critical reflection in the midst of and on behalf of it will need to be an ecclesial hermeneutic. The task of this essay is to begin to sketch the kind of hermeneutic required.

OUR INQUIRY IN THE PRESENT
THEOLOGICAL SITUATION

But why are we doing all this? If this inquiry is to be properly understood, it must be not only grasped in its own right but also seen as part of a larger quest. The search for a hermeneutic of primary thinking in the faith community is a response, not merely to the church's practical problems, but to a series of crises in the Christian theological enterprise. Every essay in this book affirms this in one way or another. But the present writer believes it makes a difference how one *comes* to the question of the faith community's practical reasoning. How and why is the traditional academic way of doing theology breaking down?

The writer was brought up theologically in a Barthian context. Hence he tends to see the present crisis—if that can be done—in Barthian terms. This essay will argue that the present deconstruction of the Christian theological edifice parallels, and may even be said to continue, the deconstruction launched by Karl Barth with his *Romans* commentary after World War I.[3] Barth's series of moves marked not only his personal intellectual development and his ongoing attempt to meet changing political and spiritual concerns, it also pointed to a series of shifts in the implied social and cultural locations for theological work. Barth journeyed from a nineteenth-century culture protestantism that had its home among educated elites and in the universities, to a theology of "infinite qualitative distinction"[4] in which the preacher proclaims the Word to a congregation of solitary existers, and finally to "theology as a function of the Church":[5] the disciplined testing of the "language about God" peculiar to a confessing community seeking its independent identity and voice in the face of worldly powers.[6]

Taken together, Barth's moves overcame the nineteenth-century marriage between theology and the spirit of the age and reaffirmed dogmatics as a "science" (in the German sense of *Wissenschaft*) in its own right. But they were worked out in a manner which assumed that both the ecclesiastical and the cultural conditions needed for confident theological construction were still relatively secure. Barth, for example, could consult the Christian past with confidence that his work stood in demonstrable continuity with it. He could presuppose the existence of the institutional church without questioning the sufficiency of his Swiss, bourgeois context for modeling its mental habits. And, above all, he could develop a "doctrine of the Word of God" without serious doubt about the nature and role of language in human life, and therefore of dogmatic constructs dependent upon it. Today each of these assumptions has been radically shaken.

We live in a crisis of sources and of our relation to them. What sources are authoritative, and why? What connects us with these sources, and how? What guarantees the identity and continuity of the faith community? We speak of appropriating tradition but we cannot (despite ecumenical achievements in this area) give a common account of what tradition is or of how it works over time. Our sense of the integrity of tradition and of its transmission has rested, Farley says, on the maintenance of a notion of the church as "house of authority" and of Christian thinking as requiring a "principle of identity."[7] But neither frame of reference is tenable under the actual conditions of contemporary Christian life on this planet.

Morever, we cannot take the institutional church we know as normative setting even for a critical "dogmatics." Instead, we face a situation of radical religious pluralism: so much so that we cannot say whether the different expressions of Christian faith across the cultures and across the globe have any single essence. Contextuality rules. Not only does Christian faith appear to have radically divergent meanings in different venues, but within Western cultures alone there have appeared theologies representing women, minority groups, groups with special interests, and the like. At this historical juncture, this is as it should be. It is in the interests of justice that different human communities come to self-awareness and achieve their voice: appropriate too that the church become a vehicle for such self-expression. But with what result for Christian faith? In what sense can all these expressions of the faith be thought to represent one church? What confessional norm or norms can be said to be present in all? Is there in fact any practical limit to such diversity? May contextually situated forms of faith diverge to the point of being beyond the possibility of mutual communications? *Is* there one gospel for the whole world?

And, finally, we face a radical loss of confidence in the means of theological conceptualization. To the extent that such conceptualization, even of the Barthian kind, depends on the integrity of the European university and literary language-worlds, it must today be called in question. The deconstructive attacks of a Foucault,[8] or of a Derrida,[9] have been devastating to the assumption that our academic discursivities place reality at our disposal. If language speaks us rather than the other way around, it cannot be the medium for a theology of the Word. We now see that language as we know it in the lecture hall or library is an expression of the human power situation, and perhaps not capable of being a medium for the expression of a Word beyond that situation.

The methods employed in *Church Dogmatics* are not workable where impassable gulfs separate past from present, here from there, language from intentional consciousness. We are left unable to account for the community of faith, or to think coherently about it. Each of the three factors of tradition, context, and contextuality has become almost infinitely variable in its own right. Any combination of these variables into a particular form of life is probably sui generis: unique, forming a class of one. To put this another way, for any given instance of the *ekklesia* we cannot confidently make connections to the Christian past, or to other contemporary forms of the church. And we cannot generalize in thought what we see. With tradition, context, and conceptuality simultaneously problematic, the ecclesio-social form of life that takes shape in any given case will probably be, at least humanly speaking, a *bricolage*, an adventitious combination of elements lashed together on the spot. The actual configuration of the faith community will seldom, if ever, reflect exactly any standard ecclesiology found in the history of Christian thought or in current denominational manuals. It will not correspond, either, to the dogmatic "Church concept" with which Barth, so his critics write, replaced the notion of God's action in history.[10]

Perhaps it is only now that the full implications of Barth's original deconstructive move can be worked out, and the question raised whether *Church Dogmatics* represents the only possible outcome of the original initiative. The issue, of course, is whether the encounter with the God of "infinite qualitative difference," which negates all human aspirations and achievements, leaves any concrete sociocultural, yet not idolatrous, place in the world for the gospel to stand. Yet if there is any act of faith inherent in the present essay, it is that God has not left the world without a witness. Despite the fact that we cannot account for them in traditional theological terms, recognizably Christian communities of faith continue to exist, in fact in many cases to thrive. Like the "subjugated knowledges" proffered by Michel Foucault[11] and the "local knowledge" analyzed by Clifford Geertz,[12] the ways of thinking worked out by thousands of Christian communities in their contexts defy academic attempts at regulation or classification. Yet, just by existing, they demand recognition. We must adopt a theological perspective through which we can be open to this demand: when, where, and as it happens. We need a perspective through which we ourselves can be open to being the ones through whom it happens.

Hence, the proposal for what could be called a "humble hermeneutic" or a "hermeneutic of recognition." We need a hermeneutic capable of detecting and identifying the forms of situational exegesis, and therefore the significative configurations, characteristic of particular forms of faith-in-situation. To see the situational shape of faith, we must bracket out, or deconstruct, the established institutional and conceptual forms in order to see what is there prestructurally. That can perhaps be done through a form of "hermeneutic phenomenology"[13] that sees the social world as "text-like" and thus can study different lived "readings" of that text. The value of semiotic method for this purpose is that it renders the world ready to be read. It helps us see how the social world, below the level of established institutions and concepts, remains "readable," and hence an arena in which human action makes sense.

Could it be that the encounter with infinite qualitative difference might be described in sociolinguistic rather than existentialist terms? The "new quest for the historical Jesus" contended that "history" in the Gospels was essentially an arena for existential encounter. Why not conjecture that such an encounter took place for the followers of Jesus as their secure frames of self-and-world reference were exchanged for a precarious, yet tangible, form of existence known as discipleship? This new form of being-in-the-world was not confined to the existential moment. It was not purely inward and dimensionless. It is describable today as a set of relationships to the powers of this world and to the forms of imagination by which the powers are sustained, such that these powers become penultimate to the power of the kingdom. There can, in short, be an exegesis of the situation that exists when the disciples leave everything to be with Jesus. The hermeneutical principles that govern this exegesis underlie the codes and rules which regulate and sustain the faith community.

The community-forming power of such a hermeneutic must rest upon the thoroughness of its inherent deconstruction and reconstruction of common "sense." Written texts are far from the only sources to be "read": the reading must penetrate to the constituent "signs" of the world, the fundamental building blocks of meaning. The coming of Jesus Christ introduces just such a radical deconstruction and reconstruction of the signs which, at that time and place, have sustained the world of power and meaning.

Is the gospel then an instrument for the "insurrection of subjugated languages"? May it be that the Word of God comes to us through signs which the forms of expression in power normally exclude and repress? May it come in messages that disrupt the structures constructed to domesticate them? Is language capable of being the vehicle of such disruption? May the Word of God speak in the wordlessness of what it *is* to be a *campesino*, or an asylum inmate? Can we reach such a level of understanding by permitting our hermeneutic of the human sign-world to be controlled by a christological metaphor: that of the Suffering Servant of God?

SEMIOTIC METHOD IN THE WORLDS OF POWER AND IMAGINATION

The emerging discipline of semiotics is the logical discussion partner for our attempt at an ecclesial hermeneutic, for it demonstrates how both society and culture are generated and maintained by human interactions involving the signifying elements in the situation concerned. Culture is, in effect, a set of codes along with the rules for using them. A hermeneutic of ecclesial existence requires semiotic analysis of the signifiers and codes among which the faith community functions as a living, expressive exegesis.

The best brief account of the theory of signs as grist for a theological method is no doubt to be found in Robert Schreiter's *Constructing Local Theologies*.[14] Semiotics is an approach to the study of the human life-world in which that world is seen as an interconnected array of "signs." Semiotic theory sees culture as a vast communication network in which virtually every element, both of the natural and of the humanmade environment, may function as the bearer of signification. Hence, the term "semiotics" from the Greek *semeion* or "sign." Different writers may use different terms: "symbols" or "signifiers" may convey approximately the same meanings, depending upon the point of view intended. Seen semiotically, a culture is a system of signs whose usage is governed by still other signs functioning to denote the relationships between signs. These usage indicators are often tacit rather than explicit. Yet they constitute much of what the culture is about. They make it possible for the signs to be understood correctly. Just as native speakers of any given language know implicitly the rules for how that language goes together, and thus can speak, for practical purposes, unlimited numbers of correct sentences, so a culture consists of signs functioning within a silent syntax so that its members can not only speak but act understandably in a vast variety of ways. The task of semiotics is to describe and explain these signs, their interaction, and the rules that govern these interactions, thereby delineating the cultural complex that emerges as a result.

But where do these sign networks come from? Each person is born into an already-existing universe of significations, but also generates his or her own inner sign network. Perhaps it is true here, as in other matters, that ontogeny recapitulates phylogeny: that the child's acquisition of signifying capacity is a product of an active and imaginative struggle for selfhood in relation to the meanings conveyed by the environment. Signs and their syntaxes arise in the individual and the collective imagination. And imagination, then and now, is preoccupied with the reality of power. Human beings form mental images of the world that are more than merely diminished or evanescent copies of what has registered on their optic nerves. Our images have to do with ourselves as actors and with the world as either inviting or resisting our actions. We see the world and ourselves in terms of what we can and cannot *do*. The slave's world image is different from the master's. If we

109

feel imploded and disempowered we form images that interpret the world, as they reflect it, accordingly. The same if we are empowered—in a position to shape our own and others' lives. The reality of power (as distinguished from mere energy or force) in human affairs is always to some degree a matter of the imagination. Political power rests on a collective sense that confers it and defines it in certain terms. To resist power that rests on shared social imagination may not only be to invite retaliation but also to violate the world image that underlies the symbolic and conceptual ordering of one's universe. It is a conjecture, but certainly an attractive one, that signs of every kind, functioning to constitute culturally maintained codes or sets of rules, rest upon each culture's reigning configurations of power and the imaginative constructs that define and sustain them.

Clearly there are different ways of construing power imaginatively, and hence different sets of culture-maintaining signs. In his book *Religion and Regime*,[15] Guy E. Swanson sets out the range of possibilities that seems to have been present in Europe at the time of the Reformation. His point is to show that the different ecclesiastical polities that settled out of sixteenth-century religio-political conflict reflected the power metaphors current in the cultures concerned. Swanson offers a spectrum from "immanental" social metaphors at one end to "heterarchic" ones at the other. In the "immanental" metaphor, power is conveyed throughout the social organism from the sovereign to whom it properly belongs. To have power is to be in symbolic touch with its source. In modern terms, it is to be "In Her Majesty's Service." The society's sign complex, then, conveys this notion even in its most apparently insignificant details. The social organism becomes a construct of corporately maintained imagination, carried by its significative liturgies, uniforms, heraldry, royal ciphers, and all the rest.

In the "heterarchic" metaphor, on the other hand, power does not flow from a royal source. It is rather the outcome of some form of adjudication of competing interests: as in the stock exchange, in litigation, or in business-contract negotiation. Again the social-cultural context for this view of power is a work of the collective human imagination maintained by a complex of signs with the rules for their use. The potent signs now tend to be the symbols of success in the conflict of interests: signs related to status, wealth, and political influence. Such signs are, as in the preceding example, both massive and subtle. Public life styles make unmistakable statements. But, lacking obvious clues, we still look for indicators of manner, dress, accent, and the like which tell us how a person has fared in the struggle. A systematic study of such sets of signs will reveal the manner in which they convey and maintain an imaginatively construed syntax of power.

In either of these semiotic contexts, or in a world which embodies some combination of them, it is possible to imagine religious communities that "read" the signs in their own either legitimating or counter-cultural ways. In the first case we have the makings of Troeltsch's "church type" and in the second his "sect type." But such ideal-typical analysis is already a form of abstraction from the notion of the faith community as itself a living exegesis. The semiotic method proposed here suggests that the faith community is a "reading" of its environment in the sense of a principled translation or paraphrase of that environment's signs. It is not just a "type," but something unique to be appreciated in its own right. Perhaps the most pertinent analogy is to an interpretation of a plot by a subplot, or the exegesis of a play by a play-within-a-play. The faith community can be made aware by its own semiotically trained theologians of *how* it is living out its subplot within the world's larger story, and hence realize what sort of sign in the world it is itself becoming.

The transformative energy of the church's lived exegesis in the sign system will depend, of course, on how close the norm or principle of this exegesis comes to the roots of signification as such. This essay has argued that significative syntaxes arise, both in the individual and in society, out of the interplay of imagination with power. An expression of the Christian message which gets at this power/imagination nexus has the potential to make a difference. Consider the possible impact in culture and society (whether of the ancient world or our own) of a community whose being rests on a situational exegesis such as this:

Who has believed what we have heard?
And to whom has the arm of the Lord been revealed?
For he grew up before him like a young plant,
and like a root out of dry ground;
he had no form or comeliness that we should look at him,
and no beauty that we should desire him.

(Isa. 53:1–2)

These words, with their well-known continuation, speak for themselves. Clearly there is a challenge here to the common power-world's fundamental meanings, to the way the sign complexes of ancient Near Eastern societies were put together. If a community of faith exists in such a power-world as carrier of such a subversive set of significations, it is in effect using the signifiers of the old world to make present a different world. To be part of such a community is to give voice to those "subjugated knowledges" that tacitly influence the manifest forms of knowledge. By reshaping human society down to the level of its foundational dialectic of power and imagination, down to the region of the origins of its signifiers, it effects a fundamental semiotic transformation at the roots of thinking and knowing.

THE SERVANT SIGNIFIERS IN THE
NEW TESTAMENT: AN ILLUSTRATION

We can infer from the Synoptic Gospels how this may have happened for the members of the early Jesus community. Consider, first, the scriptural heritage the Jesus community brought to bear. One thinks of the different ways in which the power of God *and* the resulting possibility for God's people are bodied forth in the Hebrew Scriptures: of how the early community of Israel in Canaan articulates God's rule in one way, how the monarchy does it in another, and of how the prophets recall their hearers to a covenantal sense by holding before them an imaginative vision of the blessed commonwealth. One then asks how the imaginative construal of God's power in relation to penultimate powers is expressed in the early "Jesus community." In relation to all that is going on in first-century Palestine, in relation to the various forms of symbolic valency attached to diverse elements in that social environment, what did it finally *mean* to become a follower of Jesus? What did the very existence of this "messianic" community communicate to those who knew it? Was there any relation between the meanings acted out in each disciple's membership and the messages conveyed by the faith community's public reality?

To have joined the early Jesus community must have meant experiencing an upheaval in one's symbolic world, especially where issues of ultimate and penultimate power were concerned. The signifying elements in the Palestinian Jewish tradition would have been read and acted out in new ways. The signs and signifiers surrounding the vision of the Suffering Servant now offered a vehicle for the expression of both shared and personal faith. They also made possible a "readable" public statement concerning the rule of God in history. The complex of signs embedded in the surrounding culture would have been taken up and put to new use: incorporated in fresh parable and metaphor so that the new community itself became a signifying medium for the message of the kingdom. The nascent church, by its very nature as a sign and bearer of signs, would have given the world of first-century Palestine and beyond not only something new to think about but something new to think *with:* a set of symbolic resources not previously available for wrestling with its inherent temptations and problems.

But did all this in fact happen? One reason for the elusiveness of New Testament servant imagery lies in the fact that it does not consist in a single, easily identifiable, usage. It is, rather, a perspective intrinsic to the story of Jesus and his disciples, and within that narrative takes many forms, both spoken and acted out. It has been argued by a number of scholars that the influence of this and other related passages was so taken for granted in the Jesus community that little self-conscious application of it to particular settings has survived in the Gospels. Quotations and clear allusions are surprisingly fragmentary and seem to have no consistent set of meanings. But these scattered materials may well be mere outcroppings of a massive, indeed semantically subjugated, whole.[16] The Servant Songs may have shaped the vision of power at the heart of the primitive Christian consciousness. They may have provided the initial sign set employed by the community in its exegesis of the world. The Songs may have been the imaginative form best suited to making sense of the experience the disciples shared with Jesus.

If so, these materials may have become carriers of this "sense" in a variety of subsequent expressions: each appropriate to some new situation which the New Testament also records. It appears, in fact, that the further one advances beyond the period described in the Gospels, the less intrinsic and more self-conscious becomes the usage of Isaiah 53 and related passages. Quotations become longer and more explicit. And the meanings given these excerpts become ever more clearly related to the new contexts in which they are used. While the Jesus community's original, situational, construal of power remains the meaning core, the writers of Philippians, 1 Peter, and other later New Testament writings reexpress that core in terminology suited to the new social and cultural situations in which they are involved.[17]

This process is plainly visible in Paul's Philippian letter. Here we find an instance of faith-community formation in which a semiotic deconstruction and transformation of the power world is the chosen instrument. The famous hymn of Phil. 2:5–11—a parabolized, versified, probably liturgical version of the Jesus story loaded with disempowerment and reempowerment terms—is a capsule summary of the results of earlier situational exegesis. The treatment has now become abstract enough in its hymnic versification to enable it to travel from its roots in the original Jesus community to the Pauline community. at Philippi. Particular forms of power have given way to the universal signs of power as such. The *essence* of how the world looked to those who were with Jesus is captured in a few verses on the way to becoming a confession of faith.

Paul sets this hymn in the midst of his discussion of community-forming, or community-disintegrating, relationships in the Philippian church. It is to function as confessional norm for an intepretation of the Philippians' situation that will lead to certain consequences for their life together. The Philippians are to do their practical reasoning understanding that, because they are in Christ, the power relationships characteristic of the Roman world will no longer control the forms of imagination of each other that give rise to interpersonal conduct. Factionalism, vainglory, selfishness are symptoms of the old power world. They are to be replaced by love, mercy, compassion, concern for others, the sharing of suffering. And this will be accomplished not merely by the inward transformation of individuals. It will happen because the Philippians have been led to a new kind of *thinking* based on the hymnic parable of Jesus the Servant-Lord. *Touto phroneite,* "have this mind among yourselves," the apostle writes (Phil. 2:5). The community is to be "of one mind" on these matters. To be so, we infer, is to permit all the levels or aspects of the reasoning, the *phronesis,* which attends community formation to be shaped by the imaginative reinterpretation of situation which is the great hymn.

Formed in this way, the Philippian church will be a "token" of both perdition and salvation to the world about them. Why is this so? Because by assuming the servant form of life they participate in and communicate the same hermeneutic of the world-historical situation that has called Paul to Rome, and is now being acted out through his imprisonment. The Philippians are in conflict with this world. Their conflict is the same one they have seen in the career and conduct of Paul. They thus represent a Power that the world has not yet acknowledged. The Philippian community is to embody in its current form of life the situation that will exist when all the principalities and powers bow the knee to the name of Jesus (2:9–11). This future situation will be a confessional event, even a language event. "Every tongue" will then "confess," *homologein,* that the world's scheme of identities and values has been rearranged in accordance with a new power geometry. The Philippians are to do their thinking, to work out their lives together, in accord with this new construal of the world now. So doing, they become a medium through which the gospel finds expression in the midst of time.

CONCLUSIONS

It is clear that Paul has been speaking, in this passage, of something close to what Farley calls theology as *habitus*.[18] I take this to mean a form of thought intrinsic to the fabric of life-in-faith, bred out of lived attitudes and relationships, yet capable of rising to the level of conscious deliberation. The Philippians are not merely being exhorted: they are being challenged to *think* in a certain way and to be aware that they are doing so. In them the servant form of life characteristic of the early Jesus community finds reexpression, not in literal replication but in terms of its essential characteristics as an imaginative parable. To keep living so as to act out this question in each new situation, the community must engage in shared *phronesis:* must "do" theology in its primary, confessional, form.

To see the formation of the church as a gospel-shaped and shared exegesis of any given environing sign world may be not only to think better about theology as habitus (Farley's term for the practice of theological reflection in the life of faith), but also to begin the reconstruction of theology as a method of critical reflection within, and upon, this formative activity. Such critical reflection will seek concepts that can both illuminate and regulate the church-formation process. Perhaps this search for categories will produce "rules for thought and action" which eventually become, on the one hand, doctrine, and on the other, polity or canon law. Perhaps such thinking will borrow intellectual categories that can enable it to draw metaphysical or ontological conclusions. Perhaps it will go on to consider what must be true about ultimate reality for such a community of interpretation to exist at all, thus constructing a transcendental argument. But such reflective activity, whatever its form, will arise within and build upon the active exegesis of the world that the faith community is by being present there.

The community of faith communicates. It acts as a sign in the wider world, because it takes up and transsignifies in its form of life signs that are already present in its situation. The church "speaks of God" as Karl Barth said, both in its characteristic language and in its social form.[19] It is the word of faith to some particular human situation in its living exegesis of that situation's signs, indeed of the depth dynamics of imagination and power that underlie these signs. The community of faith takes social and cultural materials to itself and transsignifies them just as the celebration of the Lord's Supper does with bread and wine.

The materials transsignified remain recognizable. But they say something new.

The messianic reconfiguration of signs sets two questions in the midst of the power/imagination world. The first asks, in ways appropriate to the time and place concerned, Who is God? The second asks, again contextually, What may we therefore do?

How to formulate the question "Who is God?" By asking what the ecclesial reality in question signifies among the operative signs in its environment with respect not only to penultimate powers but with respect to the final Power with which we have to do. In a multitude of ways, the scriptural narratives describe tests of strength between God and the idols. The Passion Narrative is in its own way a liturgical "trial of truth." Jesus is defeated in terms of the power signs of this world, and yet Christ defeats the principalities and powers of the cosmos. The community of faith is itself an answer to the question of who God is.

And the second question is thereby also set among the signs. What may we therefore do? The messianic resignifying of the power world will have opened up previously unimagined avenues for action. The world will have been opened to new possibilities through the use of metaphors that capture the reconfiguring of signs in parabolic and narrative forms. Through such metaphors, the faith community sees new openings for creative witnessing stretching ahead into the future. Paul Ricoeur suggests that in reading the parables of Jesus we can see "possible worlds" lying beyond us "in front of" the text.[20] And not only the parables told in the text, but also the great parable enacted by Jesus and his followers, could open up that way toward the future.

Does this happen, however, in a way that contributes anything to the public weal? Does the church's presence in a situation do more than witness to an alternative form of life that some may prefer? Does such presence lead to anything useful for humankind now? The faith community must ask this question if only because it remains part of the public world and needs to behave responsibly. But there is a further reason. That of which the faith community is a sign is this present world's future possibility.

We should thus be able to transcend the distinction between those versions of practical theology that focus on the *ekklesia* as such, and those for which the field of action is the whole human community. If the church *is* an exegesis of the world, it cannot leave the world behind even when the visible result of its exegesis *seems* radically sectarian. The faith community may well be determined by all that it claims that it is not. The church as an interactive form of life is more than the church as juridical institution. The institution is merely an instrument for the faithful people to use in their worldly deployment. The people are not the institution. They are, rather, a network of signifying action and interaction, both scattered and gathered, which must be understood in much more dynamic terms. The notion of a shared hermeneutic guiding situational exegeses in a world of interacting signs is designed to help make this clear.

A chorus of voices today tells us that, in the West, the public order is losing its warrants and coming apart. Hannah Arendt, in *The Human Condition*,[21] saw this almost a generation ago in respect to the res publica or polis. Alasdair MacIntyre has said it more recently with respect to moral reasoning in *After Virtue*.[22] Michel Foucault's career traced (and, some would say, helped to bring about) the deconstruction of our confidence in the great Western theoretical constructs bearing on the nature of the human.[23] In such a world, can the church's signifying presence make a difference?

That question, of course, will be answered only in the course of events. But we have already argued that the church may be situated better than any other gathering of human beings for signifying to the world the presence and meaning of what Foucault has called "subjugated knowledges," precisely those tracts of human experience which the great, yet now crumbling, conceptual constructs of the West never did bring to the point of expression: such things as what it *is* to be an inmate of the Gulag, what it *is* to be an oppressed peasant, what it *is* to be a member of a group without full access to the symbol network of social and cultural power. It takes more than occasional media attention to bring such things effectively to public awareness. It takes a community that already lives a servant paradigm, and thus can take up and body forth what such experiences mean, and how they may be vehicles for seeing beyond the values of the powerful.

In short, the church may offer the world a language for grasping its own present truths and future possibilities. The fact that the church is present as a lived parable or sign may possibly give rise to forms of thought[24] that the world desperately needs. But if this is to happen, a practical theology needs to grow up that has some awareness of this possibility, that helps shape the faith community to such ends. The proposal of this essay is that the church should thinkingly constitute its presence in the world so as to add something to humankind's capacity to envision itself whole. The faith community should contribute something to the vocabulary of human self-awareness not as "mere symbol" but as a form of "real presence." By showing the world how its own vocabulary can be taken up and redeployed around a new imaginative understanding of the final Power with which humankind has to do, the community of faith may say, more convincingly, that the possibility of salvation continues to exist.

NOTES

1. The notions of "theologia" and "habitus" are developed at length in Edward Farley's *Theologia: The Fragmentation and Unity of Theological Education* (Philadelphia: Fortress Press, 1983).

2. Robert N. Bellah, Richard Madsen, William M. Sullivan, Ann Swidler, and Steven M. Tipton, *Habits of the Heart: Individualism and Commitment in American Life* (Berkeley and Los Angeles: University of California Press, 1985), passim.

3. The possible parallel between the stance of Karl Barth's *Epistle to the Romans* (trans. Edwin C. Hoskins, 2d ed. [New York and London: Oxford University Press, 1933]) and certain features of the contemporary "deconstructionist" movement has been pointed out by Walter Lowe in an unpublished article, "Barth Contra Dualism: Reconsidering the *Römerbrief.*"

4. Barth, *Romans*, Preface to the 2d ed., 10.

5. This phrase, often used to describe Karl Barth's position in *Church Dogmatics*, may not actually appear in that text. It refers, of course, to the entire exposition in I:1—*The Doctrine of the Word of God: Prolegomena to Church Dogmatics* (trans. G. T. Thompson [New York: Charles Scribner's Sons, 1936]).

6. See ibid., I:1, p. 2.

7. Edward Farley develops the sense of these terms in *Ecclesial Reflection: An Anatomy of Theological Method* (Philadelphia: Fortress Press, 1982). The term "house of authority" is introduced on p. xiv and expounded throughout. For the "principle of identity," see pp. 34ff.

8. See Michel Foucault, *The Order of Things: An Archaeology of the Human Sciences* (New York: Vintage Books, 1973), and *Power/Knowledge: Selected Interviews and Other Writings, 1972–1977* (New York: Pantheon Books, 1981).

9. See Jacques Derrida, *Writing and Difference,* trans. Alan Bass (Chicago: University of Chicago Press, 1978), esp. chap. 1, "Force and Signification," and chap. 10, "Structure, Sign, and Play in the Discourse of the Human Sciences."

10. See, for example, Trutz Rendtorff, *Church and Theology: The Systematic Function of the Church Concept in Modern Theology,* trans. Reginald H. Fuller (Philadelphia: Westminster Press, 1971), 21.

11. Foucault, *Power/Knowledge,* esp. 81ff.

12. Clifford Geertz, *Local Knowledge: Further Essays in Interpretive Anthropology* (New York: Basic Books, 1983).

13. The term "hermeneutic phenomenology" has been used by Don Ihde and others as a characterization of the philosophy of Paul Ricoeur (see Lewis S.

Mudge, "Paul Ricoeur on Biblical Interpretation," in Paul Ricoeur, *Essays on Biblical Interpretation*, ed. L. S. Mudge [Philadelphia: Fortress Press, 1980], 9ff.)

14. Robert Schreiter, *Constructing Local Theologies* (Maryknoll, N.Y.: Orbis Books, 1985), esp. 50ff. I am indebted to Schreiter for portions of the exposition of semiotics in this essay.

15. Guy E. Swanson, *Religion and Regime: A Sociological Account of the Reformation* (Ann Arbor: University of Michigan Press, 1967); see the theological treatment of Swanson's argument in Lewis S. Mudge, *The Crumbling Walls* (Philadelphia: Westminster Press, 1970), see esp. chap. 3, "A Contextual Look at the Churches."

16. See H. W. Wolff, *Jesaja 53 im Urchristentum* (Berlin, 1949; 2d ed. 1952). Wolff argues that Isaiah 53 occupied such a central place in the life and consciousness of the apostolic band during Jesus' lifetime that seldom was it possible for the early church to use this particular passage, in the manner it used others, as a "proof text" for some particular feature of the gospel. Isaiah 53, rather, *was* the gospel. What appear to be "proof texts" are really outcroppings of a broadly held set of assumptions at the earliest stage of the history of the church.

17. It is also the case, of course, that the "Servant" Christologies which appear in the New Testament later give way to other terminologies reflecting the church's encounter with Hellenistic culture.

18. See Farley, *Theologia*, passim, and also, for a different view, Barth, *Church Dogmatics* I:1, p. 24.

19. See Barth, *Church Dogmatics* I:1, pp. 1ff. "The Church confesses God, by the fact that she speaks of God. She does so first through her existence in the action of each individual believer. And she does so in the second place through her special action as a community. . . ."

20. Paul Ricoeur, "Biblical Hermeneutics," *Semeia* 4 (1975): 101ff.

21. Hannah Arendt, *The Human Condition: A Study of the Central Dilemmas Facing Modern Man* (Garden City, N.Y.: Doubleday Anchor Books, 1959).

22. Alasdair MacIntyre, *After Virtue: A Study in Moral Theology* (Notre Dame, Ind.: University of Notre Dame Press, 1981).

23. Foucault, *Power/Knowledge*, 83–84.

24. "The symbol gives rise to thought" is the famous watchword of Paul Ricoeur's *The Symbolism of Evil*, trans. Emerson Buchanan (Boston: Beacon Press, 1969).

7 *Practical Theology and Liberation*

REBECCA S. CHOPP

As the introductory essay indicates, most of the articles in this text creatively reflect on the application of the revised correlation method for practical theology. Such application of the revised correlation method is a necessity, our various authors tell us, because theology is too far from the church, because theology is simply in our heads, because we do not reflect on intentional action, and/or because practical theology is not foundationally rooted. Together the various diagnoses suggest that the application of the revised correlation method can occur by taking the praxis of Christian witness more seriously and more concretely, and by enriching the play among text, context, and interpreter. But I want to contend that such broad and sweeping claims for the revised method of correlation must be questioned. Does the method of correlation, even when concretely applied in the many levels of discourse, set some limits on problems and possibilities for reflection and theory by its basic presuppositions? Does the method of correlation privilege certain issues and certain experiences as significant while ignoring or marginalizing other issues and other experiences? Is the method of correlation a universal method for theology that can solve all problems, offer all interpretations, meet all needs regardless of the religious issues, structural contexts, or historical realities?

Another way of putting the query of this essay in much bolder language is to argue that the method of correlation as the route for practical theology is nothing more than a new "play" on the old tag game of liberal, progressive theology that posits an underlying unity between individuals and tradition, and believes that it can reconcile, through understanding, human experience to reality. With full recognition that the liberal-revisionist project of correlation must be both

120

commended and respected for its theoretical agility as well as for its political support of the continuation of Christianity in modernity, my argument will be that the revised method of correlation and the liberal-revisionist theology to which it is linked is a discursive practice that addresses certain questions and tries to solve certain problems; like all other forms of theological reflection, liberal-revisionist theology and its method of correlation is, thus, a set of practices that, while having certain possibilities, also has certain limits. I am not interested in totally dismissing the liberal project, but I do want to suggest that liberalism construes religion and theology in a way that may not be adequate to the present situation. In sum, my argument will be that what Charles Winquist calls the fundamental rootedness of much of contemporary practical theology is the liberal project of Christianity, a project that engineers a basic identity between two abstract referents for interpretation—human experience and Christian tradition—and that expresses this unity as the meaningfulness, meaning, and truth of authentic existence, masking the compliancy of Christianity with what Johann Baptist Metz calls bourgeois existence.[1]

Having made this bold claim, I must defend my accusations and also point toward possibilities for a different model of *practical theology*, with emphasis both on practical and theology. To do this I want to take some theologies that are close to liberal-revisionist theology, those being the voices of liberation theologies including Latin American liberation theology, German political theology, and feminist theology. These liberation theologies have all been influenced by the liberal project of identifying Christianity and human freedom, but in this identification all attempt to speak for those people that liberal Christianity has ignored, forgotten, and even oppressed. Hence, there is a double relationship: as voices of victims they oppose, even contradict liberal theology, and as recipients of the tradition they are informed by and in turn transform that liberal project. This type of dialectical relationship has been suggested by Gustavo Gutierrez's distinction between historical praxis and liberating praxis.[2] Historical praxis is the project of modernity as the intentional manipulation and control, characterized by the dual values of rationalism and individualism, over nature, society, and the self. Yet historical praxis, be it in industrial, philosophical, or political revolutions, was successful only because of its dependency on massive contradictions between the "persons" and the "nonpersons" of history. This historical praxis, expressive of humanity's historical nature, is now interrupted by liberating praxis, the activity of the poor to "fashion an entirely different social order."[3] Gutierrez parallels this break-from-within history with a belief that a new form of liberating Christianity emerges out of modern Christianity. At this point, I want only to stress the status of this *new form* because, unfortunately for our liberal-revisionist correlation trajectory, this newness is finally a shift, or a dislocation from the old historical project. To take another example, feminist theology advocates not an "add woman and stir" approach to liberal Christianity, but rather a radical critique and transformation of liberal Christianity into, as Elisabeth Schüssler Fiorenza puts it, an ecclesia of women in the discipleship of equals.[4] Thus, we can bring liberation theologies into conversation with the liberal project only if we realize that we are comparing different models that are at least somewhat incommensurable in that they cannot always be evaluated against each other in a point-by-point fashion. Liberation theologians ask different questions, consider different human experiences and existences, and most of all, experience Christianity in a very different way than liberal theologians are able to conceive of or reflect upon.[5] Yet it is precisely this incommensurability, provided we remember that within each model are representations of real religious experience, that allows us to position the liberal-revisionist method of correlation as a set of discursive practices which are part of modernity's political and ideological history and not, as sometimes claimed, a universal approach to theological reflection.

It is also the case that the critique, both in the sense of understanding the presuppositions and in the sense of uncovering the distortions, of liberal-revisionist theology that I want to delineate could be argued without the aid of liberation theologies. One could use a philosophical argument, drawing upon present forms of practical reason to suggest why the method of correlation is limited for practical reflection in the present day. One could, and someone should, use a genealogical argument styled after the works of Michel Foucault to consider the structuring of the correlation method and its *correlation* with power and knowledge in our society, including how it is resisted through daily capillaries of discourse and relations among those without "power" in religious and social institutions. But I want to use liberation theology for the basic reason that besides criticizing the ideological presuppositions and structures of oppression, it also criticizes the intrinsic experiences and piety of Christianity that the method of correlation, liberal-revisionist theology, and modern Christianity both depend and reflect upon. Feminist theology, for instance, questions the religious experiences constituted in the liberal church and disclosed in liberal theology: is there a real experience of God as a generally uninvolved, uncaring, reigning power that secures the superiority of maleness, and shields the tyranny of patriarchalism under the guise of the natural order of creation? Sallie McFague has recently suggested a different religious experience among feminists, one which is described "by attending to relationships between God and human beings rather than to descriptions of God," and expressed in a variety of ways including the symbol of God as friend.[6] Metz begins his *Emergent Church* by criticizing liberal Christianity not in its method, or model, but in its piety, in its religious harmony "between the practice of religion and experience of life within society."[7] Thus liberation theologies, though not the only way to critique the discursive practices of the liberal-revisionist approach to practical theology, enable us to struggle (which is a preferable metaphor to that of play) with the way of being religious that the method of correlation presupposes and substantiates.

But is this kind of question not far from being practical? Am I not falling into the very trap, warned of by the essays, of not getting to the real facts or contexts in congregations, staying as Edward Farley's article suggests, within only one type of response to practical theology? This liberal-revisionist response to critiques such as mine reveals two important presuppositions of the revised correlation approach to practical theology: (1) that there is a progression in the hierarchy of order from fundamental through systematic to practical theology, and (2) that the congregation has some privileged primacy for correcting the errors of theologians. Both presuppositions have a great deal to do with the way theology has been structured not merely within the theological education curriculum but within the society, being located in or guaranteed by university centers of theoretical knowledge. This, in turn, is related to the larger modern project of education which inducts persons into our society and into the guilds of professions by separating them off from the actual practice of the craft or service. This social-structural critique can only be mentioned, since for our purposes we must attend to the liberal-revisionist division of theology's agenda and then to the primacy of the congregation. In dealing with these two presuppositions we can sketch, quickly, the brief outlines of liberal theology and its project to accommodate Christianity to modernity.

Practical theology dates its modern history to the restructuring of the disciplines through the now-famous encyclopedia approach. This history has been carefully documented and I only wish to underscore the fact that "regions" such as preaching, liturgy, and education were relegated to moments of clerical application worked out through systematic theology and undergirded by fundamental theology.[8] This basically deductive approach assumes that the logically important questions arise at the fundamental or foundational level, which, as the cornerstone of liberal theology, assumes that the ability to understand lies in theories that bracket daily practices to arrive at what these theologians call the "essence" of common human experience, an essence that is forthrightly entitled the religious dimension. Once the essence of common human experience is worked out, religion can be explained, at least in principle, to anyone and everyone, so that the tradition can be reinterpreted in light of human existence (since there is a fundamental relation between tradition and existence) and then reapplied to the daily practices of experience. The rhythm of this approach removes what the liberals call the essence of human experience from daily practices, in terms of both abstracting and moving to the depth of the essence of common human experience, and then reapplies this "essence" to that from which it was abstracted. As we shall soon see, this rhythm is most helpful when there is the luxury of assuming a "common" human experience and where there is the hope that theories can provide us with universal understandings that are not fallible in their claims.

The second presupposition is the question of turning directly to the congregation as a way to accomplish the "doing" of practical theology. A number of the authors decry the distance between theology and the church, as the very title of Thomas Groome's essay suggests: "Theology on Our Feet: A Revisionist Pedagogy for Healing the Gap between Academia and Ecclesia." This turn to the congregation raises the question, How did theology ever get separated from the congregation?—a question, as I mentioned before, that has to do with the structure of knowledge in our society and the need for legitimization of theology as a form of knowledge. But that question does not interest me as much as the subtle romanticization of the congregation that this critique entails. I applaud theologians being involved in the congregation, and theology does not make much sense without a relation to religious witness. But theologians will find no gnostic formulas in the congregation, indeed the questions and experiences of most congregations parallel, in a rather frightening way, the questions and experiences of liberal-revisionist theologians. One example will have to suffice, though many could be enumerated. One recent question for liberal theology has been the meaning of God, starting with the death-of-God controversy in the 1960s.[9] This question has settled on the issue of the referent and sense of language about God, including such issues as the possibility of God-talk, God-talk as illusionary, and God-talk as a function of community collectiveness. This is, it seems to me, the theological parallel to the quandary of religious language in many liberal congregations, where persons find it difficult to speak of God, Jesus, and the Spirit without, as they often put it, sounding conservative or old-fashioned. Indeed, congregational members will speak far more easily about the functional role of religion in relation to their personal needs, their quest for community, expressions of their feelings or stories, than specific religious reasons for the language of God. One of the most interesting studies that demonstrates the parallel between this problem on the congregational and the academic level is the book entitled *Building Effective Ministry*, which considers, from a variety of disciplines and approaches, a case study of the Wiltshire United Methodist Church.[10] The quite helpful essays by various consultants share one underlying assumption with the congregations: that religious language, in order to be meaningful or to have meaning, must be translated into secular categories. Theologians will discover no magic formulas, different questions, or naive religious experience in this congregation: indeed, the Wiltshire case is enough to convince anyone that secularized culture, privatized religion, and the crisis of the truth, meaning, and meaningfulness of religious language is the burden not only of modern theologians but also of contemporary congregational participants. The issue, then, is not that theology should be related in closer fashion to the church; this solution tries to reverse the first presupposition about the hierarchical order of theology. Rather, the problem lies on another level, for both the church and theology find it difficult to speak of God in a society whose ideology and politics demand strict adherence to secularistic language and that places experiences such as religion on the margins of public life in the realm of the private. As the voices of liberation theology will soon suggest to us, liberal-revisionist theology and the modern church are manifestations of their culture, twin manifestations that disclose the constitution of Christianity in bourgeois society as individualistc, existentialistic, and private.

Having examined the assumptions behind the question, Will this essay be practical? I want to answer yes, but not in relation to the assumption of the hierarchy of the fundamental-systematic-practical order or the assumption that if theologians paid attention to congregations they would be able to offer a truly practical theology. Rather I contend that the only way to consider practical theology is to look at theology quite practically, in terms of how it reflects and secures a certain form and function of religion in our culture, and how a new theology may well depend upon a quite practical fact: relating a new theological substance to a new theological method that speaks to a new experience and role of Christianity in history. In order to do this, I will, with the aid of some liberation theologians, pose three questions to liberal-revisionist theology and its method of correlation: (1) What is the point of religion for liberal-revisionist theology? (2) What is the nature of the method of correlation? and (3) What are the limits of "praxis" in liberal-revisionist theology?

WHAT IS THE POINT OF RELIGION?

The first question about the limits of the liberal-revisionist project asks of what religion basically consists, or alternatively, what is the primary experience, meaning, message of Christianity? Paul Tillich referred to this in his concept of the material norm of theology, and argued, correctly I think, that each historical age gives rise to a new norm.[11] While the symbolic constitution of the material norm is not my concern here, the issues or the problems such a norm addresses in the modern period can reveal to us the basic constitution of religion in the liberal-revisionist project.

The liberal project dedicated itself primarily to the crisis of cognitive claims, the crisis of the possibility of belief. Van Harvey's excellent book *The Historian and the Believer* suggests the seemingly contradictory position of the modern theologian who, on the one hand, must be loyal to the scientific morality of free, critical, autonomous inquiry, and, on the other hand, must remain loyal to the Christian community and its traditional belief structure.[12] Harvey locates the problem as one of morality and knowledge: as a problem of morality the theologian must either choose between or bring together two institutions—one in which authority is given only through autonomous research and arguments based on evidence; the other where authority is given through tradition and based in belief. This moral crisis depends upon a fundamentally epistemological problem since, in the crisis of cognitive claims, the theologian must attempt to make known through the human subject that which essentially lies beyond the human subject.

The liberal theologians solved or at least pacified their moral crisis by two important strategies: (1) selecting the epistemological issue as the religious question, and (2) reflecting, even supporting the continual privatization of religion in the secular world. When liberals could not know God through special privilege, they opted for discerning God in history and, most importantly, discovering God as the referent for the self. Indeed, Schleiermacher, the great father of liberal theology, represents this first strategy quite well. Remember that Schleiermacher took as the religious issue of his day the cognitive crisis of the cultural despisers. To the cultural despisers of religion, Schleiermacher argued that religion was neither knowing nor doing, but "a sense or taste for the infinite," an "intuition and feeling of the infinite."[13] Since the despisers could not know God (and thus their fundamental problem, an epistemological-moral issue) Schleiermacher asked them to look within, to discover certain feelings, and to recognize these feelings as the real seat of religion. Schleiermacher continued this basic strategy in *The Christian Faith*, accepting as the fundamental religious issue the possibility of belief, and responding to this issue by locating religion in the experience of the historical self.[14]

Liberal theology accomplished this alliance between historical knowledge and traditional belief through what revisionist theologians are prone to call a project of accommodation, an uncritical acceptance of the modern project. To be sure, out of liberalism burst neo-orthodoxy which based its origin upon a critique of liberalism's all-too-easy acceptance of the dictates and whims of modernity. Neo-orthodoxy declared a shattering no to the world, but this no was also a part of its historical age; neo-orthodoxy, in spite of its strong opposition to liberalism, continued the modern model by accepting the meaningfulness of the self as the answer to the religious question, and interpreting Christianity to represent the real essence of human freedom. Revisionist theology, while taking neo-orthodoxy as an important internal critique, is committed to continuing the liberal project, but in a postliberal age. David Tracy's early work, *Blessed Rage for Order*, is the definitive statement of the revisionist project: "In short, the revisionist theologian is committed to what seems clearly to be the central task of contemporary theology: the dramatic confrontation, the mutual illuminations and corrections, the possible basic reconciliation between the principal values, cognitive claims, and existential faiths of both a reinterpreted post-modern consciousness and a reinterpreted Christianity."[15] As Tracy suggests, the goals and loyalties of liberal and revisionist theologies are the same, though the methodological resources and substantive resources are now mutually critical in approach. The problem, at least for our purposes, is that the point of religion, or the religious question, is identical for liberals and revisionists, the question of the nonbeliever or, theologically stated, the question of the crisis of cognitive claims. All other questions—justice, liturgy, discipleship—have to be understood through this modern crisis of secularistic nonbelief.

Gustavo Gutierrez, among other theologians, has been critical of the religious question for modern theology or what he calls progressivist theology, which accepted the limits of the bourgeois nonbeliever as the religious problem that Christianity had to face. For Gutierrez, the difference between progressivist theology and liberation theology can be stated as the difference between basic questions:

> The modern spirit, whose subject frequently is the nonbeliever, questions the faith in a context of the meaning of religion. The critique from the standpoint of rationalism and the affirmation of the modern freedom prefers a debate on the terrain of religion, and the philosophical presuppositions of religion, together with the role of the church in modern, bourgeois society. The questions asked by the "nonperson" and the "nonhuman," by contrast, have to do with the economic, the social and the political. And yet this does not make for a nontheological discussion, as some seem to think. That would indeed be a facile solution. It is a matter of a different theology.[16]

While liberal-revisionist theologians respond to the theoretical challenge of the nonbelievers among the small minority of the world's population who control the wealth and resources in history, liberation theologians respond to the practical challenge of the large majority of global residents who control neither their victimization nor their survival.

Gutierrez also moves us to consider the second strategy of liberal and revisionist theologians, the privatization of religion or what he calls "the role of the church in modern society." These dual strategies are not just randomly linked for the theoretical address to the nonbeliever—who, by the way, is all "persons" and any "person" in principle—occurred through the privatization of religion and the resultant privileging of the religious dimension. Liberal, and later revisionist, theologians formulated a religious dimension to address an epistemological problem which in turn allowed for the separation of religion from other aspects of life. The church in the modern world became that institution where this private religious meaning was offered. Metz identifies the function of the church in the bourgeois world as the privatization of religion; Metz argues that as "persons" become defined by production and exchange in the evolutionary logic of modernity, the meaningfulness of life is relegated to the margins of society in the private realms of family, religion, and art.[17]

Among the most trenchant criticisms of the church in the modern world has been that of Jürgen Moltmann's in *The Theology of Hope*. In modernity, Moltmann argues, the church became the *cultus privatus*, where its first function was to be the cult of a new subjectivity.[18] Moltmann argues that both the theology of liberalism and neo-orthodoxy function to secure this privatization, securing ultimate meaning in the realm of the personal. In modern religious experience, freedom becomes largely the project of accepting oneself, and religion becomes that vehicle whereby one says yes to self and God in the private, existential encounter. Moltmann connects liberal theology and the modern church:

> A theology which settles faith in the "existence" of the individual, in the sphere of his personal, immediate encounters and decisions, is a theology which from the viewpoint of sociological science stands at the very place to which society has banished the *cultus privatus* in order to emancipate itself from it. This faith is in the literal sense socially irrelevant, because it stands in the social no-man's-land of the unburdening of the individual—that is, in a realm which materialist society has already left free to human individuality in any case.[19]

As compared to liberal-revisionist theology, the point of religion of liberation theology has to do with emancipation and enlightenment of persons in history and is formulated in a number of different ways: the option for the poor in Latin American liberation theology, the dangerous memory of those who suffer in political theology, and women's experiences in feminist theology. The radical difference of what liberation theology understands as the point of Christianity underlines the importance of dwelling at some length on the question of the point of religion since the substance of any theological model depends, to a great extent, on the issues it addresses and the historical situation in which it lives. The comparison between liberation theology and liberal-revisionist theology allows us to understand that in the liberal project, the point of religion arises out of the crisis of cognitive claims and the question of nonbelievers and becomes intertwined in a church institution which met a person's needs for meaning and ultimacy and in a theology which protected the meaning and ultimacy of the subject through a turn to the limits or depths of private, bourgeois individuals. The method of correlation, the subject of our next question, was born in the liberal-revisionist project to continue Christianity by protecting the individual and securing the individual by privatizing Christianity.

WHAT IS THE NATURE OF THE METHOD OF CORRELATION?

Having, with the aid of liberation theologians, understood the point of religion in the liberal-revisionist project, we can move directly to the second question about the nature of the method of correlation. The critical issue here is how tradition and experience are understood, and, second, how the correlation between tradition and experience occurs.

REBECCA S. CHOPP

The criticisms of liberation theology about the source of experience in liberal-revisionist theology should need only to be identified. Feminist theologians, to take one example, make clear that the experience most often reflected upon is that of white, bourgeois males. Out of reflecting upon this experience, liberal-revisionist theologians arrive at an interpretation of what they call *common* human experience. Note the basic trajectory of liberal-revisionist theology to correlate experience and tradition has been a method to elevate the experience of a certain group of men and make it universal. This is, of course, a classic example of ideology, where the experience of one group of persons is universalized, and even determined as *the* human experience. This epistemic sense of ideology joins, in liberal-revisionist theology, with a functional sense as it legitimizes the social world of the bourgeoisie.[20] The attempt to understand a *common* human experience is epistemically and functionally ideological in the method of correlation, limiting liberal-revisionist theology's ability to deal with questions of historical particularity and difference within a religion as well as between religions. For instance, this ideological bias toward a common human experience must raise questions about the liberal-revisionist concern for pluralism, since any method that already understands a common human experience from which it can extract a universal religious dimension will find it difficult to give full attention to the radical claims of pluralism. We can consider pluralism, within Christianity and within the global context, only by relinquishing our loyalty to a normative understanding of *common* human experience, as well as our fidelity to our particularistic definition of *universal* rationality.

The other source of theology has been tradition. By this theologians often mean the "classical" texts favored by the educated, male clerics and theologians of the church. Liberal-revisionist theologians increasingly appreciate Hans-Georg Gadamer's philosophical hermeneutics which allows such a tradition to be the possibility for continual engagement with a world, and allows the text to speak to us and not be limited through methods that explain the text in its historical situatedness.[21] One awareness that feminist theology can never avoid is that tradition is a living history of social practices. This means that the concept of tradition has to broaden to include other kinds of historical witnesses than those authorized by ecclesial and theological elites and that tradition must be studied in its historical situatedness and its historical effects. One of the most disturbing implications of feminist theology is the almost complete distortion of the classical tradition in relation to women. What happens when the tradition simply cannot be a source for theological reflection; when the only meanings one can retrieve from it are those of the terrible misogyny that Christianity has conceived, enforced, secured, and policed in regard to women?[22] What if, as some feminist theologians believe, we cannot be "at home" in the tradition? The method of correlation begins by assuming the at-home-ness of tradition, and while it may use experience to correct tradition, it cannot, in principle, even entertain the question of radical, systemic distortion.

Though there are other questions of the sources for the method of correlation, we can now move to analyzing just *how* the correlation occurs in this method. As Matthew Lamb has demonstrated the nature of the correlation in the liberal-revisionist approach is always a theoretical correlation.[23] The limits of this theoretical correlation lie in the dominance, and even the hegemony, of theory over praxis. Liberation theology argues for a practical correlation, which uses theories only as ways to solve problems; in this model theories can be adopted, argued, discarded in relation to the material and not vice versa. The theoretical correlation of liberal-revisionist theology must fit all human experience (which is, after all, supposedly held in common by all) into theories of depth, dimension, limit, or ultimacy. Phenomenology and phenomenological-related hermeneutical theories have been favored by the liberal-revisionist theologians because these theories depend upon bracketing out daily practices, arriving at the essence of a phenomenon, and then approaching the concrete realities. But in opposition to this attempt to give meaning via a theory of the essence of the text and of experience, one can question if meaning is not located rather in the historical practices, in what Terry Eagleton has called, "the changing, practical transactions between individuals."[24]

It is at the point of comparing the method of liberation theologians to the method of liberal-revisionists that I feel the most tension of the incommensurability problems. Liberation theology is not concerned about the crisis of cognitive claims; so it has no need for a method of theoretical correlation while, on the other hand, it is concerned with the practical crisis of the victims of history and needs a method that can critique and transform situations. Liberation theology in this sense is closer to pragmatic philosophy that begins with a problem arising out of a particular situation than to phenomenological method which begins by abstracting of meanings, giving power to the interpreter to select the "interesting" issues. It does not begin with some predetermined assumption about the essence of common human experience or about the privileged status of tradition; it begins with a need to approach different, varied, complex realities, and a willingness to privilege human emancipation and enlightenment over tradition. Indeed liberation theologies force us to wonder whose tradition the liberal-revisionists want to privilege—is the tradition of Christianity identified with the victors of history or with the prayers and hopes of the victims? Liberation theology opts for a method best called a critical praxis correlation which includes a de-ideologization of scriptures, a pragmatic interpretation of experience, a critical theory of emancipation and enlightenment, and a social theory to transform praxis.[25] That is, liberation theologians begin in what they call praxis—the practices of agents and institutions—so that practical theology names the whole rather than one special part; but with this concern of praxis, it is time to turn to our third and final question.

WHAT ARE THE LIMITS OF PRAXIS IN LIBERAL-REVISIONIST THEOLOGY?

The third question of the method of correlation considers the meaning of praxis, and now the criticisms of liberation theology can be aligned with those of current practical philosophy. These criticisms are three-fold: (1) In liberal-revisionist theology the first referent for praxis has to do with the regions of intentional application while in liberation theology the first referent of praxis is the broad matrix or web of social systems and structures, social being and doing. (2) Reflection on praxis is aimed at understanding and reconciliation with the underlying order or transcendental norms in liberal-revisionist theology, while reflection on praxis in liberation theology seeks to transform and "remake" history, thus praxis in liberation theology is future-oriented, and in liberal-revisionist theology it is present-oriented. (3) Politics is one region of activity for liberal-revisionist theology while, in liberation theology, the political is the context and condition for all reflection and action. By concentrating on the meaning and use of the popular term "praxis" in liberal-revisionist theology and in liberation theology, we can see again the vast differences in these discursive practices.

As we have already seen, liberalism moves from fundamental to systematic to practical theology, with practical theology being the application of meanings gleaned from the two prior theological realms. This is the reason that practical theology so easily slides over into regions of practice, and the discrete approaches to preaching, religious education, and the like are enumerated. It is also the reason that ethics becomes so important for practical theology in the liberal-revisionist model, for, as Don Browning has effectively demonstrated, if practice is identified with intentional human activity, then practical theology must be focused fundamentally through ethics. The underlying presupposition is that the primary referent for praxis is intentional human activity.

It is this intentional activity as the primary referent for praxis that liberation theology challenges. Liberation theologians, in a manner similar to some contemporary philosophers, wonder if praxis is not better understood in a broader sense of the web of social interactions. This web might be traced through three factors: contemporary retrievals of Aristotle and Marx, a theory of structuration combining anthropology and social structure, and attention to unintended consequences and effects. The first factor retrieves Aristotle's location of praxis in the community's continuous determination of its own becoming combined with Marx's notion of praxis involving structural relations and human interests. Here we might place the broad web of praxis not into disparate regions of praxis but in the dynamic, structural, and communal relationality of history.

The second factor concerns the recursive nature of praxis and, similar to social theorists such as Anthony Giddens, seeks to view society as composed neither of intentional individuals nor functional organisms, views that give rise to either the dominance of ethics or of sociology.[26] Giddens's model of structuration attempts to hold together the interdependency of human agency and social systems in what he calls the duality of structure. Liberation theology, like the model of structuration, assumes that human activity and social systems are co-constituted by producing and reproducing each other.[27] This factor pushes liberal-revisionist theology at its separation of the human agency and social systems, its talk of praxis either through individual intentional activity or functional social systems, its refusal to study the recursive nature of praxis and the time-space construction of history within praxis.

The third factor arises out of the first two, this factor considers the unintended effects and consequences in praxis. Activity always occurs in a complex web of relationships, within which activity rarely reaches its conscious goals. Hannah Arendt spoke of the necessity of understanding the human being as both doer and sufferer: "Although everybody started his life by inserting himself into the human world through action and speech, nobody is the author or producer of his own life story. In other words, the stories, the results of action and speech reveal an agent, but this agent is not an author or producer of his own life story. Somebody began it and is its subject in the twofold sense of the word, names its actor and sufferer, but nobody is its author."[28] One implication of this is to pay less attention, in liberation theologies, to large ethical and political theories *about* power and more attention to the capillaries and daily practices *of* power. Despite theories which talk about equality and justice, for instance, feminists become quite aware that what is really repressive are the hundreds of daily practices such as linguistic etiquette which encourages men to speak the most, media references to women as soft and round, familial relations which now expect women to manage jobs both at home and office. Thus feminists may intend to be equal, and live by promised theories of justice and distribution of power, but the "unintended" consequences of social practices are more repressive than any ethical-political theory could ever intend. In sum, praxis is not first application, formulated as intentional human activity, but, in liberation theology, first the web of relations in which the individual doing and being is enabled and contained.

The second issue of praxis has to do with the purpose of reflection on praxis in liberal-revisionist theology and in liberation theology. This issue was summarized quite well by Nicholas Lobkowicz in referring to the difference between Hegel and Marx, which, for our own purposes, can symbolize the philosophical differences between liberal-revisionist theology and liberation theology. Hegel, says Lobkowicz, understood that the order of the cosmos was disturbed and changing, but thought the only hope was to reconcile the human subject to the universe by helping the subject to understand it. Marx, argued Lobkowicz, "lost all faith in the healing and reconciling power of mere thought" and believed reflection on praxis had to be for transformation and not just acceptance.[29] Liberal-revisionist theology, stemming from what Jon Sobrino has called the first enlightenment, still wants to bring humanity into correlation with the universal order.[30] Its theoretical presuppositions orient its temporality to the present, and its reliance on transcendental arguments accents the universality of its claim. Liberation theology, concerned with the second enlightenment, understands the purpose of all reflection as transformation and thus its temporality is decidedly future-oriented.[31]

The differences in the underlying purpose of reflection accounts for a quite different view of the nature of theology. Both liberalism and liberation theology like to think of their theology as "critical reflection." Gutierrez identifies three tasks for liberation theology as "critical reflection": (1) it is a theory of definite praxis; (2) it is a critique of church and society; and (3) it is the projection of future possibilities related to the present situation.[32] For liberal-revisionist theology, critical reflection, as we have seen in the previous essays, means the correlation of meanings, meanings that are already given and at most can apply to individual, intentional action. The limits, as well as the possibilities, of the method of correlation are established by this underlying view of reconciliation to an order or normative view and thus the privileging of balancing or reconciling meanings. Transformation, future, radical conversion can only exist as deferred implications within one particular region of intentional activity.

This differentiation of praxis leads to the third criticism of praxis in liberal-revisionist theology and that is its political intent. Now, liberal-revisionist theologians prefer to talk of politics as one distinct arena of praxis and to contend that only those statements specifically intended to talk of politics are political. But liberation theology, based on its understanding of praxis as the complex web of relations that is primary for all of life, believes that all theology is political. If praxis is understood in this fashion, any theological reflection has some political implications, precisely as it shows new ways of being in the world, new relations of power, interests, knowledge, and so on. Feminist theology has observed over and over how the privatization of certain spheres of life as nonpolitical has had great political implications for women, giving rise to the feminist slogan that the personal is the political. Indeed, the limits of liberal-revisionist theology, as this essay has tried to demonstrate, are really its own political nature and effects, as liberal-revisionist theology reflects and reinforces repressive structures of consciousness and oppressive structures of social practices in the bourgeois world.

Despite revisionist appeals to liberation praxis, the political contradiction, as Gutierrez calls it, is demonstrated in the liberal-revisionist refusal to take the other requirement of critical reflection: the option for the victims of history.[33] This is not because liberal-revisionists refuse to have a subject; quite clearly its subject has been the bourgeois nonbeliever. Jose Miguez Bonino has argued that because of the contextualization of theology in the polis, theology speaks from and for a specific situation, and, Miguez Bonino argues, the goal must be to position and not simply ideologically reflect the interests of the authors of theological reflection.[34] The criticism is threefold: the method of correlation makes political choices under the guise of value-free or common existence, it denies the political import of any but a narrow range of statements, and it refuses to position itself for the oppressed.

We might conclude by suggesting that the very use of the term "praxis" in liberal-revisionist theology—despite the attempts to sound as if a serious conversation is being entertained with liberation theology—disguises yet another attempt to secure the modern project.

REBECCA S. CHOPP

This is not, I hope, to deny the worthiness of practical theology in the method of correlation. It is to suggest that this method is limited, and in spite of its rhetorics of totality and universalism, is a situated and particular discursive practice that cannot do all things for all persons. It is also to suggest that given our own historical situation of global crisis, the method of correlation may prove too limited to address the religious, human, practical needs of our age. As we deal with issues such as justice, pluralism, and other religions, the task may not be merely to understand, but to transform ourselves and our world. Liberation theology, at least in the judgment of this author, forces us to grapple with historical particularity and differences so that we may work toward a future where we can all live together. This will take theoretical and practical change and transformation, and whereas I do not think liberation theology has all the answers, I do think it addresses the issues of our present period in a way outside the limits and possibilities of liberal-revisionist theology with its revised correlation method.

NOTES

1. Johann Baptist Metz analyzes the compliancy of modern Christianity with bourgeois existence in his *Faith in History and Society: Toward a Practical Fundamental Theology*, trans. David Smith (New York: Seabury Press, 1980), and *The Emergent Church: The Future of Christianity in a Post-Bourgeois World*, trans. Peter Mann (New York: Crossroad, 1981).

2. Gustavo Gutierrez, "Faith as Freedom: Solidarity with the Alienated and Confidence in the Future," *Horizons* 2 (Spring 1975): 36–37.

3. Gustavo Gutierrez, "Liberating Praxis and Christian Faith," in *Frontiers of Theology in Latin America*, ed. Rosino Gibellini, trans. John Drury (Maryknoll, N.Y.: Orbis Books, 1974), 8.

4. Elisabeth Schüssler Fiorenza, *In Memory of Her: A Feminist Theological Reconstruction of Christian Origins* (New York: Crossroad, 1983), 343–51.

5. For one interpretation of the problems of incommensurability, see Richard J. Bernstein, *Beyond Objectivism and Relativism: Science, Hermeneutics, and Praxis* (Philadelphia: University of Pennsylvania Press, 1983), 79–108.

6. Sallie McFague, *Metaphorical Theology: Models of God in Religious Language* (Philadelphia: Fortress Press, 1982), 167.

7. Metz, *Emergent Church*, 1.

8. The best recent study of the structuring of the theological disciplines is Edward Farley's *Theologia: The Fragmentation and Unity of Theological Education* (Philadelphia: Fortress Press, 1983).

9. For an excellent description of the various problems in the language-of-God debates see Langdon Gilkey, *Naming the Whirlwind: The Renewal of God-Language* (Indianapolis: Bobbs-Merrill, 1969).

10. Carl S. Dudley, ed., *Building Effective Ministry* (San Francisco: Harper & Row, 1983).

11. Paul Tillich, *Systematic Theology* (Chicago: University of Chicago Press, 1951), 1:48.

12. Van A. Harvey, *The Historian and the Believer: The Morality of Historical Knowledge and Christian Belief* (Philadelphia: Westminster Press, 1966).

13. Friedrich Schleiermacher, *On Religion: Speeches to Its Cultural Despisers*, trans. John Oman, reprint ed. (New York: Harper & Brothers, 1958).

14. Friedrich Schleiermacher, *The Christian Faith*, ed. H. R. Macintosh and R. S. Stewart (Edinburgh: T. & T. Clark, 1948).

15. David Tracy, *Blessed Rage for Order: The New Pluralism in Theology* (New York: Seabury Press, 1979), 32.

16. Gustavo Gutierrez, *The Power of the Poor in History: Selected Writings*, trans. Robert R. Barr (Maryknoll, N.Y.: Orbis Books, 1983), 212–13.

17. Metz, *Faith in History and Society*, 36–39.

18. Jürgen Moltmann, *The Theology of Hope: On the Ground and the Implications of a Christian Eschatology*, trans. James W. Leitch (New York: Harper & Row, 1967), 311–16.

19. Ibid., 316.

20. For a discussion of epistemic and functional ideologies, see Raymond Geuss, *The Idea of a Critical Theory: Habermas and the Frankfurt School* (Cambridge: Cambridge University Press, 1981), 13–19.

21. Hans-Georg Gadamer, *Truth and Method*, trans. G. Borden and J. Cumming, 2d ed. (New York: Seabury Press, 1975). For one example of Gadamer's influence on a revisionist theologian who is also influenced by the critical theories implicit in liberation theology, see David Tracy, *The Analogical Imagination: Christian Theology and the Culture of Pluralism* (New York: Crossroad, 1979).

22. A similar concern about the ability of hermeneutical philosophy to deal with radical distortion in tradition occurs in the debate between Gadamer and Jurgen Habermas. Two interesting summaries of this debate are David Hoy, *The Critical Circle: Literature, History, and Philosophical Hermeneutics* (Berkeley and Los Angeles: University of California Press, 1982), 117–28, and Paul Ricoeur, "Hermeneutics and the Critique of Ideology," in *Hermeneutics and the Human Sciences: Essays on Language, Action, and Interpretation*, ed. and trans. John B. Thompson (New York: Cambridge University Press, 1981), 63–100.

23. Matthew Lamb, *Solidarity with Victims: Toward a Theology of Social Transformation* (New York: Crossroad, 1982), 75–76.

24. Terry Eagleton, *Literary Theory: An Introduction* (Minneapolis: University of Minnesota Press, 1983), 24.

25. For an interpretation of the method employed by liberation theologies, see my *The Praxis of Suffering: An Interpretation of Political and Latin American Liberation Theologies* (Maryknoll, N.Y.: Orbis Books, 1986).

26. Anthony Giddens, *Central Problems in Social Theory: Action, Structure*

and Contradiction in Social Analysis (Berkeley and Los Angeles: University of California Press, 1983).

27. Anthony Giddens, *The Constitution of Society: Outline of the Theory of Structuration* (Berkeley and Los Angeles: University of California Press, 1984), 374.

28. Hannah Arendt, *The Human Condition: A Study of the Central Dilemmas Facing Modern Man* (Garden City, N.Y.: Doubleday Anchor Books, 1959), 163–64.

29. Nicholas Lobkowicz, *Theory and Practice: History of a Concept from Aristotle to Marx* (Notre Dame, Ind.: University of Notre Dame Press, 1967), 340–41.

30. Jon Sobrino, *The True Church and the Poor,* trans. Matthew J. O'Connell (Maryknoll, N.Y.: Orbis Books, 1984), 12.

31. Ibid., 20.

32. Gustavo Gutierrez, *A Theology of Liberation: History, Politics and Salvation,* trans. and ed. Sister Caridad Inda and John Eagleson (Maryknoll, N.Y.: Orbis Books, 1973), 11–13.

33. Gutierrez, *Power of the Poor,* 200.

34. Jose Miguez Bonino, *Toward a Christian Political Ethics* (Philadelphia: Fortress Press, 1983), 44.

8 *Practical Theology in the Situation of Global Pluralism*

DAVID TRACY

INTRODUCTION: THE LOCAL AND THE GLOBAL IN PRACTICAL THEOLOGY

The task of contemporary practical theology grows more important and more difficult year by year. For even if, as many practical theologians in this volume and elsewhere argue, some version of a revised correlational method is essential to that task methodologically, the substantive issues grow ever more pressing and interrelated. Practical theology, after all, is a discipline which, in every local situation, attempts to be responsible to the complex needs and demands of the church as well as the ever-shifting demands of the civic order while also proving itself responsible, as all theology must, to its critical, intellectual commitments.

The particular needs and questions of particular local persons and communities should principally determine which way the "correlation" will go. Correlation, after all, is a word used to recall that, in any given situation, the demands of both the Christian tradition with its embodiment in particular ecclesial communities and the ever-shifting cultural, political, ethical, and religious situation must be allowed; hence, the phrase "mutually critical correlations." Sometimes the correlation may legitimately suggest a practical identity between those two interpretations (as in many forms of "liberal" theology). More often the correlation may suggest the presence of analogies (as similarities-in-difference) between two interpretations (as in much of the best of theologically informed pastoral counseling). At still other times, the correlation may demand the articulation not of identities or even analogies but radical nonidentities (as in the correctly confrontational style of much of political, liberation, and feminist practical theologies).

In sum, there is nothing in the "revised correlational model" that demands a "liberal" solution. There is only the demand—the properly theological demand—that wherever and whoever the practical theologian is, she or he is bound by the very nature of the enterprise as theological to show how one interprets the tradition and how one interprets the present situation and how those two interpretations correlate: as either identities of meaning, analogies, or radical nonidentities. Any one of these options is logically possible; only the particular question of particular individuals or groups in particular situations can decide what form the correlation must now take to prove both practical and theological or, more exactly, practical-theological. As always, a general method can only heuristically guide the inquiry; the subject matter alone—and that in all its particularity—must rule.[1]

So demanding a task of inquiry and practice on the local level is, as several writers in this collection make clear, no mean enterprise. It can, I realize, seem almost intellectually perverse to complicate that already complicated discussion by demanding attention to the global situation as well. Yet such complication is entirely necessary. For sociologically, there is no local situation that is not impinged upon by the wider cultural-political situation; philosophically, the concrete is never solely the particular but the particular becomes particular only in relationship to the whole; ecclesiologically, every local congregation, in whatever denomination, is implicitly related to the "great church"—the Christian church in all its cross-cultural and cross-denominational reality; theologically, the doctrine of God informing every Christian symbol, doctrine, and practice demands attention to the whole of reality—both historical reality and the reality of an encompassing nature and cosmos.

Some dialectic of the local and the global, therefore, presses upon all practical theology worthy of the name. To assume that only the "local situation" or only the "global situation" demands attention is to downplay, however unconsciously, the full demands of all practical-theological analyses of the "situation." As Rebecca Chopp correctly reminds us with her interpretation of political and liberation theologies, the reality of massive global suffering, however remote it may seem from many a middle-class American congregation, demands attention from all practical theologies. As Don Browning and Charles Winquist remind us in their different ways, the "crisis of cognitive claims" in all its permutations from "early modernity" to "postmodernity" influences all analyses of what practical inquiry is and what cognitive claims any such inquiry can make. As the editors and Edward Farley remind us, the reality of the "ecclesia" is the central reality empowering and transforming all attempts at Christian practical theology.

In this paper, therefore, I have attempted a further thought-experiment: namely, what global issues are we most likely to forget and thereby most in need of remembering? I assume, to repeat, that the global ecclesial issues of the "great church" will be to the fore of all Christian theology. I assume that the political, liberation, and feminist theologies, in fidelity to the classic prophetic trajectories of the Christian tradition, will correctly continue to insist upon the central issue of massive global sufferings of whole peoples, cultures, races, and sexes. I assume that the "crisis of cognitive claims" has not been settled and, in our "postmodern" situation characterized by increasing plurality and ambiguity, is now more difficult than ever.[2]

However, even granted these assumptions, I believe that we all need to pay more attention than most of us customarily do to three crucial facts: first, the import of the serious interreligious dialogue of our day; second, the actuality of the ecological crisis in all three worlds—especially in the rapidly industrializing Third World (e.g., Brazil); third, the possibility of nuclear holocaust and the reality of nuclearism.

These three realities, the first so promising, the second and third so disturbing, impel me to add another question to the agenda of practical theology: the need for a new practical theological understanding of nature and cosmos for our present situation. I make no claim to answer that question but only to force it upon myself and other practical theologians as a new and puzzling central practical theological issue.

I attempt to pose this question in three moves: first, sections 2 and 3 provide brief résumés of how I understand practical theology and the hermeneutical model of conversation. Section 4 provides a brief analysis of what "global pluralism" might mean as our contemporary situation for practical theology. In section 5, rather than providing further methodological reflections, I risk some tentative reflections, from within Christian theology, of the kind of thought provoked by my exposure thus far to the more cosmological interests of Eastern religions (especially as the latter are mediated through the work of Mircea Eliade).[3]

My claim is a simple but basic one: as the conversation in a situation of global pluralism proceeds, it is likely that the cosmological interests of Eastern religions will force us to recognize the relative impoverishment of those concerns in most forms of Christian practical theology. Allied to this claim is the assumption that if we are really in conversation then we are bound to respond to these "Eastern" concerns and questions via our *own* tradition—but one now informed and eventually transformed by the conversation itself.[4] I make no claims to the adequacy of the results of the conversation presented here. Indeed my own knowledge of Eastern traditions is too limited and my judgments, therefore, too fragile to make any such claim. All I do claim is that this *kind* of reflection is likely to become urgent for all of us as the fuller dimensions of our situation of global pluralism begin to dawn upon us—and to dawn, as my reflections on cosmology in section 4 suggest, in both theory and praxis.

A GENERAL MODEL OF THEOLOGY AND ITS THREE SUBDISCIPLINES

Here I wish to recall three propositions whose warrants I attempt to provide elsewhere.[5] Here I can only state them as propositions to clarify what I do and do not claim there.

Christian theology is a discipline which develops mutually critical correlations in theory and praxis between two sets of interpretations: an interpretation of the religious dimensions of the contemporary situation and an interpretation of the Christian fact.

This single discipline can be helpfully distinguished as comprised of three subdisciplines: fundamental, systematic, and practical theologies. Each subdiscipline uses the general model stated above but specifies a distinct set of criteria for developing the general model itself.

The spectrum for the three subdisciplines is not a spectrum where one of the subdisciplines (e.g., fundamental or systematic or practical theology) functions as, in effect, the general model for which the other two are more "specific" determinations (so that, e.g., praxis becomes mere applications of theories worked out elsewhere). Rather the proper understanding of the spectrum is one whereby practical theology is the most concrete exemplification of all theology whereas fundamental and systematic theologies are necessary but relatively abstract: "fundamental" to provide the necessarily abstract de facto conditions of possibility for concrete thought and action; "systematic" to provide the rhetorical and poetic claims to cognitive disclosure of transformative action; "practical" to provide the concrete praxis criteria for reflective action in the historical situation.

If this general model and general spectrum (from the abstract to the concrete, *not* from the general to the specific)[6] holds, then it follows that it becomes helpful to distinguish three subdisciplines in theology and three distinct (but not separate) sets of criteria to employ. To clarify this, recall the Aristotelian project: on the presupposition that the *Analytics* does not determine Aristotle's entire enterprise (as the Scholastics thought), the *Topics* must also be employed. This means, in turn, that there are various kinds of context-dependent criteria needed—

dependent, above all, in the particular subject matter under study. In sum, the concerns of the *Metaphysics*, the *Rhetoric, Poetics, Ethics*, and *Politics* are *all* needed at different points in the entire enterprise. No one of them can be neutralized from the concerns of the others since there is no overarching general set of criteria (e.g., in *The Analytics*) to provide surety. The recognition of this "lack" provides a relative priority to the concrete praxis criteria of the ethics and politics. But even this priority is only relative since certain cognitive issues that surface in ethics and politics may need appeals to metaphysical or hermeneutical (rhetorical and poetic) criteria as well. I understand a similar (not identical) point to be implied by Johann Baptist Metz when he states: "My criticism, then, is principally directed against the attempt to explain the historical identity of Christianity by means of speculative thought (idealism), without regard to the constitutive function of Christian praxis, the cognitive equivalent of which is narrative and memory."[7]

My own position agrees with this central, programmatic statement of Metz with the additional (and admittedly controversial) insistence that *implied* in the analysis of the "cognitive" status of "narrative" and "memory" is an analysis of the hermeneutical criteria of rhetoric and poetics (disclosure) to help determine the cognitive status of both memory and narrative. I hope I can make this rather cryptic statement clearer by turning to my second set of propositions on the model for hermeneutics which I employ in *The Analogical Imagination* and elsewhere.

WHAT HERMENEUTICS IS AND IS NOT

My first proposition must be a partially negative one. Despite widespread conceptions to the contrary, hermeneutics is not concerned only with meaning but also with truth. Indeed, the most persuasive aspect of hermeneutics on the model of conversation which Gadamer developed is, for me, its insistence that every genuine conversation with a classic is involved with the search for truth and not merely with meaning.[8] My own work in *The Analogical Imagination* tried to develop Gadamer's position in one principal way: by developing and defending the notion of the "classic" present but relatively unexamined in Gadamer's work. I hoped to show how we can publicly recognize the claim to truth of any classic as a public claim to disclosure and transformation.[9] To recall the quote from Metz: Metz or other political theologians could, in principle, employ the hermeneutical (i.e., rhetorical and poetic) criteria I develop in order to show in the wider public forum the disclosive character of the cognitive claims in memory (i.e., all the classic memories of suffering as in classic apocalyptic) and narrative (especially the classic biblical narratives disclosive of the truth of self and communal identity).[10] Such a hermeneutical move, I repeat, would not replace the concern with personal, social, and political and historical transformation via "constitutive praxis" in Metz's political theology. Indeed it could strengthen that position by clarifying and developing the disclosive-cognitive side of the claim for the public forum itself.

There is a second point to be made on hermeneutics as well—a point which I also believe can aid political theology. It is this: as hermeneutics has been employed in theology previously, it has (for example, in the so-called New Hermeneutics) largely been a matter of a hermeneutics of pure retrieval on the Gadamer model. My own position criticized this understanding on one central issue (indeed a central *praxis* issue!). First, if, as I maintain, every classic and every classic tradition (including both the Christian and the modern) is radically ambiguous and never innocent and pure, then hermeneutics itself must be a hermeneutics of both retrieval and critique-suspicion.[11] This means, in turn, that any critical theory (i.e., theory expressive of self-reflective consciousness like Lonergan's or Freud's or Dewey's or Marx's or feminist theory) is not merely appropriate but necessary for hermeneutics itself. When? Whenever we suspect (the verb is apt) that our classics include not mere errors but systematic distortions (racism, sexism, elitism, anti-Semitism, classism, etc.).

My own work in hermeneutics, in sum, has been an attempt to develop a hermeneutics for all classics that is a hermeneutics of both retrieval and critique-suspicion. At no point in this development does "theory" take over: conversation, after all, is a praxis—and a rare one in my experience; even the critical theories needed for the "suspicious" moves in a hermeneutics are *critical* theories precisely by their articulation of the processes involved in concrete self-reflective intellectual, moral, and religious praxis.[12]

What the conversation among the religions most needs, therefore, is conversation with all the classics of all the major traditions—ambiguous classics, ambiguous traditions which require hermeneutics of both retrieval and suspicion as we try to converse together in our situation of global pluralism.

THE SITUATION OF GLOBAL PLURALISM

Mainline Christian theology since the eighteenth-century Enlightenment and the nineteenth-century rise of historical consciousness has been principally concerned with the crisis of the cognitive claims of

Christianity in relationship to modernity. In my view those concerns were and are real and there is no way to pretend that they are now adequately resolved or shelved. (Indeed, the role of fundamental theology in practical theology principally addresses this issue.)

The situation has notably changed, however, in certain significant ways to relativize (and, in some ways, to radicalize) the issue of cognitive claims. Involved in this shift are, of course, the crisis of Western modernity itself—a crisis well articulated by Max Horkheimer and Theodor Adorno as *The Dialectic of Enlightenment*.[13] This crisis has occasioned a chastening (at the least) of modern Western claims to universality and a disclosure of the dialectical ambiguity (elitist arrogance, political and cultural imperialism, and sexism, racism, and classism) that are present along with its genuine virtues in the modern Western tradition.

Unlike earlier liberal and modernist theologians, many contemporary Christian theologians do not understand the modern tradition itself as cognitively untroubled. Indeed quite the opposite: we now recognize, thanks in part to the crisis of Western self-understanding and thereby to an opening to other traditions, that a global pluralism is our actuality as well. This means, in turn, that we find the question of the "other religions" not an addendum to Christian theology but somehow present from the beginning and throughout. This means that their questions and concerns should provoke us to ask the now common questions anew—both in relationship to their responses and in relationship to often forgotten or repressed aspects of our own tradition. In short, genuine conversation with the religions (perhaps heuristically guided under some such rubric as an "analogical imagination") is needed from the very beginning of theology to the end.

And yet if this conversation is not to become, in effect, simply an expansion of the traditional modern concern with cognitive claims, then the other major aspect of the global pluralism in our contemporary situation must also be addressed. That aspect is this: in any attempt to honor the pluralism of religions through genuine conversation (including argument), we cannot retreat from the praxis concerns which impinge upon all religions in all situations.[14] The fact of global pluralism is truly honored when the "global" dimension is recognized along with the pluralism. The striving for a global culture, the ineluctable drive of science and technology (especially communications) renders our planet both more pluralistic and more unified at one and the same time. We do not live yet in a "global village." But neither can we live any longer in our own "untroubled" Western village.

DAVID TRACY

Our dilemma is real: we must continue the concern with cognitive claims and theory as the conversation among the religions intensifies. Yet that conversation should not be divorced from the concerns of both theory and praxis of our emerging global community. This is, I not only admit but insist, an exceedingly difficult agenda for any Christian practical theology to take on. But I can see no way to avoid it—if we are serious that practical theology attempts to develop mutually critical correlations in both theory and praxis between an interpretation of the tradition and an interpretation of our actual contemporary situation.

For our situation is one where massive global suffering exists to interrupt all the religions and all the conversations among the religions. Our situation is one where the recognition of this suffering must be present in all the conversations on global pluralism. But rather than engaging in further reflections on the situation, allow me to try to indicate an example of the kind of Christian theological reflection that might occur if global pluralism were taken more seriously. It is something of a truism to observe that the cosmological interests (or the "manifestation" orientation) of Eastern traditions is notably stronger than that of most Western traditions.[15] And, alternatively, that the "historical" (and ethical and political) interests of Western prophetic traditions (or the "proclamation" orientation) is notably stronger than that of most Eastern traditions.

It seems plausible, therefore, to say that any conversation with the Eastern religious traditions is likely to provoke as a central question a reopening and rethinking of the issue of nature or cosmos in Christian practical theology itself. My present suggestion is that, in both theory and praxis, this reopening is sorely needed. The situation of global pluralism as described above provokes that reopening. What forms the question might take on Christian theological grounds must now be described.

COSMOLOGY AS A TEST CASE OF
GLOBAL PLURALISM

A return to the issues of cosmology seems both desirable and necessary in our present theological situation of global pluralism. That return is desirable largely because of significant shifts in the methods and contents of both theology and science. The return is necessary for two related reasons. First, there is a growing sense (occasioned by both the cosmological center of Eastern traditions and by the ecological crisis and the threat of nuclear holocaust) that the "anthropocentric" center of much contemporary theology must be challenged.[16] Second, redemption itself cannot be understood without a relationship to creation; history cannot be understood without nature; the central categories God and the self (and, therefore, society and history) cannot be fully grasped without reference to the category "cosmos" or "world." My present reflections make no claims to resolve this complex set of issues. I shall be more than content if readers come to share their sense of how urgent cosmological concerns should be for all theology in our situation of global pluralism. Above all, it is the new *status quaestionis* that must be understood before the new constructive theological work can be assessed.

Our contemporary theological situation, to repeat, has changed in both theory and praxis. In both cases, the urgency of a theological return to cosmological interests seems clear. Consider, first, the situation from the point of view of contemporary Western theory. We forget all too easily that when theologians of early modernity (seventeenth to early twentieth century) approached the relationships between science and theology the situation was, at best, deeply troubling. The scientific revolution was an intellectual event, as Butterfield remarks, which became a genuine intellectual revolution which demanded a new "thinking cap" in all disciplines. Indeed, so radical was this intellectual revolution that Herbert Butterfield does not exaggerate when he states that, in comparison, even the Renaissance and the Reformation look like "family quarrels."[17] There can be little doubt that the events symbolized by the names Copernicus, Galileo, Newton, and Darwin changed forever the landscape of theological thought.

Neither the earlier "warfare" between science and religion nor earlier "concordist" proposals of theologians and philosophers in that long period of early modernity strike contemporaries as genuine options for our radically changed situation.[18] The principal reasons for the collapse of both the confrontational ("warfare") model and the concordist model are to be found in the changed understandings of the content and the methods of both theology and science. For however alive earlier scientific models of mechanism, materialism, and positivism may be in the popular imagination (including the popular imagination of some scientists), the fact is that science itself has challenged these earlier models. It is not possible in an age where the content of science has been radically changed by evolutionary theories, relativity, quantum mechanics, the principle of indeterminacy, quarks, DNA research, and so on simply to appeal to earlier mechanist or materialist models. The content of the sciences now disallows all easy appeals to these positions. In an ironic symbol of this momentous shift, we may say that science itself no longer has need of Laplace's materialist and mechanist hypothesis! The methods of science, moreover, have themselves yielded to more modest self-appraisals. The recognition that reason too has a history has yielded, in the history of science, to proposals like those of T. Kuhn, S. Toulmin, M. Hesse, and others that earlier positivist models for scientific self-understanding cannot survive the study of the history of science nor philosophical scrutiny by philosophers of science.[19]

This shift in both the content and the self-understanding of the methods of science has occasioned, therefore, a new intellectual situation in both West and East where the relationship of science and theology seems at once more promising and more difficult. It is more difficult in the properly theoretical sense that the issues are now far more complex and often highly technical and where earlier models of sheer confrontation or easy concordism are inappropriate. It is more promising for largely the same reasons: the collapse of earlier mechanistic, materialist, and positivist models has freed science itself to a sense of the "ultimate mystery of reality" and to a chastened but real willingness to dialogue with any plausible philosophical and theological cosmological hypotheses, including those in Eastern traditions. The dialogues between many process philosophers and theologians (including, in the wider sense of process thought, the followers of Teilhard de Chardin) are merely the best-known Western instances of this increasingly fruitful dialogue.

It is equally important to recall, of course, that theological self-understanding and theological content have undergone analogous paradigm shifts in the same period. Except for fundamentalists, earlier theological models based on ahistorical and authoritarian understandings of theological claims have collapsed. Except for naive concordists, the technical complexities and tentative hypothetical character of the theologically relevant issues in contemporary science do not yield themselves to easy solutions. Indeed, all easy solutions—scientific and theological—have been unmasked as, in effect, ideologies for an intellectual elite functioning to assure the status quo.

Theologians, in sum, have learned their own form of chastened methodological and material modesty. Most now realize, as E. Schillebeeckx has observed, that theology is an interpretive enterprise that attempts to establish "mutually critical correlations" (in both theory and praxis) between interpretations of our contemporary situation and interpretations of the Christian tradition. The rise of historical consciousness in the nineteenth century and the radical sense of historicity in the early twentieth century have impelled modern theology, as B. Lonergan observed, to abandon its commitments to "classical consciousness" (including classical cosmologies).[20] Granted these gains, one still cannot avoid the impression that (with some notable exceptions) contemporary Western theology, although strong on interpretations of history and redemption, is relatively weak on interpretations of nature and creation. Part of the reason for this is undoubtedly that earlier "warfares" between science and theology and the collapse of earlier concordist proposals have rendered most theologians reluctant to reenter the dialogue with natural science. The fact that most theologians, by both predilection and training, find their most natural "conversation partners" in the human sciences has also served to encourage this same development. An allied fact is that the major gain of contemporary theology is the "deprivatizing" of theology. This deprivatizing has been best developed by political and liberation theologies faithful to a practical reason cognizant of massive global suffering. Yet those very same theologies can often encourage a relative lack of interest in strictly cosmological questions. Is this still possible, however, if the situation of global pluralism is taken seriously?

It should now be clear that a major accomplishment and a still major need of contemporary theology is to work out political and liberation theologies faithful to the demands of both theory and praxis in our grave historical situation. These theologies correctly retrieve the resources of the Christian tradition to help transform that situation of massive global suffering. Their critical analysis of the "privatization" of earlier modern existentialist and transcendental theologies can only be considered a gain for all theology. The suspicion that "cosmological" interests in theology or even the conversation among the religions *can* function as a distraction from these historical responsibilities or even as ideology for intellectual elites (as in concordist proposals) seems appropriate. The importance of these suspicions should not be domesticated. Indeed, any pure models of "progress" unable and unwilling to face the tragedy and suffering in human existence fully deserve Christian theological suspicion.

Yet another suspicion must also inform our contemporary theological consciousness. It is this: is it possible for theology to be faithful to the demands of either our situation or to the Christian tradition while continuing to ignore cosmological concerns? The question is not rhetorical. For the fact is that the rediscovery of "history" by contemporary theology has not been matched by a parallel rediscovery of "nature." A well-nigh exclusive focus on the doctrine of redemption (as related to liberation and emancipation) has not usually been paralleled by new explorations of the doctrine of creation.[21] Contemporary theology is in danger of developing interpretations of God and self (including the social self in society and history) while quietly dropping the traditional third category of "world" or "cosmos." And yet this absence would represent both a major retreat from the situation of global pluralism and a major impoverishment of the Christian tradition and possibly a major distortion of Christian understandings of salvation and history themselves.

It is, of course, necessary today to continue to demythologize and de-ideologize traditional Christian theological understandings of "world" or "cosmos." Nevertheless, it is also crucial to realize that from the New Testament period through the patristic and the medieval periods the same insight has prevailed: in John Collins's forthright statement "Human salvation cannot be divorced from our understanding of the world around us. The creation, too, is groaning in travail. . . . It is important . . . that we find a way to integrate human values with some cosmological understanding if our theology is to represent more than a fragment of existence."[22] It is especially important if the conversation with Eastern traditions is taken seriously.

The Christian tradition needs the doctrine of creation even to understand fully its own doctrine of redemption. Contemporary Christian theology needs to recover a theology of nature—even to develop an adequate theology of history. No Christian theology can claim adequacy to the Christian tradition by, in effect, retrieving only God and the self (including the social and historical self) while quietly dropping "world" out of the picture. The questions of cosmology are not properly understood as *only* concerned with the origin and natural structure of the world. Those cosmological questions include the destiny of the world, as well—including the destiny of human beings, indeed of history itself—as "inextricably bound up" with the destiny of the cosmos. The deprivatizing of theology has meant a return to real history (not mere historicity). But that return to history, in both theory and praxis, must also mean a return to nature.

These more theoretical questions, moreover, are intensified if we note two central praxis concerns of our contemporary period of global pluralism. Those two grave issues—in summary form, the ecological crisis and the threat of nuclear holocaust—must touch all contemporary theologies of history. Both issues, moreover, suggest in graphic terms the more theoretical questions expressed above. For the relationships between science and religion today or the relationships among the religions are not occasioned only by the intriguing and complex set of intellectual issues posed by the new paradigms for method in science and theology and the new content in both disciplines. The need for cosmology in theology, moreover, is not posed only by the internal theological demand that theology attempt to interpret both self and world in light of its Christic understanding of God; that theology interpret creation even to understand redemption; that theology risk interpreting nature in order to understand history. Central and pressing as these intellectual concerns undoubtedly are, they must be understood in the context of our contemporary sense of crisis. The reality of impending ecological crisis is so clear that no serious concern with historical justice can long ignore it. The struggle for justice must also include the struggle for ecology—not only to secure justice for other creatures than the human but even to secure the most basic justice of all: a livable environment for future generations of human beings. The ecological crisis forces all serious political and liberation theology to call into question, on its own praxis criteria, the possible anthropocentrism lurking in its own self-understanding. As J. Cobb suggests,[23] all cosmologically informed theologies (like Cobb's own process theology) must now be in conversation with both political and liberation theologians and with Eastern traditions in order to become a political theology. It is also the case that all political and liberation theology must now become an ecological theology as well in order to fulfill its own demands to relate to our present praxis situation.[24] This means that a reopening of cosmological concerns in contemporary theology will also become a dialogue between political theology and those forms of "postmodern" ecological science (S. Toulmin, F. Ferré) as well as Eastern traditions whose own praxis concerns are clear. All must now share a critique and suspicion of traditional scientific and theological understandings of the human right to "dominate" and exploit nature. (As Eastern traditions have consistently done.)

Allied to this sense of concern for the ecological crisis is, of course, the other central praxis issue which our contemporary situation poses: the threat of omnicide present in the possibility of nuclear holocaust.[25] The concern among scientists and theologians alike with this central dilemma imposes, besides its more obvious political concerns, a need to interpret cosmology anew. Such interpretations may help avert this overwhelming and literally final nuclear possibility for the entire planet. The issues—technical, political, and cosmological as well as theological—involved in both ecology and the possibility of nuclear war are so pressing that only a collaborative effort among all persons "of good

DAVID TRACY

will" (including scientists and theologians) can hope to find ways, in theory and praxis, to avert them as the "final solution" of a global nonpluralism. For the moment my point is a more simple and more basic one: namely, that it is now impossible for theology to understand itself as responding to the theoretical and practical challenges of our situation while ignoring the issues of cosmology. If theology is to remain a discipline establishing mutually critical correlations in theory and praxis between interpretations of the situation and interpretations of the tradition, then a global concern with cosmology must once again be accorded a central place in all theological reflection. Otherwise, we would not be faithful to either the demands of the new intellectual situation in both science and theology or the demands of East-West religious dialogue or the crises in praxis which impinge upon all. Nor could we claim, under the rubric of a theology of history, that we have adequately interpreted the full resources and demands of the Christian tradition itself: redemption *and* creation; history *and* nature; God, self, *and* world.

NOTES

1. This insistence on the purely heuristic character of a method for practical theology is one of the several strengths of the model developed in Dennis P. McCann and Charles R. Strain, *Polity and Praxis: A Program for American Practical Theology* (Minneapolis: Winston-Seabury, 1985).

2. I try to develop this theme on "postmodernity" in David Tracy, *Plurality and Ambiguity: Hermeneutics, Religion, Hope* (San Francisco: Harper & Row, 1987).

3. *Inter alia*, see Mircea Eliade, *The Sacred and the Profane: The Nature of Religion* (New York: Harper & Row, 1961).

4. See Paul Knitter, *No Other Name? A Critical Survey of Christian Attitudes Toward the World Religions* (Maryknoll, N.Y.: Orbis Books, 1985).

5. The works in question are David Tracy, *Blessed Rage for Order: The New Pluralism in Theology* (New York: Seabury Press, 1975), *The Analogical Imagination: Christian Theology and the Culture of Pluralism* (New York: Crossroad, 1981), and "The Task of Practical Theology," in *Practical Theology: The Emerging Field in Theology, Church, and World*, ed. Don S. Browning (New York: Harper & Row, 1983).

6. The same model (from the abstract to the concrete, not the general to the specific) informs Schleiermacher's *Glaubenslehre*—despite Barthian attempts to read it otherwise.

7. Johann Baptist Metz, *Faith in History and Society: Toward a Practical Fundamental Theology*, trans. David Smith (New York: Seabury Press, 1980), 161.

8. Hans-Georg Gadamer, *Truth and Method* (New York: Seabury Press, 1975).

9. Tracy, *Analogical Imagination*, 99–154.

10. The recent work of Paul Ricoeur on narrative is especially important here: see the three-volume work on *Time and Narrative* (Chicago: University of Chicago Press, 1983–).

11. For the categories, see Paul Ricoeur, *Freud and Philosophy: An Essay on Interpretation* (New Haven: Yale University Press, 1970), 3–59, 494–553.

12. Raymond Geuss, *The Idea of a Critical Theory: Habermas and the Frankfurt School* (Cambridge: Cambridge University Press, 1981).

13. Max Horkheimer and Theodor Adorno, *The Dialectic of Enlightenment* (New York: Seabury Press, 1975).

14. This "praxis" concern should include, in my judgment, both ethical-political-religious concerns (especially for justice) and also the religious praxis traditions of spirituality and piety.

15. See Paul Ricoeur, "Manifestation and Proclamation," *Journal of the Blaisdell Institute* (Winter 1978), and my own version in *Analogical Imagination*, 154–231.

16. For a strong critique of this anthropocentrism in theology, see James M. Gustafson, *Ethics from a Theocentric Perspective*, vol. 1 (Chicago: University of Chicago Press, 1981).

17. Herbert Butterfield, *Origins of Modern Science* (New York: Free Press, 1965).

18. For historical and systematic theological analyses of these traditions, see Nicholas Lash and David Tracy, eds., *Cosmology and Theology, Concilium* (Edinburgh: T. & T. Clark, 1983). The present section of this article is, in fact, a revised version of my introductory essay to that volume—the entire issue forced me, as I hope it may persuade others, to face this cosmological issue anew.

19. See Thomas Kuhn, *The Structure of Scientific Revolutions* (Chicago: University of Chicago Press, 1962); Stephen Toulmin, *Human Understanding, vol. 1: The Collective Use and Evolution of Concepts* (Princeton: Princeton University Press, 1972); and Mary Hesse, "Cosmology as Myth," in *Cosmology and Theology*, ed. Lash and Tracy.

20. For an example, see Bernard Lonergan, "Aquinas Today: Tradition and Innovation," in *A Third Collection: Papers by Bernard J. F. Lonergan, S.J.*, ed. Frederick E. Crowe, S.J. (New York: Paulist Press, 1985).

21. One exception here is Jürgen Moltmann, *The Future of Creation* (Philadelphia: Fortress Press, 1979).

22. John Collins, "New Testament Cosmology," in *Cosmology and Theology*, ed. Lash and Tracy, 7.

23. John B. Cobb, Jr., *Process Theology as Political Theology* (Philadelphia: Westminster Press, 1982).

24. Schubert M. Ogden, *Faith and Freedom: Toward a Theology of Liberation* (Nashville: Abingdon Press, 1979), 97–114.

DAVID TRACY

25. The recent works on "nuclearism" of Susan Brooks Thistlethwaite (ed., *A Just Peace Church* [New York: United Church Press, 1986]) and Gordon Kaufman (*Theology for a Nuclear Age* [Philadelphia: Westminster Press, 1985]) are especially relevant here.

Editors' Epilogue

Our symposium has ended. We began with a much-asked, yet surprisingly intractable question. How is academic theology related to actual, living communities of faith? The essays in this book have pursued this issue directly enough. But they have also uncovered many of its implications, taking us into questions of situational hermeneutics, ministry in relation to theological understanding, metaphors for theological practice, revisionist pedagogy for seminary and parish, the levels of practical ethical reflection, the semiotic mode of thinking about thinking, and so forth. And our dialogue has produced two challenges to the customary frame of reference for the debate as such. One essay has questioned our book's dominant liberal "correlation" methodology. Another has challenged the self-sufficiency of Christian tradition as such in a deeply threatened global civilization, calling for dialogue with other faiths. At the very least, the theme of "practical theology" has shown its capacity to lead us into issues which stand at the center of contemporary debate. Whether the way we have traveled shows "promise," as our subtitle suggests, and if so, what kind, is now the question.

THE SEMINARY AS "SITUATION"

One can only pose this, or any other, query from the standpoint of the "situation" one is in. Most of us are in one way or another theological educators. Our inquiry began, let us not forget, with a grant from the Association of Theological Schools. The vantage point from which we look out upon the human world is one of syllabi and classes, curriculum committees and constituencies, of the latest articles and books noticed, reviewed, and sometimes read. Is the North American theological school a credible setting in which to wrestle with the questions this book asks? After all, there are other possibilities: the parish, the ecumenical agency, the issue-oriented action group, the base community, and many others. But we are where we are and must take responsibility, as no one else can, for the task of practical theologizing in that place.

On reflection, we think that the theological school is far from being the worst place to work at grasping what is going on in our world. The impression persists that other professional schools and university departments are often, by comparison, remarkably narrow-minded and self-interested: temptations, of course, not unfamiliar to us either. Theologians, of course, can and do draw gratefully upon the insights of the different disciplines of the university. The seminary, however, is different: it is a place where profound tradition with its interpretations meets the reality of communities of faith in a setting of creative visioning of what could be or should be in the life of the human race. This task requires the seminary to take into account both the newly rising perspectives of the disempowered and the variety of religious cultures which have been on earth for thousands of years, to delve deeply into what has been repressed, and also to range broadly across the whole spectrum of cultural possibilities, in a situation of deep threat to the human experiment itself. Theological situationality is by nature inclusive in character.

But the potential for intellectual leadership inherent in this crossroads social location remains for the most part unfulfilled. Neither pure scholarship, nor the "how-to-do-it" mode, nor pure prophetic idealization are in themselves enough. No doubt we are still looking for the new paradigm of theological knowledge (it is twenty years since this term first entered our vocabulary) to hold it all together. So much jostles together in the life of the typical theological school that the first requisite may simply be to keep the pieces of the puzzle on the tabletop long enough to begin to see how they could fit together.

The competing energies of theological educators tend to tilt the table in different directions at different times. Scholarly efforts vie with programs oriented toward the operational needs of the churches, and both confront a strong desire of many to think prophetically, globally, or interculturally. The seminary is in fact a bundle of academic departments, a professional school, *and* a visionary think tank all at once. The great danger is that institutions will simply decide (for reasons of fund raising, constituency building, or just plain focusing of faculty effort) to specialize, with university-related faculties going one way, church-related institutions another, and action-committed bodies—many of them ecumenical—still another. Yet such fragmentation could impoverish the theological debate. In the face of such centrifugal pressures, and with sympathy for the different engagements they represent, the editors maintain that interaction among these concerns, with their characteristic conceptual vocabularies and methods of inquiry, is essential for progress in theological understanding today. The promise of practical theology, if it is to be fulfilled, will depend on it.

PROMISE IN THE PRACTICAL FIELD

What, then, can hold all this together? The most likely institutional location for continued pursuit of this conversation is precisely the "fourth sector" of the curriculum, the practical area. Our authors agree that "the practical field" should do far more than teach techniques for the delivery or application of what the academic departments produce. The ministry area is not simply the marketing subdivision for an enterprise that sees "real" theology as biblical, historical, or systematic. Practical theology may actually turn out to be the place of meeting of all the different disciplines and experiences that make up "theology" in the larger sense of the term. If the practical field were strong enough politically and intellectually to stand at the heart of the theological enterprise, its members together might call upon (even hire and fire) specialists in the other areas as they seemed needed for whatever inquiry was afoot at the time!

The practical area is often the source of curricular initiatives which can serve as testing grounds for such possibilities. We think of two typical ones: the attempt to introduce the element of reflection into field education and the attempt to devise educational experiences which integrate the curriculum as a whole. We must try to provide both these things, but seldom do we do it well. Rarely do these enterprises (even when they persist for many years) get much beyond the experimental, conceptually unstable, constantly revised stage. The greatest successes seem to reflect dominant faculty personalities rather than reproducible conceptual or pedagogical breakthroughs. It is time, we think, to recognize that these unsatisfactory experiences are telling us something not only about our own inadequacies but also about the theological situation in which we live.

What issues emerge from the attempt to do better? Running through our whole book has been the question of the "method of correlation," its meaning, its implications, its applicability. There is, perhaps, agreement that the meaning of "correlation" depends on the theological and practical context in which the method is used. The original home of the term (if not of that for which it stands) is to be found in the writings of Paul Tillich with important subsequent modifications by David Tracy, hence its association with the "liberal-revisionist" outlook targeted for criticism by Rebecca Chopp. But clearly we read even in Chopp of a "critical praxis correlation" which could describe the methods for theological construction-in-situation recommended by Thomas Groome and James Whitehead. Some may feel, of course, that in Groome a method for revolutionary pedagogy developed by Paolo Friere has been domesticated for bourgeois use, and thus brought into a sphere of correlations with which it does not belong. The editors believe that it is important to unpack such issues so far as possible. Is it possible that the method of correlation has several valid forms? Let us see.

Inherent in the idea of practical theology, we think, is the notion that the theological school, with all its academic equipment, stands *within* the community of faith as an instrument *of* that community for the clarification of its thinking. Not every theological institution or faculty is free, of course, to think of itself in just this way. But the theory-practice notion by which the theologian independently articulates truths which are then conveyed to users will not wash today. Rather, the theologian stands within the ongoing stream by which the faith community has continuously interpreted its tradition-in-situation over the years. The theologian's vocation is to comment critically on this process. In that sense, her or his vocation is eminently practical. It is set within the stream of praxis. Such a vocation for practical theology suggests, we think, that it exists in three modes, each of which shows the "method of correlation" in a different light. Each mode can be expressed in the form of a question. (1) How do we initially grasp and articulate what goes on as the faith community takes form in us and through us? (2) How do we submit this formation process to appropriate theological criticism? (3) How can this theological criticism within the faith community in turn inform its life, assuming that this community wishes to be both faithful *and* responsibly involved in the modern world?

FROM SITUATION TO ARTICULATION: THE CONGREGATION AS CULTURE

The first responsibility of practical theologizing is to bring the character of the faith situation to initial, usable, expression. This will require observation and listening. How are tradition and culture, tradition and socioeconomic structure, already interacting? Correlations of various sorts have already been going on for generations before we come on the scene. The practical theologian will not be able to begin work unless he or she knows what these are.

This first step corresponds roughly to Groome's "Movements" 1 and 2, in which present praxis is named and subjected to preliminary, common-sense reflection. The problem, of course, is to bring to bear critical equipment which is not itself inherently ideological. In this volume, the essays by Edward Farley and Lewis Mudge suggest methods which might give this step more sophistication. We are called to begin with a "humble"—that is, watchful and listening—hermeneutic which can expectantly approach the signs each community of faith generates in its setting. For this purpose, it is indispensable that members of the faith community think, speak for themselves, and receive a hearing. Their "inner" appropriation of the "objective" situation is important. It is important, too, that the element of suspicion not enter before the hearing and seeing are complete. Perhaps the best model is that of the anthropologist who seeks to understand a community's culturally coded messages through a process of participant observation *before* imposing analytical categories which originate in the anthropologist's own, academic culture.

Approaches to the study of congregational life on the anthropological model are beginning to appear. One of the best works already in print is the *Handbook for Congregational Studies*, edited by Jackson Carroll, Carl S. Dudley, and William McKinney.[1] This manual proclaims at the outset that the academic disciplines as such must be bracketed out in favor of observation and listening. "Academic disciplines are not the categories that members of congregations and those who work in and with them use to organize their congregational experiences."[2] The academic world has its own culture. The congregation is a culture in its own right. The world of the congregation, or that of any other situation of faith, will inevitably escape the categories of grand theory. To use Michel Foucault's term, the shared life of faith involves "subjugated knowledge"[3] which probably cannot be translated wholly into terms other than its own.

Of paramount importance is the insight that a certain kind of *thinking* accompanies the life of faith: thinking culturally remote from that done in the academy, but thinking nonetheless. Farley would call this the foundation of theology as habitus;[4] Robert Bellah, the community's "habits of the heart."[5] This sort of thinking must be taken seriously in its own right. It is not essentially reflective, but rather anecdotal (i.e., storytelling) and deliberative. It seeks to move from the data of faith to day-to-day decision making about what it is to be faith*ful*. Many factors contribute to it. It is not linear, and it is not consciously correlative. It resembles in some ways the "social existentialism" described in the final chapter of H. R. Niebuhr's *Christ and Culture*.[6] Congregations make the best decisions they can, in the face of objective uncertainties, with the available understandings of tradition and situation. These decisions may well fall into patterns resembling one or another of Niebuhr's five forms of correlation between "Christ" and "culture." But this is for the observer, rather than the participant, to see.

BEYOND SELVES AND MEANINGS:
THE STAGE OF CRITICAL REFLECTION

Now how can the participant, who also has the vocation of theologian, reflect critically on what she or he has heard and seen? The danger here may lie in coming to this reflection with normative preconceptions, derived from "systematic theology," of the link between tradition and situation. The true force of Chopp's criticism lies in her correct observation that the dominant "liberal-revisionist" theological tradition has normed its correlation theory in advance with the view that the key categories are selves and meanings. This view, of course, rests upon the Tillichian judgment that each era in Western history has been responsive to a different theological norm, and that the norm of meaning making is ours.

No doubt, of course, each faith situation articulates or discloses its characteristic problematic. The need to theologize in the first place arises with the sense that some issue needs attention, that there is a problem to be addressed. But so various are the situations of faith today that we cannot assume in advance that we know what the problematic is. One does not send a congregation struggling with justice issues a treatise on selves and meanings. Selves, at least for the moment, find all the meanings they need in the struggle, and the struggle, rather than the selves and their meanings, has become the salient, thematic issue. While the theologian may come from one particular faith situation with its problematic, the stage of reflection requires an awareness that there are other situations. The church is inherently global. This means that practical theology cannot find its coherence in the systematic theology of one culture alone. Not, that is, if the systematic theology presumes to know in advance what the norm of the correlative relationship should be.

But this leaves us with serious problems. It is not clear, in the first place, that the array of functionally oriented disciplines in the typical North American seminary is appropriate for the analysis of every situation. And with systematic theology itself in question, we must ask how the ministry disciplines become theological in the first place. To the extent that they borrow perspectives from the different human sciences, the ministry subspecialties cannot even talk to each other, much less reliably reflect what the tradition contains. It has often been observed that the human-science disciplines—biology, sociology, anthropology, psychology, linguistics, and the like—operate with methods and perspectives so diverse that nothing even approaching a unified field theory embracing these endeavors today seems possible. Critical sociologists (let us say of the Frankfurt school) do not communicate easily with dynamic psychoanalysts (say of a Freudian or neo-Freudian persuasion). One may attempt a mediation (perhaps in a hermeneutical mode such as that of Paul Ricoeur), but the result will probably please no one but the mediator. If the different ministry disciplines remain tied to these warring perspectives on the human, they will scarcely find the means for moving toward a convergence of interpretive styles. Each of the different subfields will continue to have its own eyes and ears. At best, we will end up with a jostling of regional hermeneutics, each with its own method and angle of vision.

Farley has likened practical theology in this aspect to the pseudo-science of "ecology." Organized study of the global environment is not a discipline in itself, but rather employs a range of other disciplines (let us say from minerology to agronomy to atmospheric sciences and much more) without relying on any actual or supposed theoretical unity among these fields save use of the scientific method itself. And scientific method is, in fact, not one method but many, depending on a community of honest investigators and the principle of self-correctibility. The fields jostle one another, and sometimes interact. But use of them to do "ecology" is a matter of practical, if not serendipitous, judgment. One draws upon what is available, and produces some sort of plain-language policy document whose coherence is a function of the human life-world under consideration and the cognitive interests in question, not of any preexisting theoretical construct.

A strong temptation exists simply to replace older integrating norms with new ones. If existentialism and psychotherapy are out, then various forms of Marxism may be in. But we believe that normative constructs always cut two ways: they convey insights that are truly present in the tradition of faith, but they inevitably convey them tendentiously. Can there possibly be an integrating perspective that simply draws attention to the relation between content and praxis without contributing systematic distortion to both? Could it be that some form of philosophical pragmatism (drawing on the thought of Charles Peirce, Thomas Dewey, and William James, and also on such neo-pragmatists as Richard Rorty) could function for our time as a vehicle for the critical confrontation between the tradition and practice? Pragmatism states, in simplest terms, that the meaning of a proposition consists in the concrete results, the actions, which follow if the proposition is held to be true. Here, possibly, is a conceptual bridge on which we could move from liberalism's focus on selves and meanings to a new focus on the practical forms of faith in the midst of the modern world.

RECONSTITUTING THE FAITH COMMUNITY: FROM PROMISE TO POLITY

We come, then, to a final step. Can thinking of the sort described, pursued as a special vocation by certain members of the community of faith, illumine the calling of the community as a whole? It is one thing to think *about* the formation of the community. Does such thinking have value *in* and *for* the community?

Living a faith tradition in the modern world—is that still possible? Where does the real issue now lie? Whatever liberation theologians may say, Charles Winquist is right: the question of faith's cognitive status will not go away. The cultured despisers are still around, and some of them are ourselves! Yet the terms in which the problem is posed have shifted. It is one thing to debate faith's cognitive status when tradition is still firmly embedded in the culture, when the social role of the churches remains relatively unchallenged, and when the main issue is some particular emergent intellectual development such as the rise of biblical criticism, the growth of positivism, or the challenge of evolution. It is quite another matter to do so when the culture no longer transmits the tradition, the society no longer supports the churches, and intellectual developments, whatever they may be, count for little in a society given over to a war of ideologies fueled by power seeking and greed. In an age when all this is true and when many church members derive their knowledge of the faith mainly from portrayals in the media, the first requisite is not to defend the faith conceptually but to reconstitute it from the beginning as a lived reality, a form of life.

The questions of selfhood and meaning need now to be inscribed within a larger set of issues. How is authentic Christian formation possible? How can we conceive a lived context of faith in which some form of critical correlation between tradition and situation can even begin to take place? How can the community of faith be both responsible to the tradition and responsibly present in a pluralistic world? In the wake of the Enlightenment we asked about the status of "religion." Where, among human faculties and capacities, could it fit in? Today "religion" is everywhere and not only in fundamentalisms old and new. Civil religion lives in official rhetoric. In practice, it has become a piously acquisitive creed. But *where* is the blessed fellowship, the covenantal commonwealth, the community called church? The question of meaning has become the question of faith community as such: the tangible sign of the human oneness this world so desperately needs.

Practical theology today must ask how and where there can exist a *polity*, an ecclesial form, for the life of faith. The churches in their continuing existence at least pose the *question* of "church"—without them, the question itself would be forgotten. The churches do not give answers, but they do offer social space in which answers may be sought. One supposes that the faith polity we need now would combine some form of ordered life embodying small-scale democratic virtues with the poverty and simplicity of the early church. It would be so conceived and led so as to bear testimony to the gospel not only by its words but by its manifest social form. The thinking required to form and maintain such communities in faithful being would be their working, eminently practical, theology.

In the much-quoted closing of his book *After Virtue*,[7] Alasdair MacIntyre suggests something of this sort. Historical parallels are perilous, MacIntyre says, but we could be facing something like a new dark age, in which the best we could do would be to form communities of civility for keeping the human virtues alive. We may need such communities also to keep the Christian faith alive in ways ultimately meaningful to the human race. "This time . . . the barbarians are not waiting beyond the frontiers; they have been governing us for quite some time." Could we, too, then be waiting, as MacIntyre suggests, "not for a Godot, but for another—doubtless very different—St. Benedict"?[8]

NOTES

1. Jackson Carroll, Carl S. Dudley, William McKinney, eds., *Handbook for Congregational Studies* (Nashville: Abingdon Press, 1986). See also James Hopewell, *Congregation: Stories and Structures* (Philadelphia: Fortress Press, 1987).

2. Carroll et al., *Handbook*, 9.

3. Michel Foucault, *Power/Knowledge: Selected Interviews and Other Writings, 1972–1977* (New York: Pantheon Books, 1981), 81ff.

4. Edward Farley, *Theologia: The Fragmentation and Unity of Theological Education* (Philadelphia: Fortress Press, 1983), passim.

5. Robert N. Bellah, Richard Madsen, William M. Sullivan, Ann Swidler, and Steven M. Tipton, *Habits of the Heart: Individualism and Commitment in*

American Life (Berkeley and Los Angeles: University of California Press, 1985), passim.

6. H. R. Niebuhr, *Christ and Culture* (New York: Harper Torchbooks, 1956).

7. Alasdair MacIntyre, *After Virtue: A Study in Moral Theology* (Notre Dame, Ind.: University of Notre Dame Press, 1981).

8. Ibid., 244–45.